# Non-Native Language Teachers

# Educational Linguistics

## Volume 5

General Editor:

Leo van Lier
*Monterey Institute of International Studies, U.S.A.*

Editorial Board:

Marilda C. Cavalcanti
*Universidade Estadual de Campinas, Brazil*

Hilary Janks
*University of the Witwatersrand, South Africa*

Claire Kramsch
*University of California, Berkeley, U.S.A.*

Alastair Pennycook
*University of Technology, Sydney, Australia*

The *Educational Linguistics* book series focuses on work that is: innovative, trans-disciplinary, contextualized and critical.

In our compartmentalized world of diverse academic fields and disciplines there is a constant tendency to specialize more and more. In academic institutions, at conferences, in journals, and in publications the crossing of disciplinary boundaries is often discouraged.

This series is based on the idea that there is a need for studies that break barriers. It is dedicated to innovative studies of language use and language learning in educational settings worldwide. It provides a forum for work that crosses traditional boundaries between theory and practice, between micro and macro, and between native, second and foreign language education. The series also promotes critical work that aims to challenge current practices and offers practical, substantive improvements.

*The titles published in this series are listed at the end of this volume.*

Enric Llurda
Editor

# Non-Native Language Teachers

### Perceptions, Challenges and Contributions to the Profession

 Springer

Enric Llurda, Universitat de Lleida, Spain

Library of Congress Cataloging-in-Publication Data

Non-native language teachers: perceptions, challenges, and contributions to the profession
/ Enric Llurda, editor.
    p.cm.—(Educational linguistics; v. 5)
    Includes bibliographical references and index.
ISBN-10: 0-387-24566-9       (alk. paper) -- ISBN 0-387-24565-0  (EBOOK)
ISBN-13: 978-0387-24566-9
  1. Language and languages—Study and teaching. 2. Language teachers. I. Llurda, Enric.
II. Series.

P53.85.N66  2005
418'.0071—dc22                              2005043069

Printed in the United States of America.

9 8 7 6 5 4 3 2 1       SPIN   11386186

springeronline.com

# Dedication

*To Dolors, Àngels and Roger*

# Contents

viii

# Contributing Authors

**Eszter Benke**
Budapest Business School, Hungary
e.benke@axelero.hu

**George Braine**
The Chinese University of Hong Kong, Hong Kong
georgebraine@cuhk.edu.hk

**Vivian Cook**
University of Newcastle upon Tyne, UK
vivian.c@ntlworld.com

**Josep M. Cots**
University of Lleida, Catalonia / Spain
jmcots@dal.udl.es

**Tracey M. Derwing**
University of Alberta, Alberta / Canada
tracey.derwing@ualberta.ca

**Josep M. Díaz**
University of Lleida, Catalonia / Spain
dtorrent@gmx.net

**Ofra Inbar-Lourie**
Beit Berl College, Israel
inbarofra@bezeqint.net

**David Lasagabaster**
University of the Basque Country, the Basque Country / Spain
fiblahed@vh.ehu.es

**Jun Liu**
University of Arizona, Arizona / USA
junliu@u.arizona.edu

**Enric Llurda**
University of Lleida, Catalonia / Spain
ellurda@dal.udl.es

**Ernesto Macaro**
University of Oxford, UK
ernesto.macaro@educational-studies.oxford.ac.uk

**Arthur McNeill**
The Chinese University of Hong Kong, Hong Kong
amcneill@cuhk.edu.hk

**Péter Medgyes**
Eötvös Loránd University, Hungary
medgyes@ludens.elte.hu

**Marko Modiano**
University of Gävle, Sweden
mmo@hig.se

**Murrray J. Munro**
Simon Fraser University, British Columbia / Canada
mjmunro@sfu.ca

**Dorota Pacek**
University of Birmingham, UK
a.d.pacek@bham.ac.uk

**Kanavilil Rajagopalan**
State University of Campinas, Brazil
rajan@iel.unicamp.br

**Juan M. Sierra**
University of the Basque Country, the Basque Country / Spain
fipsiplj@vc.ehu.es

# Acknowledgments

As a non-native teacher of English, I have always been sensitive to the cause of the thousands of teachers of English who, like me, have had to struggle with the language and overcome the threats to their self-confidence posed by the perceived inferiority of non-natives in lieu of native teachers. Fortunately, excellent recent work—a good deal of which led by the TESOL NNEST Caucus—has helped to increase the status and professional self-esteem of non-native teachers, bringing them to the forefront of research in educational linguistics. This book is an attempt to move further in this direction by gathering several works by leading researchers with the explicit goal of contributing serious discussions and empirical studies on the role of non-native teachers in the language teaching profession.

I am indebted to all of the book's authors for their enthusiastic support of the project and their unfaltering willingness to participate in it. Their commitment kept me going in those few moments when despair seemed to be imminent. I am also indebted to the authors who broke the ice with research dealing with non-native teachers: Péter Medgyes, George Braine, Vivian Cook, and Jun Liu are among the contributors to this volume. A few other names must be mentioned here as well: Lia Kamhi-Stein, Janina Brutt-Griffler, Keiko K. Samimy, Cecilia Tang,, Nuzhat Amin, Thea Reves, Valéria Árva, Paul K. Matsuda, Barbara Seidlhofer, and many others. Their work provided inspiration for my own research and stimulated my embarking in this adventure, although it is quite likely I would not be involved in research dealing with non-native teachers had it not been by the initial push and the sensible advise given by Tracey M. Derwing, an excellent friend and advisor.

xii

I would also like to thank my colleagues at the University of Lleida for key help in the course of the preparation of this book: Eva Alfonso, Lurdes Armengol, Elisabet Arnó, Ester Baiget, Francesc Català, Josep M. Cots, Josep M. Díaz, Montse Irún, Xavier Martín, and Olga Rovira invested part of their time to help me with the project. The University itself was supportive in various ways by allowing me to develop the necessary contents and contacts.

I am very grateful to Leo van Lier, the general editor of this series for his support and guidance; the two anonymous reviewers of the whole manuscript for their thorough and very useful comments; the three academics who agreed to back my initial proposal: Brock Brady, Paul K. Matsuda, and Jasone Cenoz; and all the staff at Springer who at one point or another guided me and answered all my questions: Renee de Boo, Marianna Pascale, Marie Sheldon, and the people at Author Support.

Finally, I am most grateful to my wife, Dolors, my two children, Àngels and Roger—always sweet and patient with their busy father—, their grandparents, Carme, Antoni, Lluïsa and Tomàs, and all the rest of my family.

Chapter 1

# LOOKING AT THE PERCEPTIONS, CHALLENGES, AND CONTRIBUTIONS... OR THE IMPORTANCE OF BEING A NON-NATIVE TEACHER

ENRIC LLURDA
*Universitat de Lleida*

## 1.    INTRODUCTION

When in 1999 George Braine's book on non-native speaker (NNS) English teachers appeared, a lot of NNS professionals in TESOL, including myself, felt that an important area of study was finally becoming visible. After reading the book, I immediately wanted to be part of the shared effort to bring to the forefront of educational linguistics the task carried out by thousands of non-native language teachers all over the world. A few years earlier, Medgyes (1994) had opened the floor for a debate on this issue, bringing together experiential facts and theoretical principles in a rigorous and clear manner. Braine's volume consolidated the work in the area by gathering a unique collection of papers written by a group of authors actively involved in the contribution made by NNSs to the language teaching profession. Those were the seminal books that somehow prompted the recent interest in NNS teachers. However, it must also be acknowledged that during the 1990s, a portion of research on educational linguistics was turning to the social context in which language teaching took place. Thus, without explicitly addressing NNS and NS issues, the works of Holliday (1994, 1996), Ballard (1996), and Cortazzi & Jin (1996), significantly contributed to the understanding of the complex relationship between NS teachers

E. Llurda (Ed.), *Non-Native Language Teachers. Perceptions, Challenges and Contributions to the Profession*, 1—9.

(BANA, in Holliday's terminology, standing for *B*ritish, *A*ustralasian, and *N*orth-*A*merican) and NNS teachers (TESEP, standing for *Te*rtiary, *Se*condary and *P*rimary education in non-English speaking countries), and addressed power relationships in language teaching as well as differences in teaching cultures. Cortazzi & Jin (1996: 192) reported on a study based on 105 university students' essays on the theme 'Western ways of teaching and Chinese ways of learning', which showed a remarkable coincidence with the results of research specifically addressing the characteristics of NS and NNS teachers. Although the above studies is rarely mentioned in bibliographical lists devoted to research on NNS teachers, they well deserve being acknowledged here as part of the initial efforts to assert the status of NNS teachers of English in the world.

Now, ten years after Medgyes' pioneering work, research on non-native teachers has become widely accepted and several authors have gained respect for their active involvement in academic forums. Furthermore, research on NNS teachers has moved beyond the former *ghetto* of non-native authors. A look at the list of contributors to this volume will suffice to illustrate that although non-natives still greatly outnumber natives writing on this topic, native speakers are also involved in the study of NNS teachers. The work of authors such as Vivian Cook, Marko Modiano, Arthur McNeill, Tracey Derwing, and Murray Munro is indicative of the growth of interest among NSs in NNS issues, and also demonstrates that research on NNS teachers is increasingly conducted by NNSs and NSs alike. A further confirmation of this increasing interest in NNS issues is Bailey's (2001) explicit identification of research about non-native teachers as necessary for teacher preparation and development. And it is very indicative of the importance of this area in language teaching research that the TESOL International Research Foundation (TIRF) 'Call for Research Proposals 2003-2004' identified the following research priority:

> The relationship between teachers' proficiency in English, effectiveness in teaching English as a second or foreign language or as a medium of instruction, and student achievement.
> (retrieved from: http://www.tirfonline.org/AboutTIRF/pages/callforproposals.html)

All of the above point to a great momentum for studies about NNS teachers. Although the need has probably always been there, the interest has only recently appeared. Unfortunately, many authors still have difficulties finding widely read publication channels to disseminate their studies, which lie hidden as 'unpublished manuscripts' (see Braine, this volume). Thus, important findings remain unknown to the research and language educational community. Another limitation thus far is the fact that research on the topic has been conducted mainly in North America. One of the necessary conditions of research on NNS issues is that it should take into account the specific characteristics of the local setting where the teaching will take place. The local component determines to what extent and in what way being a NNS teacher may affect a language teacher's identity. More work is needed that takes into consideration the relevance of the local context in any analysis of the implications of being a NNS language teacher, thus moving from global perspectives to locally meaningful settings. With the exception of Medgyes' work, very few authors have seriously dealt with NNS teachers in EFL contexts. This volume's aim is therefore twofold: it helps to disseminate research about NNS teachers, and it also fills a gap by bringing in research conducted in EFL settings, such as the Basque Country, Brazil, Catalonia, Hungary, Israel, and Sweden, in addition to some innovative research in the more deeply studied ESL contexts.

## 2. OVERVIEW OF THE VOLUME

This book contains 14 more chapters, which are organized in five sections that attempt to deal with NNS teachers from a range of different perspectives. The first section provides a set of introductory works by George Braine and Marko Modiano. Braine, from his position as the initial driving force in the constitution of the *TESOL Caucus on non-native English speaking teachers* (NNESTs) and the editor of an influential volume (Braine, 1999), writes a historical review of research on NNS teachers, structured around the two main approaches in existing research: self-perceptions of NNS teachers, and students' perceptions of NNS teachers. Braine's critical review of recent research about NNS teachers concludes with the acknowledgment of an emerging recognition of studies in this area, which he states is becoming a *global phenomenon*, and the identification of a paradoxical finding that appears in most of the reviewed studies: the realisation of NNSs' lower proficiency in English is combined with the increase in appreciation of NNS teachers' characteristics by students who have had longer contact with those teachers.

Braine's chapter is followed by Modiano's account of the impact of the increasing role of English as an international language in the language teaching profession. Modiano is a NSs of English who is based in a northern European EFL setting (*i.e.*, Sweden), in which a vast majority of citizens can speak English (81% of the population, according to data published in the *Eurobarometer 54 on Europeans and languages* - INRA, 2001), and where this language is becoming increasingly present in everyday life, and more specially in academic life (see Phillipson & Skutnabb-Kangas, 1999, for an account of how English is penetrating domains in Scandinavia that used to belong to national languages). Modiano develops a coherent account of cultural studies in the light of the role of English as a Lingua Franca. He compares NNS teachers who are 'supportive of the NS norm' with those who are committed to the promotion of English as a lingua franca (pages 25-43). Taking Sweden as an example, Modiano argues that models of English in Europe are evolving from NS-dominated to linguafranca-oriented. Although, this shift may be partially impeded by the slowness of educational materials to adapt, change is in progress, and the increasing influence of cultural studies programs can facilitate NNSs to embrace the notion of English as the European (and global) lingua franca.

The second section of the volume is devoted to aspects of language teaching, with a look at NNSs' performance in language classrooms. The four contributions in this section range from the more theoretical (Cook, Macaro) to the more experiential/experimental (Cots & Díaz, McNeill).

Cook builds on his previous work on multi-competence (Cook, 1991) and on the idea of the *L2 user* (Cook, 2002) as opposed to the *L2 learner*, more traditionally used in applied linguistics. His chapter presents the main characteristics of L2 users, as opposed to native speakers, and the implications of these characteristics for language teaching, emphasizing the unique contribution NNS teachers can make to language teaching in their undisputable condition of L2 users.

Chapter 5 takes one of the aspects considered in Cook's paper and looks into it in a more detailed manner. Ernesto Macaro builds his text around the following eight questions:

- Why is codeswitching in the L2 classroom such a contentious issue?
- Is codeswitching contentious as classroom behaviour just for the teacher or also for the learners?
- What do language teachers think of the practice of codeswitching?
- For what purposes (or communicative functions) do language teachers codeswitch and how much codeswitching goes on?
- What do learners think about teachers codeswitching during lessons?
- What are the effects of codeswitching or not codeswitching on classroom interaction?
- What are the effects of not codeswitching on the learner's strategy development?
- Can codeswitching be a systematic, principled and planned part of the L2 curriculum?

Macaro's questions explore the uses of codeswitching in the L2 classroom from a wide range of perspectives. Four questions concern the diverse attitudes towards codeswitching in the classroom, whereas three more questions are about the causes and consequences of codeswitching. Finally, the last question comes as a conclusion, indicating some guidelines for the use of codeswitching in the classroom, which according to Macaro, should not be used in a random or haphazard fashion, but restricted by clearly articulated principles, since otherwise L1 use might become 'a discourse carried out entirely in L1 with only a marginal reference to the L2' (page 72).

The use of functional linguistics to account for classroom performance is the link between Macaro's chapter and Cots & Díaz's micro-analysis of six classes taught by different teachers: four NNSs and two NSs. In chapter 6, Cots & Díaz open an innovative perspective by applying standard discourse analysis tools to the study of NNS teachers' classroom performance. The authors look into the six lessons to find out how teachers construct social relationships and how they convey linguistic knowledge discursively. In their analysis, social relationships are built through power strategies and solidarity strategies, whereas linguistic knowledge can be conveyed through categorical knowledge strategies and non-categorical knowledge strategies. A parallel analysis is carried out on the use made by different teachers of personal pronouns (*i.e.* I, you, we) and the verbs that are used after each of these pronouns.

If, as we said above, chapter 6 represents an innovative attempt to apply standard discourse analysis procedures to the study of NNS teachers, the next paper contributes to the field with a quantitative study comparing NS and NNS teachers' capacity to predict learners' vocabulary difficulties in reading texts, as well as the effect of expertise in developing this capacity. In chapter 7, McNeill presents a study involving sixty-five teachers, divided into four groups according to nativeness and expertise, which were asked to identify difficult vocabulary, and contrasted their answers to the actual results obtained by students in a vocabulary test, thus empirically establishing which group of teachers was better at predicting vocabulary difficulty.

Teachers-in-training are considered in section three. Although the three papers in this section deal with TESOL students in North American graduate programs, the perspectives are rather different. Llurda, in chapter 8, presents the results of a survey conducted among practicum supervisors in graduate TESOL programs. The survey was conducted with thirty-two supervisors from a wide variety of institutions. Based on their experience observing student teachers in the practicum, supervisors had to respond to questions regarding their language skills and teaching skills. One of the main findings in the study is that it is very difficult to characterise all NNSs as a single group given the wide range of variation in language skills of NNSs attending graduate TESOL programs. It is claimed that such variation is at the heart of the problems experienced by NNS teachers in asserting their status as competent language teachers.

In contrast to the overview of TESOL student teachers given by Llurda, Liu opts for an intensive approximation to the experiences of four Chinese Graduate Teaching Assistants teaching freshman composition, with the particularity that their students are native speakers. In Chapter 9, Liu refers to some of the fundamental topics in research about NNS teachers: teachers' own perceptions towards their teaching; the challenges and difficulties encountered by NNS teachers; the problem of establishing credibility as NNS teachers; the strategies for teaching; and students' perspectives. Liu advocates establishing support networks, and facilitating peer mentoring, as possible ways to help NNS student teachers cope with such potentially stressful situations as the teaching of composition to NSs.

In Derwing & Munro's contribution, their experience as teacher educators in two TESOL programs in Canada is outlined. They adopt a pragmatic view that allows them to consider teacher education requirements regardless of their students' native or non-native status. They point to the challenge created by 'the wide variation in English proficiency' among their students, both native and nonnative. The authors identify some aspects that are important for ensuring the preservice teachers' success, such as language proficiency, personality, past experiences of the cooperating teacher, gender, cultural background of ESL students, and the hosting school characteristics. Derwing & Munro thus present a set of practical reflections that should be kept in mind by coordinators of TESOL programs in North America with both NS and NNS students.

Although students' preferences have been repeatedly cited as the reason why many school administrators prefer to hire NS teachers over NNSs, to our knowledge no studies had been conducted examining students' attitudes towards NNS teachers until recently. It was as though researchers felt they already knew what the result would be, and so there was no need to conduct such research. Only very recently some researchers started eliciting students' views (Cheung, 2002; Lasagabaster & Sierra, 2002; Liang, 2002; Moussu, 2002). Somehow, section 4 of this book further covers this inexplicable gap in research, as it focuses exclusively on students' perceptions of NNS teachers.

In chapter 11, Eszter Benke & Péter Medgyes present the results of a survey among Hungarian students regarding their perception of their NNS teachers. The authors point to several advantages and disadvantages of both native and non-native teachers, which confirm previous statements by Medgyes (1994), such as NNSs' advantage in grammar teaching and—in EFL settings—their greater familiarity with the local educational environment. On the other hand, NNS teachers seem to be more prone to use the students' L1 in class, which is often perceived as a disadvantage. The authors warn readers of the complexity of the picture and the high degree of variability among different students' preferences

Chapter 12 presents David Lasagabaster and Juan Manuel Sierra's study questioning Basque students about their preferences with regard to native or non-native teachers. The results of their closed questionnaire tend to confirm that EFL students have a preference for NS teachers over NNSs, but they also show that a combination of NSs and NNSs is even more appreciated. Some interesting differences among students of different ages can be observed, as university students seem to be more inclined towards NS teachers than younger students. The authors also conducted an open questionnaire, in which students had to indicate the main pros and cons they would associate with native and non-native teachers. Responses support previous statements, particularly those made by Medgyes (1994) in his characterisation of the bright and the dark sides of being a NNS teacher, and are therefore consistent with the findings reported in Benke & Medgyes' chapter.

Chapter 13 aims at the same type of question but employs a very different methodology. Instead of questioning a wide number of students about their preferences, Dorota Pacek has chosen to conduct a case study with two groups of international students taking ESL classes in a British university. Of particular relevance is the observation that the attitudes of many students towards their NNS teacher evolved positively as the course advanced and students gradually became used to the teacher.

The last section of the book is devoted to NNS teachers' self-perceptions. Although this is probably the most extensively developed area of study in NNS teacher research (see, for example: Reves & Medgyes, 1994; Liu, 1999; Llurda & Huguet, 2003), Ofra Inbar-Lourie and Kanavilil Rajagopalan offer two original approaches. In chapter 14, Inbar-Lourie explores the self and perceived identities of EFL teachers and places her study within a social-psychological framework. EFL teachers had to 'ascribe themselves as NSs or NNSs of English' and specify whether they thought other teachers and students perceived them to be NSs or NNSs. Students were also asked about their teachers' identities as NS or NNSs. A gap was found between self and perceived identities, showing that EFL teachers find it natural to function in a multi-identity reality that is accepted as a natural part of their professional life.

The book concludes with a look at NNS teachers' anxieties. In a study involving Brazilian teachers, Rajagopalan analyses the causes underlying negative self-perceptions by NNS teachers', and proposes a 'pedagogy of empowerment' that will help NNS teachers 'overcome their lack of self-confidence'. Rajagopalan's paper brings us back to the point of departure in this book, as he links his discussion to the present role of English as an international language.

It is the intention of this volume to provide readers with a broader understanding of what it means to teach a language that is not the teacher's L1. One of the premises is that NNS teachers are ideally endowed with the capacity to teach a language that belongs to the wide community of its speakers worldwide. Most contributors to this volume have openly committed to the establishment of NNSs as legitimate language teachers. In addition, this book also gives clues that may ultimately help identify NNS teachers' qualities, improve teacher training programs, and guide administrators in their selection of the best possible teachers for a given setting.

## 3.    REFERENCES

Bailey, K. M. (2001). Teacher preparation and development. *TESOL Quarterly, 35* (4), 609-611.

Ballard, B. (1996). Through language to learning: Preparing overseas students for study in Western universities. In H. Coleman (Ed.), *Society and the language classroom.* Cambridge: Cambridge University Press. 148-168.

Braine, G. (Ed.) (1999). *Non-native educators in English language teaching.* Mahwah, NJ: Lawrence Erlbaum Associates.

Cheung, Y.L. (2002). The attitude of university students in Hong Kong towards native and non-native teachers of English. Unpublished M. Phil. thesis. The Chinese University of Hong Kong, Hong Kong.

Cook, V.J. (1991). The poverty-of-the-stimulus argument and multi-competence. *Second Language Research, 7* (2), 103-117.

Cook, V.J. (Ed.) (2002). *Portraits of the L2 user.* Clevedon: Multilingual Matters.

Cortazzi, M. & Jin, L. (1996). Cultures of learning: Language classrooms in China. In H. Coleman (Ed.), *Society and the language classroom.* Cambridge: Cambridge University Press. 169-206.

Holliday, A. (1994). *Appropriate methodology and social context.* Cambridge: Cambridge University Press.

Holliday, A. (1996). Large- and small-class cultures in Egyptian university classrooms. A cultural justification for curriculum change. In H. Coleman (Ed.), *Society and the language classroom.* Cambridge: Cambridge University Press. 86-104.

INRA (2001). *Eurobarometer 54 special: Europeans and languages.* A report produced for The Education and Culture Directorate-General.

Lasagabaster, D. & Sierra, J.M. (2002). University students' perceptions of native and non-native speaker teachers of English. *Language Awareness, 11* (2), 132-142.

Liang, K. (2002). English as a second language (ESL) students' attitudes towards non-native English-speaking teachers' accentedness. Unpublished M.A. thesis. California State University, Los Angeles, CA.

Liu, J. (1999). Non-native-English-speaking professionals in TESOL. *TESOL Quarterly, 33* (1), 85-102.

Llurda, E. & Huguet, A. (2003). Self-awareness in NNS EFL primary and secondary school teachers. *Language Awareness, 12* (3&4), 220-233.

Medgyes, P. (1994). *The non-native teacher.* London: Macmillan. (1999) 2nd edition. Ismaning: Max Hueber Verlag.

Moussu, L. (2002). English as a second language: Students' reactions to non-native English speaking teachers. Unpublished M.A. thesis. Brigham Young University, Utah.

Phillipson, R. & Skutnabb-Kangas, T. (1999). Englishisation: One dimension of globalisation. *AILA Review, 13,* 19-36.

Reves, T. & Medgyes, P. (1994). The non-native English speaking EFL/ESL teacher's self-image: An international survey. *System, 22* (3), 353-367.

Seidlhofer, B. (2000). Mind the gap: English as a mother tongue vs. English as a lingua franca. *Views (Vienna English Working Papers), 9* (1), 51-68.

Seidlhofer, B. (2001). Closing a conceptual gap: The case for a description of English as a lingua franca. *International Journal of Applied Linguistics, 11* (2), 133-158.

PART I

# SETTING UP THE STAGE: NON-NATIVE
# TEACHERS IN THE TWENTY-FIRST CENTURY

Chapter 2

# A HISTORY OF RESEARCH ON NON-NATIVE SPEAKER ENGLISH TEACHERS

GEORGE BRAINE
*The Chinese University of Hong Kong*

## 1.      INTRODUCTION

Research on the self-perceptions of non-native speaker (NNS) English teachers, or the way they are perceived by their students is a fairly recent phenomenon. This may be due to the sensitive nature of these issues because NNS teachers were generally regarded as unequal in knowledge and performance to NS teachers of English, and issues relating to NNS teachers may have also been politically incorrect to be studied and discussed openly.

Despite the pioneering work of Medgyes (1992, 1994), it took nearly a decade for more research to emerge on the issues relating to NNS English teachers. In fact, there has been a surge of such studies recently, partly as a result of the establishment of the Non-native English Speakers' Caucus in the TESOL organization in 1999 (see Braine, 1999, or go to http://nnest.moussu.net/ for more information on the Caucus). At the recently concluded TESOL 2003 conference in Baltimore, USA, more than 20 presentations included the acronym NNS in their titles, and most of these presentations were made by NNS English teachers themselves. This not only indicates that NNS English teachers appear to have a powerful new voice through the Caucus, but also that they are no longer reluctant to openly acknowledge themselves as NNS speakers.

A movement in an educational context could be relevant and popular, but it cannot grow without the backing of sound research and pedagogy. The purpose of this opening chapter is to critically examine the recent studies on

E. Llurda (Ed.), *Non-Native Language Teachers. Perceptions, Challenges and Contributions to the Profession*, 13—23.

NNS English teachers. One characteristic of these studies is that they have been conducted mainly by NNS researchers. Another is that only a few have covered students' attitudes and preferences—probably the most crucial factor in the study of NNS teachers. A third characteristic is that these studies have been conducted in both ESL and EFL contexts. Because most of these studies were conducted for the purpose of Masters' theses or doctoral dissertations, most are yet to be published.

This chapter will describe the objectives, methodologies, and findings of the following studies: Reves & Medgyes (1994), Samimy & Brutt-Griffler (1999), Inbar-Lourie (2001), Llurda & Huguet (2003), Moussou (2002), Liang (2002), Cheung (2002), and Mahboob (2003). Based on their objectives, the studies have been classified into two categories: self-perceptions of NNS teachers and students' perceptions of NNS teachers. Although every effort has been made to examine all recent studies on NNS English teachers, some may have not been included for the obvious reason that many theses and dissertations are difficult to access because they remain unpublished.

## 2.      SELF-PERCEPTIONS OF NNS ENGLISH TEACHERS

No review of research into NNS English teachers could begin without reference to Péter Medgyes, himself a non-native speaker, who appears to be the first to have brought the issues concerning NNS English teachers to the open. His two articles in the *ELT Journal* titled 'The schizophrenic teacher' (1983) and 'Native or non-native: who's worth more?' (1992), were also the forerunners of his groundbreaking book *The Non-native Teacher* (first published by Macmillan in 1994 and reissued by Hueber in 1999), in which Medgyes mixed research with his own experience as a NNS English teacher and first-hand observations of other NNS teachers, and boldly discussed previously untouched topics that would be considered controversial even today: 'natives and non-natives in opposite trenches,' 'the dark side of being a non-native', 'and who's worth more: the native or the non-native'. Medgyes also advanced four hypotheses based on his assumption that NS and NNS English teachers are 'two different species' (p. 25). The hypotheses were that the NS and NNS teachers differ in terms of (1) language proficiency, and (2) teaching practice (behavior), that (3) most of the differences in teaching practice can be attributed to the discrepancy in language proficiency, and that (4) both types of teachers can be equally good teachers on their own terms.

Reves & Medgyes (1994) was the result of an international survey of 216 NS and NNS English teachers from 10 countries (Brazil, former Czechoslovakia, Hungary, Israel, Mexico, Nigeria, Russia, Sweden, Yugoslavia, and Zimbabwe). The objective was to examine the following hypothesis: NS and NNS English teachers differ in terms of their teaching practice (behaviors); these differences in teaching practice are mainly due to their differing levels of language proficiency, and their knowledge of these differences affects the NNS teachers' 'self-perception and teaching attitudes' (p. 354). The questionnaire consisted of 23 items of which 18 were addressed to both NSs and NNSs and five to NNSs only. Most of the questions were closed-ended and meant to elicit personal information of the subjects and their teaching contexts. The open-ended questions were meant to elicit the subjects' self-perceptions and their opinions relating to the three hypotheses. The overwhelming majority of the subjects, by their own admission, were NNSs of English. In their responses, 68% of the subjects perceived differences in the teaching practices of NS and NNS teachers. Eighty-four percent of the NNS subjects admitted to having various language difficulties, vocabulary and fluency being the most common areas followed by speaking, pronunciation, and listening comprehension. Only 25% of the subjects stated that their language difficulties had no adverse effect on their teaching. In view of these findings, Reves & Medgyes (1994) suggest that 'frequent exposure to authentic native language environments and proficiency-oriented in-service training activities' (p. 364) might improve the language difficulties of NNS teachers. Further, in order to enhance the self-perception of these teachers, they should be made aware of their advantageous condition as language teachers.

In their research, Samimy & Brutt-Griffler (1999) applied the Reves & Medgyes (1994) approach to survey and interview 17 NNS graduate students who were either pursuing a MA or Ph.D. in TESOL at a university in the United States. Their students, referred to as 'rather sophisticated group of non-native speakers of English' (p. 134) by the researchers, were from Korea, Japan, Turkey, Surinam, China, Togo, Burkina Faso, and Russia. In addition to using a questionnaire to collect quantitative data, Samimy & Brutt-Griffler also gathered qualitative data through classroom discussions, in-depth interviews, and analysis of autobiographical writings of the subjects. The aims of the study were to determine how these graduate students perceived themselves as professionals in the field of English language teaching, if they thought there were differences in the teaching behaviors of NSs and NNSs, what these differences were, and if they felt handicapped as NNS English teachers. Responding to the questionnaire, more than two thirds of the subjects admitted that their difficulties with the language affected their teaching from 'a little' to 'very much'. Nearly 90% of the subjects perceived a difference between NS and NNS teachers of English. They identified the former group as being informal, fluent, accurate, using different techniques, methods, and approaches, being flexible, using conversational English, knowing subtleties of the language, using authentic English, providing positive feedback to students, and having communication (not exam preparation) as the goals of their teaching. NNS English teachers were perceived as relying on textbooks, applying differences between the first and second languages, using the first language as a medium of instruction, being aware of negative transfer and psychological aspects of learning, being sensitive to the needs of students, being more efficient, knowing the students' background, and having exam preparation as the goal of their teaching. However, they did not consider the NS teachers superior to their NNS counterparts. The differences in the teaching practices of NS and NNS teachers, as stated by the subjects of this study, could be attributed to contrasting sociocultural factors embedded in Western and Asian societies. Whereas Reves & Medgyes (1994) focus on the differing levels of language proficiency and their effects on teaching practices, the differing teaching practices identified by Samimy & Brutt-Griffler (1999) may be attributed to cross-cultural differences.

The third study of the self-perceptions of NNS English teachers was conducted by Ofra Inbar-Lourie at Tel Aviv University in Israel, in one of the first studies at doctoral-level on NNSs' issues. Titled 'Native and non-native English teachers: investigation of the construct and perceptions', Inbar-Lourie's (2001) study, conducted in two phases, set out to investigate why some teachers in Israel perceived themselves as NS of English, and the effects of the native versus non-native distinction on the pedagogical perceptions of the teachers. In the second phase of the study, which is more relevant to the topic of this chapter, Inbar-Lourie specifically sought to discover if there were differences in perceptions between teachers who claim to be NS of English and those who do not, with regard to the following factors: differences between NS and NNS English teachers; the teaching and status of the English language; English teaching in Israel; and English teaching and assessment methods. Further, Inbar-Lourie also sought to determine the effect of personal and professional background variables on the pedagogical perceptions of the teachers regarding the above issues.

In the first phase, data was gathered through a self-report questionnaire distributed to 102 English teachers in Israel. In the second phase, self-report questionnaires were distributed to 264 English teachers (93 NSs and 171 NNSs) followed by semi-structured interviews with nine teachers. Results from the first phase indicated that the teachers' native speaker identity could be explained by nine variables, two of which could best predict this identity:

having spoken English from the age of 0 to 6, and others' perception of them as native speakers of English. Results from the second phase of the study indicated that differences between NS and NNS teachers could be detected only in some categories, mainly the superiority of the NS teachers (as espoused by the NS teachers themselves), the degree of confidence in teaching specific language areas, and in student-teacher relations. No differences were found in perception categories relating to teaching and assessment practices, defining students' knowledge of English, the status of the English language, and goals of teaching English. In fact, perception differences in these areas arose not from the teachers' status as NS or NNS but from personal and professional variables such as country of birth, length of residence in the country, school level, and perceived type of school. NNS teachers reported having better relations with students and feeling more confident in using the L1 to facilitate teaching. Interviews with nine teachers confirmed the results from the self-reports.

In a more recent study, Llurda & Huguet (2003) investigated the self-awareness of 101 non-native English teachers in primary and secondary schools in a Spanish city. Through a set questionnaire (partially inspired by Medgyes, 1994) administered orally in one-on-one interviews with the subjects, the researchers aimed to determine how the subjects perceived their own language skills, how these skills affected their teaching, and how the skills had evolved over time; the subjects' teaching ideology as expressed through their preferences for designing a language course and their goals as language teachers; and the subjects' position in the NS-NNS debate, specifically with regard to the preference for NSs or NNSs as language teachers, and the need for cultural knowledge on the part of English teachers.

Although the research approach was qualitative, Llurda & Huguet relied heavily on statistics in the analysis of their data. In the case of language skills, they found that the secondary teachers showed more confidence in their skills than primary teachers, especially in general proficiency, grammar, knowledge of grammatical rules, and reading comprehension. Although primary teachers admitted that they did experience certain difficulties in teaching English, they did not attribute these difficulties to their proficiency in English. As for language improvement over time, the primary teachers displayed a greater awareness of their language improvement and believed that this improvement came through conscious study of the language.

In terms of language courses and language teaching goals, the majority of primary teachers (81.6%) chose communicative functions and topics as the foundations for language courses. Only half the secondary teachers did so, although more of them (38.1%) opted for language structures and habit creation than their primary counterparts. In the case of teaching goals, almost all the primary teachers (97.2%) preferred communicative strategies, while only two-thirds of the secondary teachers did so.

In the NS or NNS debate, the primary teachers appeared to be more influenced by the native speaker fallacy, half of them stating that they would hire more NSs than NNSs for a language school, although the other primary teachers did state that they would hire equal numbers of NS and NNS teachers. As for secondary teachers, nearly two thirds chose the balanced option of hiring teachers from both groups. In fact, most of the secondary teachers (65.6%) believed that being a NNS was an advantage. As for the need for cultural knowledge, the teachers clearly preferred British culture, with situations involving the English language being closely associated with British NS.

## 3.      STUDENTS' PERCEPTIONS OF NNS ENGLISH TEACHERS

The research described so far has focused on the self-perceptions of NNS English teachers. Research on students' perceptions of these teachers, as crucial as the self-perceptions if not greater, has a more recent history. One of the first studies in this area was by Lucie Moussu, whose M.A. thesis at Brigham Young University, USA, was titled 'English as a second language students' reactions to non-native English-speaking teachers' (2002). Moussu's research questions were as follows: (1) What feelings and expectations did the students have at first when taught by NNS English teachers, and why? (2) What other variables (such as gender, age, first language, etc.) influence the students' perceptions of their NNS teachers at the beginning of the semester? (3) How do the variables of time and exposure to NNS teachers influence the students' perceptions of their teachers?

Moussu's subjects were four NNS English teachers from Japan, Argentina, Ecuador, and Switzerland, and 84 ESL students above the age of 17, both males and females, from 21 different countries. All the students were enrolled in an intensive English program attached to a US university. The students responded to two questionnaires, one given the first day of class the second given fourteen weeks later on the last day of class. Over the 14-week semester, three separate sets of interviews were also conducted with six students. Analysis of the data shows that from the beginning of the semester, the students had positive attitudes towards their NNS teachers. For instance, 68% of the students said that they could learn English just as well from a non-native speaker as from a native speaker, and 79% expressed admiration and respect for their non-native speaker teachers, and as many as

84% of the students expected their class with a such a teacher to be a positive experience. The Korean and Chinese students expressed negative feelings toward their NNS teachers more frequently than other students. Time and exposure to the teachers only made their opinions more positive by the end of the semester. For instance, to the question 'Would you encourage a friend to take a class with this non-native English-speaking teacher?' only 56% of the students had answered 'yes' at the beginning of the semester. By the end of the semester, 76% had answered 'yes' to the same question.

Kristy Liang's Master's research (2002) at California State University, Los Angeles, also investigated students' attitudes towards NNS English teachers. Specifically, the study was designed to investigate 20 ESL students' attitudes towards six ESL teachers' accents and the features of these teachers' speech that contribute to the students' preference for teachers. Five of the teachers were NNSs from different language backgrounds and the other was a NS.

The students listened to brief audio recordings delivered by the six NNS English teachers and rated and ranked the teachers' accents according to a scale of preference. Data was collected through questionnaires which included information on the students' background, their beliefs about teaching, and their ranking and preferences. The results showed that, although the students rated pronunciation/accent in the ESL teachers' speech as very important, pronunciation/accent did not affect the students' attitudes towards their previous NNS English teachers in their home countries. In fact, the students held generally positive attitudes toward the teachers in their home countries, and believed that pronunciation/accent was not as relevant as it appeared in the first place. Further, personal and professional features as derived from the teachers' speech, such as 'being interesting', 'being prepared', 'being qualified', and 'being professional', played a role in the students' preference for teachers. In conclusion, Liang (2002) suggests that, instead of focusing on ESL teachers' ethnic and language background, the discussion on NNS English teachers should focus on their level of professionalism.

So far, what has been missing is an investigation of both teachers and students in a single study, and Cheung (2002) filled this need with her Masters' research conducted at The Chinese University of Hong Kong. Cheung's objectives were to determine the attitudes of the university students in Hong Kong towards NS and NNS teachers of English, the strengths and weaknesses of these teachers from the perspective of students, and their capability of motivating the students to learn English. She also attempted to determine if there was any discrimination against NNS English teachers in Hong Kong.

Cheung triangulated her data collection with the use of questionnaires, interviews, classroom observations, and post-classroom interviews. The questionnaire was distributed to 420 randomly selected undergraduates from a variety of majors at seven universities in Hong Kong. Most of the students (98%) were Cantonese or Putonghua speakers, and 99% of them had learned English either in Hong Kong or China. Ten students from three universities, were also interviewed. In an unusual approach, Cheung also sought the opinions of twenty-two university English teachers, ranging from head of department to instructor, at six universities. A majority of these teachers were expatriates with about 60% being NS of English. Nearly 90% had been resident in Hong Kong for more than 6 years. The results showed that both students and teachers saw NS and NNS teachers having their respective strengths. A high proficiency in English, ability to use English functionally, and the awareness of the cultures of English speaking countries were the strengths observed in NS teachers. In the case of NNS teachers, the ability to empathize with students as fellow second language learners, a shared cultural background, and the emphasis they placed on grammar were seen as their strengths. As for teacher competency, both students and teachers stated that teachers should be well-informed about the English language, able to make learning relevant and fun, good at motivating students, able to encourage independent learning and thinking, sensitive and responsive to students' needs, and able to respect students as individuals with their own aspirations. Not all students and teachers were of the opinion that there was discrimination against NNS English teachers in Hong Kong.

All the studies of students' perceptions of NNS English teachers described so far have been conducted at the Masters' level. The only doctoral research into this issue was just completed by Ahmar Mahboob (2003) at the Indiana University in Bloomington, USA, under the title 'Status of non-native English teachers as ESL teachers in the USA'. Mahboob's study was conducted in two phases. First, using a questionnaire, he examined the hiring practices of the administrators of 118 college-level adult English language programs, the demographics of the English teachers in these programs, and the demographics of the students enrolled in the programs. Mahboob found that the number of NNS teachers teaching ESL in the United States is low (only 7.9% of the teachers employed at these programs), and that this low figure is disproportionate to the high number of NNS graduate students enrolled in MA TESOL and similar teacher-education programs. Mahboob attributes the low figure to the preference given by most (59.8%) program administrators to 'native English speakers' in hiring practices.

The second phase of Mahboob's study is more relevant to this chapter because it examined students' perceptions of NNS teachers. Instead of using questionnaires to survey the students, Mahboob used the novel and more insightful 'discourse-analytic' technique, asking 32 students enrolled in an intensive English program to provide written responses to a cue that solicited their opinions on NS and NNS language teachers. The student essays were coded individually by four readers who in turn classified the students' comments according to linguistic factors (oral skills, literacy skills, grammar, vocabulary, culture), teaching styles (ability to answer questions, teaching methodology), and personal factors (experience as an ESL learner, hard work, affect). The analysis of these comments showed that both NS and NNS teachers received positive and negative comments. In the case of NS teachers, the majority of positive comments related to oral skills, with vocabulary and culture also being viewed positively. Negative comments on NS teachers related to grammar, experience as an ESL learner, ability to answer questions, and methodology. In the case of NNS teachers, experience as an ESL learner earned the most number of positive comments, followed by grammar, affect, oral skills, methodology, hard work, vocabulary, culture, ability to answer questions, and literacy skills. NNS teachers received negative comments with regard to oral skills and culture.

## 4.    CONCLUSION

The most obvious factor to emerge from the above description of research is that issues relating to NNS English teachers have now become a legitimate area of research. As noted at the beginning of this chapter, despite the pioneering work of Medgyes in the early 1990s, studies on these issues began to be published in the United States only a decade later. The gap may be due to the fact that Medgyes' research was published in a journal which is not widely read in the US, and that his book *The non-native teacher* was published only in the UK and was difficult to obtain in the US until it was reprinted by another publisher.

Although the influence of Medgyes on issues relating to NNS English teachers is in the area of teachers' self-perceptions, his research has stood the test of time and will form the benchmark for many more studies to come. More recently, he has also embarked on the study of NNS teachers' classroom behavior (Árva & Medgyes, 2000 and learners' observations of the differences in teaching behaviour of NS and NNS teachers (Benke & Medgyes, this volume) that are bound to become models for future research.

As mentioned earlier, the study of NNS English teachers is a global phenomenon. The research itself has been conducted in Asia (Hong Kong and Israel), Europe (Hungary and Spain), and North America (USA). The

English teachers who have been the subjects of the research have come from no less than 20 countries worldwide, including Africa and South America. In the future, researchers from more countries will be drawn to such studies, and English teachers from more countries will become research subjects. It will be a healthy trend.

An unmistakable characteristic of the studies described in this chapter is that they have all been conducted by NNSs. This, no doubt, is an indication of the empowerment of these researchers, who are no longer hesitant to acknowledge themselves as NNSs and venture into previously uncharted territory. On the other hand, research by NNSs on issues that are critical to themselves may cast a shadow of doubt on the validity and reliability of the data. It must be pointed out that most of these researchers had not removed themselves, as they should have, from the data gathering process. Instead, some had designed and distributed the questionnaires, conducted interviews, and analyzed the data by themselves. When a NNS teacher questions NNS students on preferences for teachers, the responses are likely to be favorable to NNSs. Likewise, when a NNS asks a NS sensitive questions regarding NNS issues, the responses could be more politically correct than accurate.

So, what does the research reveal? The research on self-perceptions, spanning over a decade, indicates that NNS English teachers from more than 20 nationalities and even more L1 backgrounds acknowledge that they are NNSs of English, and that differences exist between themselves and NS teachers in terms of language proficiency and teaching behavior. Many of these NNS teachers also affirm that this (lower) proficiency in English exerts an adverse effect on their teaching. As far as students are concerned, they appear to be largely tolerant of the differences between their NS and NNS teachers, including accent. In fact, evidence suggests that students become more tolerant and supportive of NNS teachers the longer they are taught by these teachers.

In the case of students' perceptions, one factor deserves careful attention in future research. That is, how do students define NS and NNS? Anecdotal evidence suggests that, from some students' viewpoint, all Caucasians (including Finns, Germans, Russians, and Swedes, for instance) are NS of English. Other students, especially Asian-Americans, may not consider American-born Asians to be native speakers of English simply because they are not Caucasian. Hence, when pilot testing questionnaires for use in survey research, or when planning interviews, researchers should ensure that their student informants have a reasonable understanding of the terms NS and NNS.

The relative merits of NS and NNS English teachers have been extensively discussed by, among others, Davies (1991), Widdowson (1994), Boyle (1997), Cook (1999). As the power of the English language spreads, more and more English teachers will be needed. They will continue to outnumber their NS counterparts simply because the vast majority of English users are NNSs. The supply of NS English teachers, especially those willing to teach under difficult conditions for a meager salary, is limited. Especially in foreign language contexts, the teaching of English may become the exclusive domain of NNSs in time to come.

# 5.    REFERENCES

Árva, V. & Medgyes, P. (2000). Native and non-native teachers in the classroom. *System, 28* (3), 355-372.

Boyle, J. (1997). Imperialism and the English language in Hong Kong. *Journal of Multilingual and Multicultural Development, 18* (2), 91-104.

Braine, G. (1999). *Non-native educators in English language teaching.* Mahwah, NJ: Lawrence Erlbaum Associates.

Cheung, Y.L. (2002). The attitude of university students in Hong Kong towards native and non-native teachers of English. Unpublished M. Phil. thesis. The Chinese University of Hong Kong, Hong Kong.

Cook, V. (1999). Going beyond the native speakers in language teaching. *TESOL Quarterly, 33* (2), 185-209.

Davies, A. (1991). *The native speaker in applied linguistics.* Edinburgh: Edinburgh University Press.

Inbar-Lourie, O. (1999). The native speaker construct: Investigation by perceptions. Unpublished doctoral dissertation. Tel-Aviv University, Tel-Aviv, Israel.

Liang, K. (2002). English as a second language (ESL) students' attitudes towards non-native English-speaking teachers' accentedness. Unpublished M.A. thesis. California State University, Los Angeles, CA.

Llurda, E. & Huguet, A. (2003) Self-awareness in NNS EFL primary and secondary school teachers. *Language Awareness, 12* (3&4), 220-233.

Mahboob, A. (2003). Status of non-native English speaking teachers in the United States. Unpublished Ph.D. Dissertation. Indiana University, Bloomington, IN.

Medgyes, P. (1983). The schizophrenic teacher. *ELT Journal, 37* (1), 2-6.

Medgyes, P. (1992). Native or non-native: who's worth more? *ELT Journal, 46* (4), 340-349.

Medgyes, P. (1994). *The non-native teacher.* London: Macmillan. (1999) 2nd edition. Ismaning: Max Hueber Verlag.

Moussu, L. (2002). English as a second language students' reactions to non-native English speaking teachers. Unpublished M.A. thesis. Brigham Young University, Utah.

Reves, T. & Medgyes, P. (1994). The non-native English speaking EFL/ESL teacher's self image: An international survey. *System, 22* (3), 353-367.

Samimy, K. & Brutt-Griffler, J. (1999). To be a native or non-native speaker: Perceptions of 'non-native' students in a graduate TESOL program. In G. Braine (Ed.), *Non-native educators in English language teaching.* Mahwah, NJ: Lawrence Erlbaum. 127-144.

Widdowson, H. (1994). The ownership of English. *TESOL Quarterly, 28* (2), 377-389.

Chapter 3

# CULTURAL STUDIES, FOREIGN LANGUAGE TEACHING AND LEARNING PRACTICES, AND THE NNS PRACTITIONER

MARKO MODIANO
*Gävle University*

## 1.    INTRODUCTION

Jenkins (2000), in her discussions of English as an International Language (EIL), approaches 'mutual phonological intelligibility' from the perspective of the non-native speaker (NNS). Critiquing traditional ELT, Jenkins notes that conventional programs 'involve elements that are unnecessary, unrealistic, and, at worst, harmful for preparing teachers to equip their learners with pronunciation skills appropriate to an international use of English' (2000, 1). Her focus is on the cross-cultural aspects of English language usage among non-native speakers. Moreover, Jenkins establishes a basis, not only for the legitimization of non-native norms for pronunciation, but also for English language teaching and learning practices which are lingua franca oriented. Here we see the first signs of an important break with conventional ELT ideologies and practices.

Seidlhofer, also skeptical of traditional views of ELT, is concerned that some English instructors 'have interpreted their task . . . as that of getting their students to ape native speakers as faithfully as possible, or rehearsing them in patterns of native-speaker behaviour, with all the cultural baggage that comes with this unquestioned, even unnoticed' (1999, 237). Unfortunately, those who advocate the replacement of traditional ELT practices and educational standards with an EIL or Euro-English framework

E. Llurda (Ed.), *Non-Native Language Teachers. Perceptions, Challenges and Contributions to the Profession*, 25—43.

are challenged by two fundamental obstacles (for comprehensive discussion see Modiano, 2001a; Seidlhofer, 2001); one, ELT programs which strive to showcase an international or pan-mainland European conception of the tongue are forced to do so without a legitimate and codified standard, and two, as yet there is no established platform for a 'cultural studies' component in ELT which is international as opposed to native-speakercentric. Without a *lingua franca* educational standard, an international perspective in the 'cultural studies' module for ELT amounts to little more than a sampling of various varieties and possibly literary texts in such varieties, a review of the 'deviation' of language features from 'standard English', and scrutiny of the 'periphery culture' as it can be characterized for being 'different' from the culture of center-positioned speech communities. Focus all too often falls on *comprehension* as opposed to *communicative language ability* (see Llurda, 2000). The utilization of educational standards based on non-native varieties such as EIL, however, would not only bring the learning of English more into line with the actual linguistic environments which the NNS inhabits, it would also set the stage for an international cultural studies component.

ELT programs organized around educational standards and cultural studies regimes which tone down the role of the native speaker (NS) and instead concentrate on NNS varieties of English establish a foundation for the proliferation of a cross-cultural communicative perspective for *NNS to NNS* interaction. Here, the NNS practitioner has certain advantages over the NS instructor—not only because they have knowledge of the linguistic complexities of the mother tongue and the target language in contact—but more importantly because the NNS practitioner is well suited to provide students with a *pluralistic* cultural perspective (see Braine, 1999; Cook, 1999; Davies, 1991; Kramsch, 1998; Llurda, 2004a; Medgyes, 1992; Modiano, 2001b; Paikeday, 1985; and Rampton, 1990). In contrast, the 'traditionalist' NS practitioner, in promoting the legacy of the West, does not engage cultural pluralism from the perspective of the Other, (who in Braj Kachru's concentric circles of world Englishes are by default on the periphery). EIL ideologies, the notion of the language as the property of the L2 speaker, presuppose not only that prescriptive, culture-specific notions of 'standard English' play subordinate roles in the development of NNS standards, but also that the cultures of the native speaker are given less weight in comparison to the importance of the cultural contexts in which L2 speakers communicate cross-culturally.

The *essence* of the cultural studies modules which are offered in English language education, something constructed by educational materials, pedagogical methodology, and by the contexts in which language is realized, can be differentiated. For instance, ELT practices in nation states where the population is predominantly of European descent and English speaking are radically different from ELT platforms for second-language speakers living in nation states which have a colonial history. Foreign-language learners residing in developed countries, as well, require ELT practices, educational standards, and cultural studies programs which are especially designed to meet their needs. For learners living in English-speaking nation states, traditional ELT will be protocol for the vast majority of learners[1]. Post-colonials are now turning to the new Englishes in increasing numbers. With mainland Europeans, however, while there are learners who find EIL less appealing because they accept and prefer conventional ELT platforms, the students who reject the ideologies underpinning conventional ELT and as a consequence engage a lingua franca conceptualization of English will not find what they need in traditional institutionalized English language teaching and learning programs[2].

If we look at the ideologies promoted in the cultural studies programs that accompany the teaching and learning of a foreign tongue in the EU, it is apparent that foreign languages are often associated with nation states perceived as the homeland of the tongue, and the study of the literature, culture, and society of such political entities is an essential component of language education. Moreover, traditional foreign language programs follow well established pedagogical platforms. For example, the educational standard is prescriptive and targets the use of an idealized and supposedly prestigious speech community. NS teachers are models of correct usage, and as such there are considerable demands on the NNS instructor to appear to be a native speaker. The students strive to achieve near-native proficiency in the standard presented in the instruction. It is understood that the study of the culture of the target speech community, as well as societal organization, geography, religious makeup, etc., will result in a literacy which goes hand in hand with the attainment of near-native proficiency. As Llurda notes (2004b), in such settings there is no questioning of 'the cultural stereotypes that may be transferred to students eager to become as English-like as possible'. Many students who succeed in such educational programs become (auxiliary) members of the speech communities which they study.

For some, educational programs based on conventional practices are experienced as *culturally intrusive* and detrimental to the maintenance of indigenous identities rooted in the ancestral culture and language. For those who speak endangered languages and who are members of endangered cultures, the large-scale acquisition of languages of wider communication, while beneficial in some respects, can be the decisive event which sets into motion the demise of moribund languages and subsequently the cultural distinctiveness of the individual and the group to which the individual belongs. Here, linguistic imperialism is seen as a process which, through foreign language teaching and learning, results not only in the death of many languages and cultures, but also in a transformation of the cultural identity of the learner. The role of English is especially significant in this respect (for discussion of linguistic imperialism see Parakrama, 1995; Pennycook, 1998; and Phillipson, 1992).

It is clear that traditional foreign-language educational programs need to be revised. This is because they do not promote cross-cultural communication in the *NNS to NNS* context. Most importantly, however, they do not provide learners ample opportunity to construct an 'identity' in the foreign tongue which reflects their L1 personality, (promoting, instead, a rendition of an idealized NS model). Thus, it is no longer possible to assume that traditionally run cultural studies modules in foreign language learning programs, and the configurations of cultural identity which accompany language learning in such contexts, can be promoted in institutionalized language-learning settings without first questioning the pros and cons of such activity. In this paper I will discuss the current lack of a viable platform for the study of *culture* in English language-learning programs, and describe how new conceptualizations of English can give rise to language teaching and learning practices which take into consideration the multi-cultural nature of English in the world. This positioning, moreover, indicates that the NNS practitioner, not only in language studies but also in cultural studies, has certain advantages over the NS teacher.

## 2.      THE CONSTRUCTION OF IDENTITY IN NON-NATIVE VARIETIES

In post-colonial settings where English serves linguistically pluralistic communities, the emergence of second-languages varieties of English indicates that the tongue is now evolving in a manner somewhat removed from the control of native-speaker based standardization functions. Braj Kachru, in establishing the notion of *world Englishes*, argues convincingly that cultural identities characteristic of members of second-language speech communities, such as, for example, Nigeria and India, support communicative expediency, and are often more appropriate, in context, in comparison to L2 identities developed through training to master standard English in the guise of prescriptive British English (BrE) or American English (AmE) (Kachru, 1982). This is because of the value of a sense of community which can be created by the use of indigenous culture-specific codes. Moreover, in second-language forums, some forms of language, such as BrE with Received Pronunciation, establish destructive class divisions and forcefully substantiate foreign ideologies. The same can be said of AmE when it is used as the educational standard in places such as the south Pacific, where those critical of Americanization are quick to point out the disruptive nature of the American ideologies transferred to pupils in their studies and through their exposure to English. Indeed, the current post-colonial movement for greater sensitivity on the question of cultural identity and linguistic human rights has led to a better understanding of the role which second-language varieties play in the creation of cultural identities. It is high time that we begin to examine more closely the same questions as they apply to foreign language speakers.

Many ESL programs have been modified as a result of increased awareness of the role which second-language usage plays in the development of cultural identity. For example, instead of studying BrE with RP pronunciation, reading Shakespeare, learning about Parliament, organizing role-playing exercises targeting tourist activities in London, etc., while pursuing proficiency in English, many people in developing nations are now receiving English language education in their own varieties, and their teachers are actively working to bring indigenous intellectual properties into the instruction. Thus, the study of the work of writers who are members of the learners' community, the use of domestically produced teaching and learning materials, a focus on local histories and the study of the nation state in and through the English language, is found to be a viable platform for many second-language speakers of English who are engaging the lingua franca in an effort to come to terms with life in the aftermath of British rule. English, in such capacities, is expedient for the simple reason that many developing nations are made up of a myriad of diverse speech communities. A language of wider communication is a necessity in the nation-state building processes. English, as a supranational language, provides peoples with divergent linguistic backgrounds an opportunity to come together in the celebration of national identities. Thus, instead of holding the language in high esteem because it can function as a gateway to Western lifestyles and ideologies, ESL speakers can instead focus on the expediency of the tongue in its various functions as a lingua franca.

Mainland Europe, on the other hand, appropriates the English language in an entirely different manner. Much of the social and cultural distinctiveness of English is familiar territory to western Europeans, who in most cases speak languages which, like English, have considerable spread in the world. For mainland Europeans, the ideological imposition of English language learning is far less resolute. Nevertheless, while there is awareness that English is fast becoming Europe's lingua franca, there is much less acknowledgment of the fact that, for mainland Europe, English is evolving into a variety in its own right (see Jenkins, Modiano & Seidlhofer, 2001). The emergence of this new European form of the tongue has far reaching implications for the pedagogy utilized in institutionalized language-learning settings, for the framework of educational materials such as textbooks, dictionaries, and grammars, for the cultural studies programs which accompany foreign language learning, and for the cultural identities which are constructed in the process.

## 3.       TRANSCULTURALISM, INTERCULTURALITY AND BICULTURALISM

In a discussion of language teaching and European integration, Karen Risager notes that the blurring of national borders in the EU 'actually undermines a [foreign language] teaching which is still decidedly influenced by the idea of the national language and the national culture' (1998, 242). Asking, '[h]ow does language teaching in Europe respond to this development?' (242) Risager reports on foreign-language teaching trends in Denmark which suggest that teaching and learning strategies have shifted from a *foreign-language* and *intercultural* approach, to one which is *multi-cultural* and *transcultural*. Internationalization, Risager reports, is the decisive force behind this change. Dismissing the foreign-language approach because it promotes the transference of ethnocentrism from an idealized foreign culture to the learner's culture, Risager claims that such ideologies in language teaching have declined since the 1980s. Unfortunately, however, there are practitioners who persist in promoting a foreign language, foreign culture vision of the target language in mono-lingual, mono-cultural contexts (and this is especially true for English)[3]. The intercultural approach is an improvement in the sense that there is some focus on the learner's cultural distinctiveness in the negotiation of the target language and culture(s), but as the language is nevertheless 'taught as if it were a first language' (Risager, 244), such programs for foreign-language learning are also found to be deficient.

The multicultural dimension of social life is regarded as the norm in human interaction when foreign languages are taught from a lingua franca perspective. With transculturalism, moreover, there is the global dimension. Here it is possible to center the learning of a language on a broad range of NNS to NNS interaction functions. Thus, the cultural context for language learning is the site in which a myriad of actors representing various languages and cultures, as well as differing levels of competence and comprehensive ability, come together in any number of constellations. Here, the lingua franca allows individuals competent in the language rights of *access* and *participation*. While it is evident that the NS constituency will be taking part in this activity, the cultural distinctiveness and particular manner of language use which distinguishes the native speaker will be simply one point of departure among many in the broad spectrum of lingua-franca-using peoples.

McKay, in a discussion of cultural studies in ELT (2000), builds upon Kramsch's views of 'culture' in language education (Kramsch, 1993). Here, it is clear that McKay and Kramsch adhere to the notion that the teaching of language and culture require a keen respect for the learner's cultural orientation. In their view, one target of the instruction will be to encourage learners to position themselves as members of their own culture who understand their own and other cultural positioning, and not as prospective members requesting acceptance/admittance of a foreign group of L1 speakers. McKay finds Byram's (1998) distinction, that biculturalism presupposes identification *with*, and perhaps acceptance *of* the culture of the target language, as opposed to interculturalism, which merely signifies awareness of other cultures, to be useful. As English is defined as an international language, one which is owned by those who have knowledge of the tongue, the cultural distinctiveness of the language cannot be represented by any one speech community. Thus, the cultural dimension of ELT, among other things, must be presented in a manner which encourages learners to come to terms with those peoples who in one capacity or another use the English language in their dealings with others, as well as with their own cultural distinctiveness in and through the English language.

McKay stresses the 'need to acknowledge the value of including information about the students' own culture' because such information is needed by students who will want to be able to explain their own culture to others (McKay, 2000: 11). This is a new and refreshing vision of the cultural studies component in ELT. Devising curriculum, developing ELT strategies, and compiling language education materials with such goals in mind becomes something entirely different in comparison to the traditional orientation of much present-day ELT activity. Moreover, if the goal of the instruction is to promote the learner's distinct identity in and through the English language, and if the reason for doing so is because there is a firm belief that such activity results in EFL/ESL speakers who are better equipped to engage a multi-cultural world, it is expedient, surely, that the training is carried out by someone who has experience expressing her or his own culture in a foreign language. The NNS practitioner is especially well suited to meet such challenges.

On the other hand, when training learners to engage native speakers in native-speaker contexts, ELT programs need to provide instruction in the cultural contexts of NNS to NS interaction, especially in those educational settings where learners have integration motivation. For such students, the NS practitioner is certainly expedient when the goal of the instruction is to navigate in the environments which native speakers inhabit. With students who buy into traditional notions of foreign language learning, and who are at advanced levels of proficiency, it is reasonable to expect that such students will want to gain knowledge, for example, of American and British culture, and the NS practitioner will no doubt continue to be appreciated among such learners. The value of utilizing such instructors in such capacities, however, does not undermine the importance of promoting the NNS practitioner in EIL educational programs.

A program for EIL must by definition include scrutiny of the contexts in which English is used in NNS to NNS cross-cultural contexts. Moreover, while one important aim of EIL language-learning programs is to inform students of how they can represent their own cultures and identities in and through the English language, they also prioritize the need to provide students an opportunity to gain knowledge of the wider environment in which they will operate. Here, knowledge and understanding of all of the English-using peoples is beneficial. Such training and knowledge is not based on a belief that native-speaker standards have more value in comparison to de-nativised standards. Just as second-language varieties are more expedient forms of communication in communities which are defined as being in the 'outer circle' in Kachru's taxonomy, foreign-language varieties are appropriate for foreign-language speakers who aspire to learn English without giving others the impression that they are auxiliary members of Anglo-American society (see Kachru, 1985).

While many NNS practitioners working in mainland Europe are supportive of the NS norm, the NNS practitioner committed to the promotion of English as a lingua franca can be seen to have advantages in all forms of institutionalized foreign language training. The NNS practitioner, for obvious reasons, understands the manner in which their pupils perceive 'foreignness' in others, and the way one can come to terms with this knowledge, in an entirely different manner when compared to a monolingual NS practitioner. Thus, if one assumes that one aim of the instruction is to encourage if not acceptance then at least respect for the practices and beliefs of others, the NNS practitioner, having been effectively the Other to native speakers, is better able to share with their pupils various communicative strategies for overcoming obstacles between peoples with differing linguistic, cultural, and social orientation. Such processes of *reception* and *negotiation* are perhaps better understood by the NNS practitioner for the simple reason that they have lived through similar thought processes, and such experience aids them in their efforts to assist their students on their journey into the English-using world. It should be noted, however, that having lived through the same processes does not guarantee a higher degree of tolerance. It is my opinion, however, that where instructor and pupil share common ground, a better foundation for EFL/ESL education is established. Thus, interculturalism, as a conceptualization of the goals of the linguistic and cultural component in ELT, is best achieved, in my opinion, when the practitioner shares the learners' cultural orientations. The alternative is to fall back into the trap of elevating the NS (and NS cultural contexts) at the expense of local identities. Without the promotion of local identities in ELT, there is a danger that the teaching and learning of English will continue to be an instrument of cultural and linguistic imperialism. On the other hand, with the promotion of local identities in ELT, there is the possibility that English will become a more 'democratic' lingua franca.

Kramsch offers a useful distinction here in her proposal for a convergence of the merits of the brand of linguistic human rights as they are proposed by Skutnabb-Kangas & Phillipson (1994) and the notion of communicative competence. 'A pedagogy of the authentic' as it is proposed by Kramsch, presupposes an awareness of the actual contexts in which English is used by learners (1998, 24). Such positioning illustrates an attempt to come to terms with the imposition, or linguistic imperialism functions of foreign language learning. It also establishes a frame of reference for an investigation of the various discourse strategies which distinguish the NNS from the native speaker and the cultural distinctiveness which the NS constituency is believed to represent. Thus, it is plausible, certainly, that NNS practitioners will take a leading role in the construction of platforms for legitimizing, codifying, and standardizing non-native varieties which reflect the mindset of the NNS who in the utilization of the lingua franca realizes linguistic and cultural realities which are distinctly different from the frames of reference which characterize the native-speaker. This is the true nature of the lingua franca conceptualization of English. While the majority of native speakers primarily use English in their contact with other native speakers, it is the NNS constituency which represents the avant-garde in the development of the language as a vehicle for global linguistic and cultural integration.

## 4.     SWEDEN AND THE GENESIS OF EURO-ENGLISH

My concern has primarily been with the manner in which lingua franca perceptions of English can benefit the development of English language teaching and learning strategies for mainland Europe. For the discussion presented here on the cultural studies component in ELT, and the role which the NNS practitioner can play in the teaching of cultural studies modules, it would be helpful if some mention is made of the special mainland European conditions of English language teaching and learning. A focus on Sweden is presented here for the simple reason that I am most familiar with English language education in this country, but also because English language programs in this EU member state are very similar to educational programs utilized in northern Europe and as such are representative of EFL for this region of the EU. In Sweden, the tradition at all levels of education, up until the early 1990s, was to promote standard BrE with Received Pronunciation, and for the students to work toward the achievement of near-native proficiency. Cultural studies programs targeted British culture and social organization, with some space reserved for American studies.

As a result, prior to the 1990s the majority of Swedes were in possession of a British accent and followed the conventions of BrE grammar, spelling, and lexis. Many users of English from other parts of the world made associations, when interacting with Swedes, to a British cultural and social context. While previously, for example, Swedish educators adhered to the notion that it was unacceptable to mix features of British and American English, and their students showed signs of compliance with this practice, with linguistic Americanization, a *Mid-Atlantic English* spoken form of the tongue has become common in Sweden, perhaps more common than either AmE or BrE (see Axelsson-Westergren, 2002; Mobärg, 2002, and Söderlund & Modiano, 2002). Linguistic Americanization, which has been on the increase in both Sweden and Europe throughout the post-war period, with a radical upswing in the late 1980s and 1990s, has rendered consistency in one variety nearly impossible. The advent of the Internet, developments in telecommunications, the proliferation of American media in several manifestations (film, global television networks, interactive computer applications, etc.) has accelerated the spread of AmE, as well as the manner in which AmE impacts on other varieties. Moreover, in the last ten years or so there have been signs that BrE, in itself, is no longer comprehensive enough to meet the needs of both Swedish and mainland European students[4].

Consequently, the English language usage of many Swedes is now more pluralistic, more in line with the Swede's self-perception as a world citizen who relies on the English language to communicate across cultures. The shift away from the BrE perspective on English, however, and toward a more culturally pluralistic understanding, has not been acknowledged in many institutionalized language-learning settings. While in college-level education we have seen curriculum development which demonstrates awareness of the changes which have taken place, primary and secondary schools, as well as teacher training programs, have not adequately readjusted their curriculum to accommodate the changes in our understanding of learner motivation and the cultural contexts of EFL. This is unfortunate, seeing as the need to teach English as a lingua franca is becoming a pressing concern in those educational settings where the learners themselves prefer to use international forms of the tongue.

## 5.     EFL IN SWEDEN

In the recruitment of teachers for the primary and secondary schools (and in some instances, in institutions of higher learning), the fundamental tenet of administrators responsible for hiring has long been to highly value native speakers of 'prestige' varieties. When individuals with such abilities are not available, natives who aspire to achieve such goals are perceived to be the next best thing going, and consequently the majority of English teachers in Sweden speak the stylized British vernacular, albeit at times with somewhat of a Swedish accent. In the instruction, traditional foreign-language pedagogy is the order of the day. The teacher, the model, drills their pupils in a prescriptive grammar, enforces consistency, and unfortunately in the process sometimes deems incorrect features of the language which are acceptable in other varieties, especially AmE. Moreover, along with a belief in the supremacy of BrE is the understanding that British intellectual property is also more valued in comparison to what is on offer from other English-language domains.

The assumption, naturally, is that the pupils are being trained to operate in Britain. That is to say, the exercises are designed to accommodate the ease of communication between the pupil and a native speaker of BrE. The instructor, in such contexts, is expected to 'represent' the native speaker, to 'recreate' the social environment in which the native speaker thrives. Many of the standard social conventions, the polite behavior, are brought to the fore in such ELT settings. The use of tag questions and allusions to the weather, for example, are taught as a means of 'breaking the ice' in polite conversation. Beyond social protocol, much emphasis is placed on a Swedish perception of British history, culture, and society. Such knowledge is supposedly required of those who want to be viewed as being 'in the know' by their prospective British interlocutors. The British themselves are reduced to stereotypes. Education programs often culminate in Swedes actually travelling to the UK. This 'closure ceremony' brings home the value of knowing English in a British context and reinforces the pupils' faith in the wisdom of learning BrE. Such training, it is believed, is invaluable as a means of preparing pupils to not only engage the British but also other English speaking peoples.

## 6.    BRITISH ORIENTATION IN THE SWEDISH EDUCATIONAL MATERIALS

The educational materials utilized in the instruction reflect this conservative view of the language. British dictionaries are standard issue in Sweden (most commonly *Longman* and the *Oxford*), as are the textbooks and grammars, which are often written by British people living and working in Sweden, or by Swedes schooled in the British fashion. While we are seeing greater space in the materials being devoted to other varieties of the tongue, these activities are often slanted so that they read as examples of an individual with a British orientation encountering someone who is effectively the Other. Speakers of other varieties of English, native speaker as well as second-language speaker based, are patronized at the expense of the British perspective. Americans are often downplayed while the British themselves are invariably depicted as individuals who demonstrate what proper language and appropriate social protocol are all about. Thus, stereotypes abound in discussions of the 'typical' American as unrefined, while the stereotypical British individual is perceived as someone living out a more sophisticated and idealized British life. Moreover, while a liberal and culturally pluralistic atmosphere is often created in the materials as well as in the instruction, it is apparent that the language is presented as the property of the British, and the contexts which are utilized in most of the texts illustrate how one perceives the world from an Anglophile vantage point.

This order is in the process of breaking down as a result of changes taking place both inside and outside of the classroom. For example, in recent years we have seen an upswing in the use of American materials, not especially in textbooks, dictionaries, and grammars, but more noticeably in reference works. Much of the information technology available to Swedish school children is in AmE, as is media exposure. Books and interactive computer applications are often in AmE, and present an alternative to BrE orientation This movement away from a BrE perspective is further enhanced by the reading of books written by authors from developing countries. The emergence of 'literatures in English' as opposed to 'English literature', is challenging the traditional cultural context of ELT. Thus, ELT practices, as well as educational materials, while promoting standard British English as the model in the instruction of grammar, lexis and speech skills, are augmented by student exposure to a wide range of varieties. Indeed, it is becoming increasingly apparent to a growing number of ELT practitioners in Sweden that the belief in a cultural studies program which is totally focused on a British conceptualization of the world is decidedly old-fashioned. If we take into account the actual materials utilized in the instruction, it is apparent that native speakers of BrE, and NNS practitioners who embrace the BrE standard, have a platform which supports their efforts to promote traditional ELT ideologies. The NNS practitioner in Sweden eager to implement new approaches to the teaching of English will look for other materials, materials which focus on multiculturalism and on cultural diversity.

## 7.     CULTURAL STUDIES PROGRAMS AND CULTURAL PLURALISM

It is clear that traditionalist programs have been and are primarily concerned with British social and cultural phenomena. Nevertheless, a number of new discourses are currently being promoted. A fascination with ethnicity and the post-colonial movements, for example, effectively shifts the cultural context of English language learning away from traditional renditions of the canon (from a British perspective) toward interest in the discourses being created by people living in developing countries as well as minorities living in the West. The focus on hyphenated identities, on people discriminated for any number of reasons, is capturing our attention while the intellectual properties of the mainstream in Britain as well as in the United States are losing ground. It is logical to assume that the reading and study of canonized authors is an important academic activity for those L1 speakers who are eager to learn more about their own cultures. However, for the EFL enterprise, such texts are less pedagogically appropriate when compared to narratives that focus on cross-cultural contact, and this is especially true when those involved in the action utilize the English language as a lingua franca. As a result of this shift in interest, it is becoming accepted among ELT practitioners to target social interaction among non-native speakers as opposed to the traditional view of the non-native learner encountering the native speaker. This cultural context, NNS to NNS, creates social protocol which is an interesting field of study in its own right. Thus, in cultural studies and literature programs in Sweden which are designed to support the language learning process, an alternative to BrE orientation is to envision English language usage from a non-native perspective, and to promote the intellectual properties of post-colonials and minorities.

The reading of 'literatures in English' as opposed to 'English literature' presupposes that literatures from throughout the English-using-world are studied. At Gävle University, for example, freshman students read world literatures in English and study the language as a culturally pluralistic medium of communication. It should be noted, however, that the cultural studies programs, in order to be efficient, require an EIL educational standard for the actual teaching of the language. To enforce an educational standard in the instruction which is AmE or BrE, and to then superimpose a 'culturally pluralistic' rendition of the English language in the cultural studies and literature modules, is not consistent, and while superior to conventional programs, brings us merely half way along our journey.

## 8.    IDENTITY, CULTURAL STUDIES, THE NNS, AND ELT

The issue of cultural identity is of primary importance, as is the expediency of the target variety in communicative terms. ELT, in order to be an agent in the promotion of linguistic human rights, needs not only a lingua-franca vision of standard English but also a cultural studies platform which promotes the development of non-native speaker identities (see Canagarajah, 1999; Modiano, 2001b; and Rajagopalan, 1999). As a first step, international dictionaries should be used in the instruction. Lexical knowledge must go beyond the simple description of meaning. Instead, lexical knowledge should include not only awareness of where terms are readily used, but also where such terms are uncommon. Beyond this knowledge, students of the various manifestations of EIL will want to learn about words which are 'core English' and as such are readily used and understood among the majority of users of English. As an example, BrE *public school* for *private boarding school* and *stone* as a measurement of weight (6.3 kilograms) are culture specific. A great many people in North America are not aware of these distinctions (indeed, many users of English throughout the world are not familiar with these terms in any capacity). Students with a cross-cultural perspective on English are made aware, not only of the terms themselves as well as where these terms are used, but also of the fact that the term *private boarding school*, or the designation of weight in kilos, is more readily used and understood internationally. Thus, in the study of vocabulary, students of English as a lingua franca are made aware of such complexities of lexical usage. The alternative, to target a culture-specific rendition of lexis, is less communicatively expedient and also more culturally intrusive. Moreover, the NNS practitioner, one who has no loyalties to any NS constituency, is in a better position to promote pragmatism in such matters.

The same can be said of pronunciation. Either learners are given instruction in standard English, and are expected to 'master' the spoken language on such terms, or else they can be encouraged to target other pronunciation standards. It is envisioned that students of EIL are exposed to, and provided instruction, in many different varieties. In their pursuit of awareness of the myriad of Englishes, such learners will gain knowledge of many different ways in which words can be pronounced. However, in order to assist the learner in the development of their own accent, one which is communicatively expedient, the ELT practitioner will need to have special knowledge of the pronunciation 'difficulties' that are particular to the language group of which the learner is a member. Moreover, it is certainly acceptable, in the ideologies of EIL, that learners can retain traces of their mother-tongue accent. In this respect, Jennifer Jenkins has carried out extensive work on the parameters of pronunciation for the NNS, and offers in her work a proposal for NNS pronunciation guidelines which have substantial functional value in the communicative act (see Jenkins, 2000). Thus, it is conceivable that the proficient EIL speaker is someone who has mastered the English language, is an excellent communicator in the cross-cultural context, and has an accent which reveals the native tongue of the speaker. In time, however, conceptualizations such as the *non-regionally identifiable*, or *non-geographically identifiable accent*, which presuppose a NNS pronunciation that has a great deal of value in the communicative act, will become a viable choice. This sense of L2 English usage being difficult to locate geographically can already be observed in the English which is spoken by many mainland Europeans. Such usage is very much what I have attempted in my work to describe as a form of Mid-Atlantic English or Euro-English.

As a native speaker, however, I find it difficult to teach my students how to speak with a non-regionally or non-geographically identifiable accent. Surely, individuals who speak without a NS accent are better equipped to teach learners how to speak English in this capacity. Once again, we see the wisdom of promoting the NNS practitioner in ELT, especially in those educational settings where the dominance of a so-called 'prestigious' NS variety is in the process of being replaced by ELT ideologies sensitive to the cultural imposition of foreign language learning.

The focus on an EIL conceptualization of lexis and pronunciation goes hand in hand with the reading of literatures in English, where texts are introduced in the instruction which have their roots in a broad cross-section of English-using communities. In such readings students not only have an opportunity to observe how English acts as a language of wider communication, they can also witness how various forms of social protocol operate in diverse cultural contexts. The social and cultural ideologies which flourish in literatures in English provide students with an opportunity to engage a culturally pluralistic world, something which acts as a counterweight to the Anglo-American vision promoted in much traditional English and American literature. Instead of reading Shakespeare, Austen, Dickens, the Brontë sisters, Hawthorne, and Poe, students pursuing English as a lingua franca can read texts by writers such as Achebe, Gordimer, Kincaid, Kingston, Tan, and Walker[5]. Both the NNS practitioner and learner, in the study of such texts, are on equal terms with the materials. The alternative is the NNS as the Other, observing from the periphery the cultural artifacts of the center-positioned NS constituency.

With the study of the English language, students are given an introduction to sociolinguistics where world Englishes, major varieties and their regional accents and dialects, second-language varieties, and pidgins and Creoles are scrutinized. Students learn more about how English operates in a diverse number of nation states so that they can gain a better understanding of the wide range of English language usage. Here, it is conceivable that English language studies can be the basis for an investigation of mainland-European societal organization, with mainland Europe, for example, getting the type of attention that the UK receives in traditional programs. Furthermore, the workings of organizations such as the European Union, the International Red Cross, the United Nations, and the World Bank, can be studied. Such activities are alternatives to the traditional emphasis on British and American institutions and social organization.

Cultural studies programs could just as well focus on the artifacts of any nation state or region. Such exposure, as well as efforts to better comprehend the ideologies which underpin intellectual properties produced by non-native speakers of English, can act as an avenue into global awareness, something which supports the NNS in the effort to construct an understanding of the English language as a lingua franca and not as the medium of Anglo-American cultural and socioeconomic hegemony. The study of cultures (in contact) in and through the English language provides learners with an awareness of their role in global integration and internationalization. Here, under the guidance of the NNS practitioner, both student and teacher can position themselves centrally in the development of English as a global lingua franca.

## 9.    CONCLUSION

It is clear that the vision of globalization and cultural integration, not only for Europe but also for people throughout the world, is dependent on a language of wider communication. If, for the EU this language is English, and if, furthermore, the European NNS is eager to participate in the globalization movements, it is expedient, certainly, that ELT programs provide mainland Europeans an opportunity to learn the tongue as a lingua franca. Indeed, programs loyal to an Anglo-American perspective on English, with NS hegemony in defining proper use, cultural orientation, and social protocol, will not be deemed ideologically sound in the years to come. As an alternative, Mid-Atlantic English, Euro-English, and EIL visions of English for mainland Europe are better suited to support the NNS in the effort to construct identities in and through the lingua franca which best represent mainland European cultural orientation. Such a stance presupposes that the NNS practitioner plays an important role in the development of the English language. The first step must be to establish lingua franca platforms for the educational standard, and moreover, to implement a cultural studies supplement to foreign language teaching and learning which is culturally pluralistic as opposed to being loyal to a proposed native-speaker perception of reality.

## 10. NOTES

[1] It is of course conceivable that non-native learners living in nation states where English is the majority language will reject integrative motivation and instead chose to acquire English in much the same manner as foreign-language learners who, for instance, pursue English-language studies in mainland Europe with utilitarian motivation.

[2] This is because traditional English language learning programs are designed to further the interests of the native-speaker constituencies. For non-native speakers to become liberated from the hegemonic positioning of the native-speaker, a rejection of native-speaker definitions of standard English must take place (see Modiano 1999).

[3] With the reservation, naturally, that it is customary in such quarters to recognize two dominant cultures in ELT, the American and the British constituencies.

[4] In 1994, the official state educational policy was changed from requiring the teaching of standard BrE to the choice of teaching either educated forms of BrE *or* AmE (with AmE being treated as an unwanted cousin by many educators). At the same time, the English which the Swedes themselves used evolved into an English which has more in common with AmE, other native-speaker based varieties such as Irish or Australian English, and international forms of the tongue such as Mid-Atlantic English, Euro-English, and EIL.

[5] In the freshman English course at Gävle University students read the following novels: Chinua Achebe, *Things Fall Apart*, London: Heinemann 1958, Nadine Gordimer, *July's People*, New York: Viking Press 1981, Jamaica Kincaid, *The Autobiography Of My Mother*, New York: Farrar Straus & Giroux 1996, Maxine Hong Kingston, *The Woman Warrior*, London: Picador (1975) 1981, Amy Tan, *The Joy Luck Club*, London: Vintage (1989) 1998, Alice Walker, *The Color Purple*, Cambridge: Cambridge University Press (1983) 2000.

## 11. REFERENCES

Axelsson-Westergren, M. (2002). 'Refined' or 'relaxed' English pronunciation: Usage and attitudes among Swedish university students. In M. Modiano (Ed.), *Studies in Mid-Atlantic English*. Gävle, Sweden: HS Institutionens Skriftserie Nr 7. 132-146.

Braine, G. (Ed.) (1999). *Non-native educators in English language teaching.* Mahwah, NJ: Lawrence Erlbaum Associates.

Byram, M. (1998). Cultural identities in multilingual classrooms. In J. Cenoz & F. Genesee (Eds.), *Beyond bilingualism.* Clevedon: Multilingual Matters. 96-116.

Canagarajah, A.S. (1999). On EFL teachers, awareness, and agency. *ELT Journal, 53* (3), 207-13.

Cook. V.J. (1999). Going beyond the native speaker in language teaching. *TESOL Quarterly, 33* (2), 185-209.

Davies, A. (1991). *The native speaker in applied linguistics.* Edinburgh: Edinburgh University Press.

Jenkins, J. (2000). *The phonology of English as an international language.* Oxford: Oxford University Press.

Jenkins, J., Modiano, M. & Seidlhofer, B. (2001). Euro-English. *English Today, 17* (4), 13-19.

Kachru, B. (1982). Models for non-native Englishes. In Braj Kachru (Ed.), *The other tongue.* Urbana, IL: University of Illinois Press. 31-57.

Kachru, B. (1985). Institutionalized second-language varieties. In S. Greenbaum (Ed.), *The English language today.* Oxford: Pergamon Press. 211-226.

Kramsch, C. (1993). *Context and culture in language teaching.* Oxford: Oxford University Press.

Kramsch, C. (1998). The privilege of the intercultural speaker. In M. Byram & M. Fleming (Eds.), *Language learning in intercultural perspective.* Cambridge: Cambridge University Press. 16-31.

Llurda, E. (2000). On competence, proficiency, and communicative language ability. *The International Journal of Applied Linguistics, 10* (1), 85-96.

Llurda, E. (2004a). Non-native-speaker teachers and English as an international language. *The International Journal of Applied Linguistics, 14* (3), 314-323.

Llurda, E. (2004b). 'Native / non-native speaker' discourses in foreign language university departments in Spain. In B. Dendrinos & B. Mitsikopoulou (Eds.), *Policies for linguistic pluralism and the teaching of languages in Europe.* Athens, Greece: University of Athens Press. 237-243.

McKay, S.L. (2000). Teaching English as an international language: Implications for cultural materials in the classroom. *TESOL Journal,* Winter, 7-11.

Medgyes, P. (1992). Native or non-native: who's worth more? *English Language Teaching Journal, 46* (4), 340-49.

Mobärg, M. (2002). RP or GA? On Swedish school students' choice of English pronunciation. In M. Modiano (Ed.), *Studies in Mid-Atlantic English.* Gävle, Sweden: HS Institutionens Skriftserie Nr 7. 119-131.

Modiano, M. (1999). Standard English(es) and educational practices for the world's lingua franca. *English Today, 15* (4), 3-13.

Modiano, M. (2001a). Ideology and the ELT practitioner. *The International Journal of Applied Linguistics, 11* (2), 159-173.

Modiano, M. (2001b). Linguistic imperialism, EIL, and cultural diversity. *ELT Journal, 54* (4), 339-346.

Modiano, M. (Ed.) (2002). *Studies in Mid-Atlantic English.* Gävle, Sweden: HS Institutionens Skriftserie Nr 7.

Paikeday, T. (1985). *The native speaker is dead!* Toronto: Paikeday Publishing Inc.

Parakrama, A. (1995). *De-hegemonizing language standards: Learning from (post) colonial Englishes about 'English'.* London: Macmillan.

Pennycook, A. (1998). *English and the discourses of colonialism.* London: Routledge.

Phillipson, R. (1992). *Linguistic imperialism*. Oxford: Oxford University Press.

Rampton, M. B. H. (1990). Displacing the 'native speaker': Expertise, affiliation and inheritance. *ELT Journal, 44* (2), 97-101.

Rajagopalan, K. (1999). Of EFL teachers, conscience, and cowardice. *ELT Journal, 53* (3), 200-6.

Risager, K. (1998). Language teaching and the process of European integration. In M. Byram & M. Fleming (Eds.), *Language learning in intercultural perspective*. Cambridge: Cambridge University Press. 242-54.

Seidlhofer, B. (1999). Double standards: Teacher education in the expanding circle. *World Englishes, 18* (2), 233-245.

Seidlhofer, B. (2001). Closing the conceptual gap: The case for a description of English as a lingua franca. *The International Journal of Applied Linguistics, 11* (2), 133-158.

Skutnabb-Kangas, T. & Phillipson, R. (Eds.) (1994). *Linguistic human rights*. Berlin: Mouton de Gruyter.

Söderlund, M. & Modiano, M. (2002). Swedish upper secondary school students and their attitudes towards AmE, BrE, and Mid-Atlantic English. In M. Modiano (Ed.), *Studies in Mid-Atlantic English*. Gävle, Sweden: HS Institutionens Skriftserie Nr 7. 147-171.

PART II

# NNS TEACHERS IN THE CLASSROOM

Chapter 4

# BASING TEACHING ON THE L2 USER

VIVIAN COOK
*University of Newcastle upon Tyne*

## 1.     INTRODUCTION

This paper argues that the starting-point for language teaching should be the recognition that the second language (L2) user is a particular kind of person in their own right with their own knowledge of the first language (L1) and the L2, rather than a monolingual with an added L2. An L2 user is a person who uses another language for any purpose at whatever level (Cook, 2002a), and thus is not covered by most definitions of either bilinguals or L2 learners. They might be writers like Nabokov or Conrad creating novels, ethnic minority children acting as translators for their parents in medical consultations, tourists travelling on holiday, terrorists training for action, journalists plying their trade, businessmen doing deals on the internet, jockeys giving television interviews. Some L2 users acquired their second language through practical living, others after long study in the classroom; some need it for survival in everyday existence, others for amusement, pleasure to education. In short L2 users are as diverse as the rest of humanity. Their needs and uses of language are as wide as monolinguals, if not wider.

## 2.     THE L2 USER CONCEPT AND MULTICOMPETENCE

The L2 user concept is based on the multicompetence view of second language acquisition, which has been developed as an overall approach to L2

E. Llurda (Ed.), *Non-Native Language Teachers. Perceptions, Challenges and Contributions to the Profession,*
47—61.

learning since Cook (1991). Multicompetence means the knowledge of two or more languages in one mind. The term thus encompasses the concept of interlanguage, which has been used only for the second language component, and the first language component. It treats the mind of the L2 user as a whole rather than as having separate L1 and interlanguage components. It argues that studying second language acquisition means accepting this totality, not just the interlanguage component.

The main question for multicompetence research is how the two languages relate in the same mind. At some level the two languages must co-exist. The question is the level at which they separate or indeed if they separate at all. This has been seen as an 'integration continuum' (Cook, 2002a), going from total separation between the languages at one end to total integration at the other. This continuum might represent development over time or it may be that particular individuals are more or less integrated however long they have been learning a second language. It might represent different aspects of language: pronunciation and vocabulary might be more likely to be integrated, grammar less likely. The position on the continuum might also vary according to Grosjean's concept of language mode, the integration of the two languages depending on the extent to which the speakers perceive that they are in monolingual mode (using one language, whether L1 or L2) or bilingual mode (using both languages together) (Grosjean, 2001).

The term 'L2 user' is then crucial to the approach. Chomsky (*e.g.* 1986) insists that linguistics has to account for the linguistic knowledge of the adult native speaker; only after this has been described can it go on to see how it is acquired and explain what this knowledge is. The study of the first language does not start by looking at how children acquire it: it is the mature L1 user that counts.

Similarly L2 research is about the minds of people who have successfully reached a usable level of the L2, not just how they learn it. Some L2 users may also be L2 learners who are still acquiring language: an immigrant using the second language in the street becomes a student learning the language when they step through the classroom door. But we are no more justified in saying that an L2 user is a perpetual L2 learner than we are in saying an adult native speaker is still learning their first language. When L2 research talks about everything to do with the L2 as 'acquisition' or talks about people who speak second languages as 'L2 learners' it implies that no person using a second language succeed in getting to a state of using the language properly. A person of fifty who has used a language all their lives is not called an L1 learner; why should their use of a second language for, say, thirty years still be deemed learning? The term only people who escape the label of 'L2 learner' are balanced bilinguals, equally native-like in both languages, like a double monolingual rather than an L2 user.

## 3. THE NATIVE SPEAKER CONCEPT IN SECOND LANGUAGE ACQUISITION AND LANGUAGE TEACHING

The crucial relationship that has been changed in multicompetence is then that between the native speaker and the person acquiring or using a second language. L2 research from the 60s onwards made use of the interlanguage concept to describe the independent language of the L2 learner. The aim was to describe learners in their own right—look at their grammar, their phonology and their vocabulary as things of their own. Yet the research methods employed consistently involved measuring the L2 learner against the native speaker, whether in terms of Error Analysis (errors being things natives wouldn't say), obligatory occurrences (contexts where natives have to have particular forms), or grammaticality judgements (sentences natives reject). The model against which the learner was measured was how a native speaker performed.

This led to a pervasive air of failure and gloom: the interesting thing about people acquiring second languages was why they were so bad at it, few if any achieving the levels in a second language any monolingual can attain in the first language. To take some representative quotations, which could be repeated from virtually every general book about second language acquisition, 'failure to acquire the target language grammar is typical' (Birdsong, 1992: 706), 'children generally achieve full competence (in any language they are exposed to) whereas adults usually fail to become native speakers' (Felix, 1987: 140), and 'Unfortunately, language mastery is not often the outcome of SLA' (Larsen-Freeman & Long, 1991: 153). No criterion is proposed for L2 success other than being like a native speaker. Success means getting as close as possible to this target.

Is the native speaker target in fact attainable? A few people have been found who can pass for native speakers, so perhaps it could be valid for some. But their numbers are so small that they are as relevant to SLA as Michael Schumacher's driving skills are to my daily drive to work. The reasonable definition of a native speaker is a person speaking the language they learnt first in childhood. By this definition it is impossible for any L2 learner ever to become a native speaker without going back in time to their childhood; nothing learnt in later life could qualify you as a native speaker.

   The problem with using the native speaker target is that two groups of native speakers and L2 users are being compared as if one were intrinsically trying to become the other. The comparison is loaded because one group is defined in terms of the other. This does not occur in other areas of language study, following Labov's powerful arguments for linguistic differences between groups rather than deficits (Labov, 1969). Thus it is no longer felt to be proper to talk about the language of Black citizens of the USA being deficient with regard to that of whites, about the language of working-class children being deficient compared to that of middle-class children, or the language of women being a deficient version of men's language, though all of these were claimed at one time or another. Does measuring L2 users against L1 native speakers amount to falling into the same trap? Some insist that second language acquisition is a unique case where we are justified in seeing one group of human beings in terms of another; while we don't treat women as failed men, we may legitimately treat L2 users as failed native speakers. The reasons why L2 users should be treated as different rather than deficient will be elaborated below. L2 users have the right to speak English as L2 users rather than as imitation native speakers, as exemplified by the French wine-grower who said 'I speak English very badly but my French accent is perfect'. L2 users should be judged by what they are, L2 users, not what they can never be by definition, native speakers.


## 4.      THE NATURE OF THE L2 USER

   If L2 users are indeed unique users of language in their own right, not imitations of native speakers, what are their characteristics?

   **1) The L2 user's knowledge of the second language is typically not identical to that of a native speaker.** Controversy has raged over whether a small proportion of native speakers can use language identically to monolingual native speakers. Some pointed to 'balanced' bilinguals whose second language is still different from native speakers in grammaticality judgments tests (Coppieters, 1987), others to a small group of L2 students who cannot be distinguished from monolingual native speakers (Bongaerts, van Summeren, Planken & Schils, 1997). As we saw above, the fact that a few untypical people are able to run a hundred metres in less than ten seconds does not tell us the normal running speed of the human race.
   The knowledge of the second language of the vast majority of learners is different from that of native speakers. Much effort in SLA research has been devoted to seeing why this is the case, whether through Error Analysis, access to Universal Grammar or L1 interference. Given that

multicompetence means having two languages present in the same mind, it is hardly surprising that the knowledge of the second language is not like that of a monolingual. The L2 learner has had the first language always present while acquiring the language; the L2 user has it in their mind whichever language they happen to be functioning in. The interlanguage component of multicompetence forms part of a system with another language and so is bound to be different from the L1 grammar of a monolingual who has only ever had one system.

But this does not mean that difference is deficit. The L2 user language may be a perfectly normal language of its type; why should this more complex state of the mind be measured against the comparatively simple L1 language of a monolingual? If the target is not to imitate the native speaker, the question of whether the eventual state should be like a native speaker is a side issue, no more relevant than discussing how many men can pass for women, even if both topics provide stimulating discussion and amazing anecdotes.

The proper goal for an L2 user is believed to be speaking the second language like an L2 user, not like an L1 user, with the exception, say, of those who want to be spies. This is easier said than done. We do not at present have any descriptions of what successful L2 usage might be. Perdue (2002) describes the basic grammar that all L2 learners seem to acquire in the early stages, regardless of L1 or L2. Jenkins (2000) has shown what a syllabus would look like that was based on the comprehensibility of English among L2 students. It may be that there is not a single successful end-point to L2 acquisition as there is for L1 and so many models of successful use are needed. It may also be that for the time being the native speaker model will have to do as a rough and ready approximation until there are the descriptions of L2 user grammar, L2 user frequency and L2 user phonology to put in its place. But this does not alter the fact that we should not expect the language of an L2 user to approximate that of a native speaker; we should not penalise deviations from the native speaker in the students.

**2) The L2 user has other uses for language than the monolingual.** At one level there are uses which involve both languages more or less simultaneously such as translation and code-switching. Some see these as extensions to the monolingual's ability to paraphrase and change style (Paradis, 1997); others see the monolingual uses as limited versions of the full range available to L2 users (Cook, 2002a). But L2 users employ a wider range of language functions than a monolingual for all the needs of their lives. An L2 user can be seen in terms of *métissage*—'the mixing of two ethnic groups, forming a third ethnicity' (Canada Tree, 1996).

At another level everything the speaker does is informed by the second language, whichever language they are using. Few L2 users can so compartmentalise their languages that they effectively switch one off and function solely in the other. Their everyday use of language is subtly altered by their knowledge of other languages. Furthermore the L2 user never gets to function in the same situation as the L1 user because the very presence of an L2 user changes the perceptions of the participants. The language used by the L2 user may perhaps be more polite than that of the natives, say 'Thank you very much indeed' rather than 'Thanks' (Cook, 1985) but may be mirroring the native speaker's expectations: we don't expect L2 users to speak like us and regard near-nativenesss as suspicious, perhaps spy-like. Native speakers do not talk in the same way to non-natives as they do to natives, partly in terms of syntax, partly in terms of how information is presented. Again the practical situations such as shopping and going to the doctors are different when an L2 user is involved. The ones that are depicted in language teaching coursebooks are then quite misleading if they involve only natives and native-to-native speech. For the majority of learners non-native speech to non-native-speakers may be far more relevant and valuable.

**3) The L2 user's knowledge of their first language is in some respects not the same as that of a monolingual.** A recent volume (Cook, 2003) brought together a variety of investigations into the effects of the second language on the first. The speaker's knowledge of their first language is undoubtedly influenced by the other languages they learn, whether in terms of:

- *syntax*: Japanese speakers of English are more prone to prefer plural subjects in Japanese sentences than Japanese who don't know English (Cook, Iarossi, Stellakis & Tokumaru, 2003).
- *the lexicon*: experienced Russian speakers of Hebrew use a less rich vocabulary in Russian than comparative newcomers (Laufer, 2003).
- *stylistic complexity*: Hungarian children who have learnt English use stylistically more complex Hungarian (Kecskes & Papp, 2000).
- *pragmatics*: Russian learners of English begin to rely on expressing emotions as states rather than as process (Pavlenko, 2003).
- *phonology*: French users of English pronounce the /t/ sound in French with a longer Voice Onset Time (VOT) than monolinguals (Flege, 1987).

It seems clear that the syntactic processing of people who know another language is no longer the same as monolinguals, even if the differences are small and need complex techniques to establish. The relationship between the two languages in the mind of the L2 user goes in both directions, not just one.

**4) L2 users have different minds from monolinguals.** The effects of the more complex system of multicompetence extend outside the area of language. Research over the past forty years has confirmed the effects of the L2 on the minds of the users, heralded by such traditional goals of language teaching as brain training. Children who have learnt a second language:

- have a sharper view of language if they speak an L2 (Bialystok, 2001).
- learn to read more quickly in their first language (Yelland, Pollard & Mercuri, 1993).
- have better 'conceptual development', 'creativity' and 'analogical reasoning' (Diaz, 1985).

Current research by my students and myself is exploring whether certain basic concepts are modified in those who know a second language. Athanasopoulos (2001) found Greek speakers who knew English had a different perception of the two Greek words covered by English *blue*, namely γαλαζιο (*ghalazio*, 'light blue') and μπλε (*ble*, 'dark blue'), than monolingual Greek speakers. Bassetti, *et al* (2002) found that Japanese people who had had longer exposure to English chose shape rather than substance more in a categorisation experiment than those with less exposure. Some concepts may then move towards the second language of L2 users, some may perhaps have forms that are the same neither as the first language or the second. This does of course assume that people who speak different languages think to some extent in different ways, a revival of the idea of linguistics relativity that has been gaining ground in recent years (Levinson, 1996).

To sum up, L2 users have different language abilities and knowledge and different ways of thinking from monolingual native speakers. Rather than encouraging the students to get as close to the native speaker as possible, teaching should try to make them independent L2 users who can function across two languages with mental abilities the monolingual native speaker cannot emulate.

# 5. IMPLICATIONS FOR LANGUAGE TEACHING

## 5.1 The language user and the native speaker

An implicit goal of language teaching has often been to get as close to the native speaker as possible, recognising the native speaker as having the only acceptable form of the language. If the arguments above are accepted, a more achievable goal is to make students into successful L2 users. The native speaker target has been more a matter of exerting the power of the native speaker than a recognition of what students actually need.

One perennial justification is that the students themselves want to be like native speakers. As Grosjean (1989) points out, L2 users are part of the same social climate as monolinguals and have come to accept that native speakers rule the roost. I couldn't count how many times a perfectly fluent L2 user has apologised to me for their level of English; yet they were doing something I could not possibly do in their language: why wasn't I apologising? Because as a native speaker I had the right to impose my standards on others. People who have spent their language learning lives trying to speak as much like native speakers as possible become upset when you say that such a target is meaningless: what they want to hear is praise that they have almost got there and could be mistaken for natives.

What is required is then a proper description of L2 users to form the basis for teaching. Here comes the major problem: once a goal is defined in L2 user terms it is no longer a single putatively unified target like the native speaker. What is a successful level of L2 use for a particular individual or a particular country may not apply to others. An immigrant who wants to practices medicine in an English speaking country needs very different L2 use from say a medical researcher who wants access to the medical literature and the web through English. A child in Shanghai who may never encounter a live native speaker of English needs different L2 use from a Chinese child in Vancouver. This is the dilemma that confronted ESP: as soon as you start looking at individual needs for a second language you need to think of specialised goals.

Obviously many situations do generalise for large numbers of L2 users: travelling in English in non-English-speaking countries may be useful for large numbers of users who will never have conversations with native speakers. The description of such contact situations may be a valuable part of the syllabus, rather than the typical native to native or native to non-native speaker ones usually found in textbooks. Jenkins' (2000) account of the phonological needs of multilingual students in classrooms for talking to each other is an interesting example of this approach, though it does go outside a classroom environment. Eventually we may have descriptions of the language of successful L2 users on which to base our teaching. Meanwhile because of their long tradition and their availability, descriptions of the native speaker such as grammar-books or corpora of native speaker texts may be what we have to fall back on. But this is a temporary expedient; what is needed is proper descriptions of successful L2 users which can show their unique characteristics of grammar, vocabulary and pronunciation, rather than relegating them to deviation from the language of the native speaker

## 5.2 External and internal goals of language teaching

It is convenient to divide the goals of language teaching into *external goals* relating to the students' present or future use of the L2 outside the classroom and *internal goals* relating to the students' mental development as individuals (Cook, to appear).

Getting rid of the native speaker target changes the external goals of language teaching. The students' goal is to be able to use both the L2 and the L1 in the appropriate situations and for the appropriate uses. It is not necessarily to be like a native speaker or to mingle with native speakers, even if for some people this may be an appropriate goal. One of the unfortunate side effects of the communicative revolution in language teaching was its emphasis on external goals in an almost behaviourist way rather than on the internal development of the learners' minds. Hence for many years textbooks and syllabuses were concerned with how students should use the language in conversation and how they could convey ideas to other people—Wilkins' function and notions (Wilkins, 1976) not with internal goals

Yet a traditional benefit of language teaching was the internal goal of improving the students' mind within a humanitarian education. As we saw earlier, there are indeed cognitive changes in L2 users' minds compared to monolinguals, mostly to their benefit. At the level of national curricula, the UK Modern Language Curriculum (DfEE, 1999) expects pupils to 'understand and appreciate different countries', to 'learn about the basic structures of language' and how it 'can be manipulated'. The curriculum for Israel (1998) divides language teaching into domains: the domain of *appreciation of literature and culture* 'addresses the importance of fostering understanding and developing sensitivity to people of various cultural backgrounds' and the domain of *language* helps 'pupils develop their language use as well as gain further insight into the nature of their mother tongue' At the level of the students themselves, Coleman (1996) found that popular reasons for learning a modern language among UK university students were 'because I like the language' and 'to have a better understanding of the way of life in the country or countries where it is spoken'—internal goals.

So the consequence of an L2 user approach for the goals of language teaching means on the one hand basing the target on the external needs of L2 users, on the other focussing on desirable internal changes in the student. L2 users can add the ability to use a second language to their existing abilities so that they can behave as no monolingual can do. They may change the contents and processes of their minds in a way no monolingual can match.

Education has as always to balance the external value of a subject to the future social and career needs of the students with the internal value of the changing ways in which the students' minds can function.

## 5.3     Native speaker teachers

If the native speaker is no longer the standard against which L2 users are measured, what does this do to the position of native and non-native speaker teachers? Successful students will never become like the native speaker teacher since the vast majority of them will not get remotely near native speaker speech and will not think in monolingual ways but L2 user ways. They are much more likely to become like the non-native speaker teachers who are using a second language efficiently for a particular purpose. The only asset of the native speaker teacher is precisely that they are native speakers: if this is now immaterial to the goals of language teaching, then it is no longer an asset. And of course this is a waning asset since the L1 is progressively changed in a native speaker in an non native speaking environment (Porte, 2003).

This approach ties in with the debate over the merits of native speaker and non-native speaker teachers in language teaching (Cook, 1999). In many parts of the world it is simply taken for granted that native speakers are best. Language teaching institutions stress this in their advertisements and in their employment policies. A trawl of the web immediately finds a school in Brazil that wants 'Native English speaker, bilingual, university degree', one in Italy that wants 'experienced, qualified professional native speaking English Language Teachers', one in Indonesia that needs 'Native EFL teachers' and one in China looking for 'Enthusiastic NATIVE English Teachers'. It is obviously felt to be a major selling point for an institution to have native speaker teachers.

Students are not necessarily as impressed by native speaker teachers as one might suppose. I conducted a questionnaire survey of L2 students of children aged on average 14 and adults in six countries; the main objective was to evaluate their attitudes to monolingualism but at the same time I slipped in some questions about other topics. So one question asked whether they agreed or disagreed with the statement 'Native speakers make the best language teachers'. The students in the six countries I had access to were either adult learners of English or child learners aged on average 14, and are obviously not a representaive sample of countries or ages. Still, as seen in Figure 1, the approval rating for native speaker teachers converted to scores out of a hundred ranges from 72% for children in England down to 33% for children in Belgium and from 82% for adults in England to 51% for adults in Taiwan. While this indeed confirms a preference for native speakers, this is not overwhelming preference with the exception of England. L2 students do not feel that strongly about having native teachers. Given that students are just reflecting the knee-jerk reactions of the societies in which they dwell and the beliefs of their teachers and parents it is surprising that they are luke-warm about native speaker teachers.

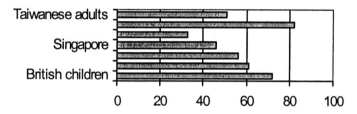

*Figure 1.* Average approval rating of 'Native speakers make the best language teachers' out of 100.

The pros and cons of native and non-native speaker teachers from the L2 user perspective are then:

- *non-native speaker teachers provide models of proficient L2 users in action in the classroom.* Here is a person who knows two languages using the second language effectively, showing that it is possible to do this in a language that is not one's own. The native speaker teacher who does not know the first language of the students is only a model of something alien which the students can never be. Here also is a person who can speak from personal experience of the difference that L2 learning has made to their mental lives, to their appreciation of other cultures and to their feeling for language, something that the monolingual native speaker cannot do and probably does not even appreciate that it exists.
- *non-native speaker teachers present examples of people who have become successful L2 users.* The non-native teacher has been through the same route as the students and has acquired another language, a living demonstration that this is possible for non-native learners. They have shared the student's own experience at some time in their lives and have learnt the language by the same route that the students are taking. The native speaker teacher cannot appreciate their experiences and problems except at second hand.
- *non-native speaker teachers often have more appropriate training and background.* Expatriate native speakers come in from outside the

country and do not necessarily see the culture of the classroom and the values of the educational system in the same way; they usually do not have as deep a knowledge of the educational system as the indigenous teacher. Many native speaker teachers have not had the same level of teacher training as the native or have not been trained in the systems and methods of that country. Though these are accidental by-products—not all native speakers are handicapped by ignorance of the local situation and by lack of training—this certainly applies to a large proportion of the expats teaching English as a Foreign Language in different parts of the world

- *non-native speaker teachers may have the disadvantage of lesser fluency etc.* The above is predicated on the non native speaker teacher indeed being an efficient L2 user who can speak fluently and communicate within the classroom. It may be for one reason or other that some teachers do not attain this level; in many countries teachers do not feel their command of English is adequate for the demands of their task. But this is only relevant if it reflect shortcomings in being L2 users, not shortcomings in being like a native speaker: the type of English needed for successful use as a language teacher may be different from that of the native speaker; several times one has heard of successful teaching by teachers who were effectively going through the course one step ahead of the students in terms of learning, perhaps giving them an even greater feel for the students' problems.

## 5.4    The first language in the classroom

If the first language is always part of the L2 user's multicompetence, then we have to re-examine its role in language teaching. Current language teaching has mostly tried to minimise the use of the first language in the classroom (Cook, 2001). A typical view is that in the UK National Curriculum (DfEE, 1999)—'The natural use of the target language for virtually all communication is a sure sign of a good modern language course', a prevailing view for the past hundred years—'It is assumed throughout that the teacher's success is judged by the rarity of his lapses into the foreign tongue' (Thorley, 1918). If the L2 user has two languages available in the same mind, teaching should make systematic, deliberate use of the first language, partly by developing methods that incorporate both languages, partly by evaluating when the L1 can be used effectively within the L2 classroom, both as part of a true L2 user situation and to help the students' learning. This means recognising the classroom as a true L2 use situation, not an imitation L1 situation, so that the first language can be used:

- *as a way of conveying L2 meaning.* In many circumstances the first language is as effective a means of conveying meaning as any other, provided it does not lead to treating the meanings of the second language as translation equivalents of the first language.
- *as a short-cut for explaining tasks, tests etc.* If the point of a teaching activity is the task itself, not the way of getting people to do the task, then the teacher has to find the quickest and most effective way of getting the task underway, which may well be to use the first language of the students. Rather one minute of instructions in the L1 and 9 minutes in the L2 doing the task than 9 minutes of instructions in the L2 and 1 minute in the L2 doing the task.
- *as a way of explaining grammar.* If the goal is for students to understand the grammar itself rather than to benefit from the incidental language involved, again the teacher has to choose the best vehicle for conveying this, which may be the first language, as indeed many teachers already prefer (Franklin, 1990). This also has the advantage of building on grammatical models and terminology familiar to the students rather than on the Latin-based concepts and terms of the English-speaking world's tradition of school grammar.
- *for practising L2 uses such as code-switching.* Mostly frowned on within communicative teaching, the use of code-switching in the classroom is nevertheless almost inevitable when the students know each other's first language. rather than being shunned this might be deliberately controlled by the teacher as a gain for the students as recommended in the New Concurrent Method (Jacobson & Faltis, 1990).

Obviously the use of the first language in the classroom should not be taken to an extreme. The teacher has a duty to provide as much input in the L2 as possible simply because the class may be the only time when the students encounter the second language and in particular when it is actually being used for real classroom and social functions. But it is wrong to try to impose a total ban on the L1 in the classroom, partly as this makes teachers feel guilty in not observing it, partly because it ignores the very real ways in which the first language can be used, partly because it does not take account of the classroom as an authentic situation of L2 use, rather than pseudo-native speaker use.

## 6.    CONCLUSIONS

We see that starting from the L2 user has multiple consequences for language teaching. Many of these may be incompatible with other features of the teaching situation and the syllabus or even with the students own perceived needs and so can be ruled out once a wider picture of teaching is taken into account. Nevertheless this approach by questioning existing assumptions that are taken on trust by language teaching may lead to newer, sounder and fairer teaching that treats students as successes not as failures for not becoming something they can never be—swans, not ugly ducklings.

## 7.    REFERENCES

Athanasopoulos, P. (2001). L2 acquisition and bilingual conceptual structure. MA thesis, University of Essex.

Bassetti, B., Cook, V., Kasai, C., Sasaki, M., Takahashi, J. & Tokumaru, Y. (2002). Perception of form and substance in Japanese users of English. Paper presented at EUROSLA, Basel, September.

Bialystok, E. (2001). *Bilingualism in development.* Cambridge University Press.

Birdsong, D. (1992). Ultimate attainment in second language acquisition. *Language, 68* (4), 706-755.

Bongaerts, T., van Summeren, Planken, B., & Schils, E. (1997). Age and ultimate attainment in the pronunciation of a foreign language. *Studies in Second Language Acquisition, 19* (4), 447-465.

Canada Tree (1996). Genealogy to history. http://users.rttinc.com/~canadatree/

Chomsky, N. (1986). *Knowledge of language: Its nature, origin and use.* New York: Praeger.

Coleman, J.A. (1996). *Studying languages: A survey of British and European students.* London: CILT.

Cook, V.J. (1985). Language functions, social factors, and second language teaching. *IRAL, 13* (3), 177-196.

Cook, V.J. (1991). The poverty-of-the-stimulus argument and multi-competence. *Second Language Research, 7* (2), 103-117.

Cook, V.J. (1999). Going beyond the native speaker in language teaching. *TESOL Quarterly 33* (2), 185-209.

Cook, V.J. (2001). Using the first language in the classroom. *Canadian Modern Language Review, 57* (3), 402-423.

Cook, V.J. (2002a). Background to the L2 user. In V.J. Cook (Ed.), *Portraits of the L2 user.* Clevedon: Multilingual Matters. 1-28.

Cook, V.J. (Ed.) (2002b). *Portraits of the L2 user.* Clevedon: Multilingual Matters.

Cook, V.J. (Ed.) (2003). *Effects of the L2 on the L1.* Clevedon: Multilingual Matters.

Cook, V.J. (to appear). The goals of ELT: Reproducing native-speakers or promoting multicompetence among second language users? In C. Davison & J. Cummins (Eds.), *Kluwer Handbook on English Language Teaching I.* Dordrecht: Kluwer Academic Press.

Cook, V.J., Iarossi, E., Stellakis, N. & Tokumaru, Y. (2003). Effects of the second language on the syntactic processing of the first language. In V.J.Cook (Ed.), *Effects of the L2 on the L1.* Clevedon: Multilingual Matters. 193-213.

Coppieters, R. (1987). Competence differences between native and near-native speakers. *Language, 63* (3), 545-573.

Department for Education and Employment - DfEE (1999). The National Curriculum for England: modern foreign languages. http://www.nc.uk.net/download/cMFL.pdf

Diaz, R.M. (1985). The intellectual power of bilingualism. *Quarterly Newsletter of the Laboratory of Comparative Human Cognition, 7* (1), 16-22.

Felix, S. (1987). *Cognition and language growth.* Dordrecht: Foris.

Flege, J.E. (1987). The production of 'new' and 'similar' phones in a foreign language: Evidence for the effect of equivalence classification. *Journal of Phonetics, 15,* 47-65.

Franklin, C.E.M. (1990). Teaching in the target language. *Language Learning Journal,* Sept, 20-24.

Grosjean, F. (1989). Neurolinguists, beware! The bilingual is not two monolinguals in one person. *Brain and Language, 36,* 3-15.

Grosjean, F. (2001). The bilingual's language modes. In J. Nicol (Ed.), *One mind, two languages.* Oxford: Blackwell. 1-22.

Israel Government (1998, revised). English-Curriculum for all grades. http://www.education.gov.il/tochniyot_limudim/eng1.htm

Jacobson, R. & Faltis, C. (Eds.) (1990). *Language distribution issues in bilingual schooling.* Clevedon: Multilingual Matters.

Jenkins, J. (2000). *The phonology of English as an international language.* Oxford: Oxford University Press.

Kecskes, I. & Papp, T. (2000). *Foreign language and mother tongue.* Mahwah, NJ: Lawrence Erlbaum Associates.

Labov, W. (1969). The logic of non-standard English. *Georgetown Monographs on Language and Linguistics, 22,* 1-31.

Larsen-Freeman, D. & Long, M. (1991). *An introduction to second language acquisition research.* London & New York: Longman.

Laufer, B. (2003). The influence of L2 on L1 collocational knowledge and on L1 lexical diversity in free written expression. In V.J. Cook (Ed.), *Effects of the L2 on the L1.* Clevedon: Multilingual Matters. 19-31.

Levinson, S.C. (1996). Relativity in spatial conception and description. In J.J. Gumperz & S.C. Levinson (Eds.), *Rethinking Linguistic Relativity.* Cambridge: Cambridge University Press. 177-202.

Paradis, M. (1997). The cognitive neuropsychology of bilingualism. In A.M.B. de Groot & J. Kroll (Eds), *Tutorials in bilingualism. Psycholinguistic perspectives.* Mahwah, NJ: Lawrence Erlbaum Associates. 331-354.

Pavlenko, A. (2003). 'I feel clumsy speaking Russian': L2 influence on L1 in narratives of Russina L2 users of English. In V.J. Cook (Ed.), *Effects of the L2 on the L1.* Clevedon: Multilingual Matters. 32-61.

Perdue, C. (2002). Development of L2 functional use. In V.J. Cook (Ed.), *Portraits of the L2 user.* Clevedon: Multilingual Matters. 121-144.

Porte, G. (2003). English from a distance: Code-mixing and blending in the L1 output of long-term resident overseas EFL teachers. In V.J. Cook (Ed.), *Effects of the L2 on the L1.* Clevedon: Multilingual Matters. 103-119.

Thorley, W.C. (1918). *A primer of English for foreign students.* London: Macmillan.

Wilkins, D.A. (1976). *Notional syllabuses.* Oxford: Oxford University Press.

Yelland, G.W., Pollard, J. & Mercuri, A. (1993). The metalinguistic benefits of limited contact with a second language. *Applied Psycholinguistics, 14,* 423-444.

Chapter 5

# CODESWITCHING IN THE L2 CLASSROOM: A COMMUNICATION AND LEARNING STRATEGY

ERNESTO MACARO
*University of Oxford*


## 1.     INTRODUCTION

Codeswitching (switching between two or more languages) in naturalistic discourse occurs when a speaker and an interlocutor share more than one language or dialect. It occurs because the speaker finds it easier or more appropriate, in the linguistic and/or cultural context, to communicate by switching than by keeping the utterance totally in the same language. Codeswitching occurs frequently and is widespread throughout the world's bilingual language communities. The fact that bilinguals can codeswitch is an asset and a valuable addition to their array of communication strategies.

In classroom discourse, by contrast, codeswitching is considered by many to be neither an asset nor a valuable addition. This may seem surprising given that so often, in modern approaches to language teaching and learning, teachers attempt to make the second language classroom a mirror of the outside world. Why then should there be this difference of attitude towards codeswitching?

My research on codeswitching has been carried out entirely in formal classroom settings among adolescent learners. Moreover, although I will review a variety of other classroom settings, my research has been in classrooms where the learners, by and large, share the same L1. Although in these classrooms the teacher may not necessarily share the same L1 as the

E. Llurda (Ed.), *Non-Native Language Teachers. Perceptions, Challenges and Contributions to the Profession*, 63—84.

learners (*i.e.* they will not be of the same nationality), he/she will be at least as competent in the learners' L1 as they are in the language that they are learning (usually the teacher's native language). This is therefore a different context from the one which the monolingual native speaker (usually English) teacher operates in and illustrated elsewhere in this volume (*e.g.* by Cook). For this reason I will use the terms *monolingual teacher* and *bilingual teacher* rather than *native speaker* and *non-native speaker*.

Codeswitching, by definition, is only available to the bilingual teacher. Whilst, as I shall argue, the ability of the bilingual teacher to codeswitch is to be viewed as an asset, it also brings with it a number of problems and issues.

My aim in this chapter, is to attempt to answer eight questions related to codeswitching in the second language (L2) classroom:

- Why is codeswitching in the L2 classroom such a contentious issue?
- Is codeswitching contentious as classroom behaviour just for the teacher or also for the learners?
- What do language teachers think of the practice of codeswitching?
- For what purposes (or communicative functions) do language teachers codeswitch and how much codeswitching goes on?
- What do learners think about teachers codeswitching during lessons?
- What are the effects of codeswitching or not codeswitching on classroom interaction?
- What are the effects of not codeswitching on the learner's strategy development?
- Can codeswitching be a systematic, principled and planned part of the L2 curriculum?

## 2.  WHY IS CODESWITCHING IN THE L2 CLASSROOM SUCH A CONTENTIOUS ISSUE?

In other publications (including my own) the phrase 'recourse to L1' is sometimes used in addition to or instead of 'codeswitching'. This implies *a priori* that codeswitching in the classroom is undesirable or to be regretted. Why should this be, given that codeswitching occurs naturally among bilinguals? We will note that, in the introductory paragraph, I suggested that bilinguals codeswitch because they find it easier or more appropriate for the purposes of communication. I have also argued elsewhere (Macaro, 1997, 2001a) that communication strategies, whilst being of great indirect benefit to L2 users (in that they keep the interaction going, attract greater quality input, etc.), do not in themselves lead *directly* to greater language competence. For example, word coinage does not increase the mental lexicon and syntactic avoidance does not lead to expansion of the L2 rule system. If the teacher's practice of codeswitching, therefore, is to be regarded as a communication strategy the case has to be made that the learner's indirect benefits are at least equal to if not more than the benefits of not codeswitching. If we accept that a teacher's codeswitching is (or at least can be) a communication strategy, then it has to be a better communication strategy at a certain point in a lesson than, say, repetition or circumlocution.

Thus we can begin to see how the contentious nature of codeswitching in the classroom is related to whether native speaker teachers make better practitioners than non-natives. In this aspect of the discussion it is not difficult to trace political and economic forces at play. It is in the dominant cultures' (UK, USA) interest to promote the idea that codeswitching is bad practice in the ELT classroom. Yet, the match between the bilingual teacher's brain and that of the L2 learner is much closer than that of the monolingual teacher and the L2 learner. Consequently, the former teacher's understanding of the learner's interlanguage state is likely to be much richer than that of the native speaker teacher who will, by necessity, be forced to *override* interlanguage development being unable to detect a great deal of the systematicity in it. Moreover, the teacher who has learnt more than one language is able to demonstrate that learning and using a second language is achievable and useful both to themselves and to others.

Codeswitching is also contentious because, in the past, the most desirable form of bilingualism has been one in which the individual demonstrates no interference in either language from the 'other' language. This aspiration was based on the assumption that the lexical architecture in the brain is based on a *co-ordinate bilingual model* (Weinreich, 1953) with which bilinguals develop two separate language-specific lexicons. As Libben (2000) now argues, neurological research suggests that a homogenous architecture is much more likely, one in which all closely related representations are activated by a given stimulus, regardless of whether they were originally created through one language or through another.

Codeswitching by the bilingual teacher is contentious because it flies in the face of the notion of comprehensible input (Krashen, 1987). If learners learn by adding, to their store of knowledge, just that little bit more of the new language *via inference* (i + 1), then why should they need to know what the equivalent linguistic element is in their own language? If L2 learners cannot learn new patterns of the language out of sequence from a natural order of L2 acquisition (Dulay & Burt, 1974; Bailey, Madden & Krashen, 1974), codeswitching may lead to a focus on structures 'much further up the learning line' which in turn may lead to overuse of the 'monitor' (Krashen &

Terrell, 1988). Related to this is the fact that codeswitching flies in the face of negotiation of meaning. Countless studies (see Pica, 1994, for a review) have sought to demonstrate that learners not only understand the language better but also acquire it through the negotiation of problematic breakdowns in the conversation. The fact that these breakdowns have been almost entirely semantically related (related to noun, adjectives and the *meaning* of verbs) has not led to a barrage of questions as to how all the rest of the grammar of the target language is acquired. It is possible, I would argue, that the unswerving faith in the comprehensible input—meaning negotiation—comprehensible output continuum has been entirely due to the fact that the proponents of these theories and hypotheses simply did not speak the first language of their subjects or students.

Codeswitching in the classroom is contentious because it reminds researchers and practitioners of the grammar-translation method of language teaching and this method, although it is still used in watered-down forms, is currently unfashionable.

Codeswitching by the bilingual teacher is contentious because it is believed to cut down on the amount of exposure that the learner has to the L2. However, some have argued that it is not the quantity of exposure to the L2 that is important but the quality of exposure (Dickson, 1992). In which case, the hypothesis to be tested is that large amounts of input do not necessarily lead to *take-up* of the language by the learner.

Finally, codeswitching is contentious because some national agencies attempt to control what teachers do in the classroom. As, unfortunately, teacher autonomy in the past has not been shored up by strong research evidence, people in power have tried to impose certain methodologies regardless of the lack of evidence for their propagation. One instance of this attempt to control teachers occurred in England in the early 1990s when government agencies, about to introduce a National Curriculum for Modern Languages, claimed that 'the natural use of the target language for virtually all communication is a sure sign of a good modern languages course' (Department of Education and Science, 1990: 58). This was backed up by the inspectorate who argued that 'teachers should insist on the use of the target language for all aspects of a lesson' (OFSTED, 1993: section 37) and that pupils had no difficulty in understanding lessons which were 'competently' conducted entirely in the target language (OFSTED, 1995). Exams were then introduced in which the sole method of establishing comprehension and achieving tasks was through the target language. The justification for this should make us stop and think. It rested on the claim that it was a perfectly successful practice in the TEFL world (Neather, *et al.*, 1995). In this way the sluice gate was completely shut on any debate about the value of codeswitching and at the same time it provided the inspectorate with a simple yardstick with which to judge the competence of a teacher. The measurement of success came to be to what extent could the bilingual teacher deny and overcome his/her bilingualism.

## 3. IS CODESWITCHING CONTENTIOUS AS CLASSROOM BEHAVIOUR JUST FOR THE TEACHER OR ALSO FOR THE LEARNERS?

Codeswitching by students is also contentious. Codeswitching among learners is common place in the L2 classroom where the learners share the same L1 and this is why parents, at great expense, send their children to England and America in order to sit in classrooms where they do not share the same L1. I know of no research evidence to suggest whether students learn better or worse in an 'impossible to codeswitch' type of classroom environment.

Teachers often complain that their students switch to their L1 in collaborative activities and particularly decry codeswitching in task-based oral activities such as pair work. Research suggests that codeswitching occurs not in the topic of the task but in the management of the task (Macaro, 1997) or when discussing unknown language words (Knight, 1996), or for social interaction (Tarone & Swain, 1995). Thus some teachers argue that the important aim is for the task's linguistic objectives to be achieved even if this is at the expense of codeswitching (Macaro, 2001b). Others maintain that the task's linguistic objectives should include the language needed for the task's management (*e.g.* Prahbu, 1987; Asher, 1993). I have observed (Macaro, 1997) that whereas there seems to be a fairly clear pedagogy for the topic language itself, the pedagogy for increasing the task management language is limited to phrases written on classroom walls or in students' notebooks. It is not surprising and entirely natural that students should codeswitch in order to achieve a task, the 'management language' of which they have not been taught. They are, after all, negotiating meaning by using a communication strategy in order to compensate for lack of linguistic knowledge.

Codeswitching in collaborative activities is contentious because it is considered by some teachers as evidence of off-task behaviour and, in the case of adolescents, deviant or disruptive behaviour.

Codeswitching by individual students is also regarded as evidence that they are not thinking as much as possible in the L2. For example some national agencies advocate banishing the students' L1 from the classroom in order 'to lessen any desire the pupils may have to engage in the process of translation' (Department of Education for Northern Ireland, 1985). Again, the notion is that L2 learners and users should suppress their bilingualism. Many theorists would now agree (see a review by Cohen, 1998) that the language of thought for all but the most advanced L2 learner/user is inevitably his/her L1. Yet many teachers cling to the belief that, given the right conditions, the learners in their classrooms can 'think' in the L2 when undertaking a task. This belief is not exclusive to the monolingual teacher.

## 4.        WHAT DO LANGUAGE TEACHERS THINK OF THE PRACTICE OF CODESWITCHING?

We have touched on this in trying to answer previous questions. Now let us try to answer the question in greater depth. In a review of studies of teacher beliefs (Macaro, 2000a) across age phases and educational contexts, I found a remarkable similarity of beliefs at the cross-sectional level. By far the majority of bilingual teachers regard codeswitching as unfortunate and regrettable but necessary. That is, they conceptualise it not as *codeswitching* but as *recourse to L1*. Recourse to L1 is reported by teachers as occurring across all learning contexts in which there is a choice of language use.

In all the studies one gets an overwhelming impression that bilingual teachers believe that the L2 should be the *predominant* language of interaction in the classroom. On the other hand, in none of the studies I have come across is there a majority of teachers in favour of excluding the L1 altogether. However, preference for including the L1 is not based on a perception of its value in terms of cognitive development but because teachers believe the perfect conditions, which would allow the total exclusion of the L1, do not exist. Interestingly, I have not come across any studies which specifically ask the opinions of monolingual teachers. That is, I have not come across a question such as: 'do you wish that you *were* able to make use of the learners' L1?'

The major variables in (reported) teacher recourse to L1 are the 'ability' of the learners, and the age of the learners. The findings suggest that teachers in the secondary sector use more L1 with 'less able' learners because these learners find it more difficult to infer meaning and therefore get more easily frustrated. In other words, recourse to L1 is almost entirely a comprehension issue not an acquisition issue.

In the research context I have been involved in, the nationality of the teacher is not a significant variable when it comes to teachers' beliefs about the value of codeswitching. Teachers who are foreign nationals, just like their English colleagues, soon become convinced that codeswitching is regrettable but necessary.

Lastly, many teachers report feeling guilty when they resort to the L1. This is not a healthy outcome of a pedagogical debate.

## 5. FOR WHAT PURPOSES DO LANGUAGE TEACHERS CODESWITCH AND HOW MUCH CODESWITCHING GOES ON?

Teachers, across learning contexts, report (Macaro, 2000a) that the areas in which they use the L1 are:

1. building personal relationship with learners (the pastoral role that teachers take on requires high levels of discourse sophistication);
2. giving complex procedural instructions for carrying out an activity;
3. controlling pupils' behaviour;
4. translating and checking understanding in order to speed things up because of time pressures (*e.g.* exams);
5. teaching grammar explicitly.

Systematic observation data (in the Macaro 1997 study of lower-secondary classrooms in England) confirmed some of these teacher self-reports. The L1 was particularly noted when the teacher was giving complex procedural instructions. Additionally, in this context, the L1 was used when giving feedback to students. By this is meant feedback on progress in substantial form, for example on a task just accomplished, rather than quick feedback in the standard I-R-F questioning sequence.

What is interesting about the findings above is that the L1 is used predominantly for message-oriented functions. It is interesting because one would assume that it would be used mainly for medium-oriented functions where L1/L2 comparisons might be being made. I would suggest that the reason for this is that the amount of input modification needed for certain message-oriented utterances to be successful is beyond the scope of most teachers in the time allocated to them and with the fear of the students 'switching off'. Codeswitching therefore becomes a useful communication strategy.

Two quantitative studies (Macaro, 2001b; Macaro & Mutton, 2002) found that the percentage of codeswitching that was occurring in beginner and lower-intermediate classrooms was quite small. In the first study, with six pre-service teachers (of which two were foreign nationals), the proportion of L1 use by the teachers, as a proportion of the whole lesson, was no more than 4.8% (Mean) and as a proportion of the oral interaction was only 6.9% with no lesson recording more than 15.2% L1 use (Macaro, 2001b: 537). In the second study (Macaro & Mutton, 2002), with two more experienced teachers (both foreign nationals), the results were very similar (5.5% as proportion of interaction time and 5.0% of the total lesson time). These are considerably modest figures and a lot lower than those estimated by Chaudron (1988) who put teacher L1 use at around 30%. The qualitative data gathered in the study suggested that the motive for low levels of codeswitching was largely dictated by the pressure of the National Curriculum in England (see above). In addition, as L1 speech can be delivered comparatively quickly, the discourse space allocated to it was quite small. In other words the teachers could communicate quite a lot in L1 in a very short time thus still allocating plenty of discourse space to the L2.

## 6.     WHAT DO LEARNERS THINK ABOUT TEACHERS CODESWITCHING DURING LESSONS?

The research evidence on this is scant and unfocused. Duff & Polio (1990), in a university context, found remarkable lack of consensus (and not particularly strong views) among learners as to whether their teachers should use the L1. Hopkins (1989), found that 76% of adult learners found the L1 helpful. Again, none of these studies asked students if they would prefer a monolingual teacher who would be completely unable to refer to their L1.

More recent studies have focused on the possible negative reactions of (particularly adolescent) learners faced with virtually all L2 teacher input. In the school context, the evidence we have suggests that learners may divide into two camps according to individual preferences (Macaro, 1997). Some learners get frustrated when they can't understand the teacher's L2 input and want to know the exact meaning of words and phrases. This is usually because of the consequences of not understanding—for example not being able to achieve a homework task. Others feel comfortable with the teacher's pedagogy or, at least, go along with it. For this group of students although it would be easier for the teacher to codeswitch they feel that in the long run they will learn more if he/she does not. There is no evidence pointing in the direction of higher achieving learners (or faster learners) feeling more at ease with L2 exclusivity. It seems to be more to do with individual preferences. Some like the teacher to make immediate and explicit L1/L2 connections others do not feel this is necessary.

There is some evidence that adolescent males react less favourably to teacher exclusive use of L2 (Stables & Wikeley, 1999, Jones, *et al.*, 2001) and want to know exactly what is going on. It is possible that the unequal power relationships between teacher and pupils found in most classrooms is accentuated in those L2 classrooms where the bilingual teacher excludes the L1 almost completely and this negatively affects males more than females. The Jones *et al.* study found that when some boys did not understand, exclusive use of the L2 became problematic:

> Sometimes they babble on in French and I haven't got a clue what she's going on about but the rest of them have . . . others get down with the work and I can't do it. . . I have to ask (op cit.: 24)

> Listening to the teacher go on about all the different things . . .after a while it gets boring and you lose concentration and drift off and do other things . . . (op. cit.: 37)

However this was not restricted to boys as this girl reports in a study by Clark & Trafford (1996: 44)

> 'she just yabs on and on, it gets really boring'

The problem with these studies, is that they are framed in terms of negative reactions to the bilingual teacher's discourse patterns. They do not try to pose the question: to what extent does the L1 actually help you learn? Perhaps because it is assumed that it does not. We will return to the direct impact of the L1 on L2 learning later. For the moment let us look at the kinds of discourse environments that codeswitching sets up. This discussion is based on a pre-supposition that students talking in the L2 is a good thing and relates to the tradition of research literature on interaction started by Long (1981).

## 7. WHAT ARE THE EFFECTS OF CODESWITCHING OR NOT CODESWITCHING ON CLASSROOM INTERACTION?

Other than my own studies mentioned above, I have not come across any quantitative research on the effects of codeswitching by the teacher on the general interaction. My two studies with pre-service and with experienced teachers (Macaro, 2001b and Macaro & Mutton, 2002 respectively) showed that when codeswitching was kept at a level below about 10% there was no significant increase in the learners' use of L1 in the whole group interaction.

In other words there was no correlation between teacher use of L1 and learner use of L1. Conversely, no significant increase in the students' use of L2 was detected if the teacher used the L2 exclusively or almost exclusively. In the above studies, it would appear from a quantitative and qualitative analysis of the data, that codeswitching by the teacher has no negative impact on the quantity of students' L2 production and that 'expert codeswitching' may actually increase it and improve it. Nevertheless, there may be a kind of *threshold* reached by teacher use of L1 where the codeswitching resembles less a communication strategy than simply a discourse carried out entirely in L1 with only a marginal reference to the L2. The clues to how we might accurately pinpoint and describe this threshold probably lie in discourse analysis theory (Sinclair & Coulthard, 1975; Sinclair & Brazil, 1982). It may be fruitful to pursue the notion that it is the *transaction* which determines the intent of the bilingual teacher in his/her discourse. Thus if the *transactional intent* is to communicate via the L2, the codeswitch will not push the amount of L1 use above the threshold level. The function of the codeswitch is a strategic repair.

I am now going to propose the hypothesis that if there is no codeswitching by the teacher, and very little allowed by the learners, then a number of discourse control features can come into play which are entirely manipulated by the teacher and, possibly, are detrimental to the learner.

Firstly, avoidance of codeswitching leads to greater use of input modification. In fact, in naturalistic settings, avoidance of input modification is a prime reason for the use of codeswitching. Speakers want to communicate without the time taken to modify the input. Below are listed some characteristics of teacher input modification and their effect on classroom interaction. I should point out that I am not suggesting that these characteristics have no beneficial effects, merely that they can have *some* negative effects such as increasing teacher talk-student talk ratios.

One of the potential underlying effects of input modification is that it can reduce interaction. Input modification comes out of the comprehensible input camp where it is claimed that the students will have no trouble understanding lessons conducted entirely in the L2 provided they were competently so conducted (see quote above) and that students need not be asked to speak until they are ready. What input modification actually does is to provide students with a listening text and exploitation exercises all in one—in effect a listening comprehension task. One of its functions is to reduce the need for clarification requests. This is why there was so much literature on *interaction modification* following the post-Krashen period.

| Characteristic of input modification by teacher | Negative effect on interaction |
|---|---|
| Repeating | Increases the teacher's discourse space (henceforth ITDS) |
| Speaking more slowly | ITDS and makes the discourse less realistic |
| Inserting longer pauses | ITDS |
| Stressing certain words or phrases resulting in prosodic change | ITDS; provides unnatural models for production; may result in less focus on syntax (see Harley, 2000) |
| Stressing certain words or phrases by making them louder than the rest of the utterance | Provides unnatural models for production |
| Substitute simple word for complex word | Reduces the lexical diversity |
| Substitute cognate for non-cognate | Reduces the lexical diversity and may encourage poor textual decoding strategies with an over-use of cognate search (see Macaro, 2001a) |
| Exemplifying (a week = Monday, Tuesday, Wednesday | ITDS |
| Paraphrasing | ITDS; it may also reduce lexical diversity |
| Modifying syntax (*e.g.* by using canonical forms) | Reduces exposure to complex syntactic structures and may affect complexity of response |
| Modifying syntax through fewer subordinate clauses | Reduces possibility of elaboration of discourse |

Now, I want to stress again that I am not proposing that input modification is wrong or shouldn't be used. Each of these characteristics can have a positive effect on learning, such as inferencing skills. Whereas in naturalistic discourse between two bilinguals it is often redundant (because of the codeswitching alternative), in the languages classroom it has a clear teaching function. However, it often results in the teacher hogging the discourse space and, used unsparingly, leads to 'the dumbing down' of the classroom discourse.

Input modification is not the only aspect of non-codeswitching which has a negative effect on the interaction. I am again particularly drawing from adolescent classrooms here. In order to avoid a codeswitch teachers use mime to put across the meaning of a linguistic item. In a sense this is a kind of codeswitch-switching from a verbal code to signed code. Although this may help with communication, the focus is taken away from the language in the interaction. Eventually, if the same mime is repeated long enough, the students may stop listening to the spoken language altogether and just understand from the mime.

In order to avoid a codeswitch the teacher demonstrates to the pupils what they have to do. For example they may position learners in a particular way in order to show them how not to see each other's information in an information-gap activity. Again, this is a substitute for language which helps with communication but does not help with acquiring new language.

## 8.     WHAT ARE THE EFFECTS OF NOT CODESWITCHING ON LANGUAGE LEARNER STRATEGY DEVELOPMENT?

Research on cognition, whatever the model of working memory adopted (see Myake & Shah, 1999 for a review), points to problems associated with the limitations of working memory components. For example in the Baddeley & Logie (1999) model the limitations of the phonological loop and the visuo-spatial sketchpad (seen in terms of capacity limitations and duration limitations) are what can impede or facilitate coding and processing in working memory and storing and retrieval in and from long term memory. I want to argue that codeswitching is used by beginner and intermediate learners (but also to some extent by advanced learners) in order to lighten the cognitive load problems in working memory. This strategy of lightening the cognitive load can be activated in a number of language learning tasks.

Kern (1994), for example, attempted to elicit the language of thought during a reading comprehension task and concluded that learners were using their L1 as the language of thought, to their advantage, in order to:

- reduce *working memory* constraints;
- avoid losing track of the meaning of the text;
- consolidate meaning in *long term memory*;
- convert the input into more familiar terms (thereby reducing anxiety);
- clarify the syntactic roles of certain lexical items.

Thus the L1 was being used by the students to lighten the cognitive load as they were trying to process the text. If we can consider classroom discourse as text to be decoded and understood, we can perceive how the teacher's codeswitching can help counter the cognitive constraints imposed by working memory limitations. A codeswitch can reduce the selective attention dedicated to a single communication breakdown, freeing up working memory capacity to work on the meaning of larger chunks of input whilst at the same time offering the hearer the opportunity of quick storage of an L1-L2 equivalent they were previously not aware of.

Teachers, deprived of codeswitching from their tool kit, cannot act as a bilingual dictionary for the learners. In fact, the diktat that there should be no recourse to L1 by the teacher makes bilingual teachers behave like monolingual dictionaries. Most learners report finding bilingual dictionaries (Bishop, 2000) a useful tool in carrying out reading and writing tasks. It is true that some learners use dictionaries too much (particularly in exams) thus pre-empting the possible deployment of other important strategies, for example top down processing in reading comprehension. Nevertheless, taking away the bilingual teacher's right to codeswitch is like taking away the student's right to use a bilingual dictionary. The use of a bilingual dictionary in a reading comprehension task is a way of lightening the cognitive load by, for example, reducing the number of unknown elements the reader is asking working memory to keep activated at any one time. In fact it could be argued that judicious use by the teacher of codeswitching is a way of modelling, in an implicit way, judicious dictionary use whilst at the same time lightening the cognitive load brought about by constant high speed inferencing in the spoken medium. As well as modelling a cognitive strategy, the bilingual teacher therefore offers the learner a metacognitive learning strategy: evaluation of when it is appropriate to use a dictionary and when it is appropriate to make the cognitive effort to infer from context.

Teachers, deprived of codeswitching from their tool kit are unable to offer learners translation as a learning task. Monolingual teachers, of course, cannot offer this kind of task. Banning translation from the L2 classroom deprives learners of the possibility of developing a valuable language skill that they are very likely to need in the outside world, particularly the world of work. Moreover, and following on from the previous paragraph, banning translation deprives teachers of the possibility of modelling reading strategies (see Macaro, 2001a for a fuller explanation) and training the students to use them. Not only does it model appropriate dictionary use as a strategy, but it also draws the learners' attention to how to look for contextual clues, syntactic clues, text design clues, how to make decisions of which bits of language to skip and when to return to them once more in-text evidence has been gained. It is also an appropriate vehicle with which to give learners negative evidence of the transferability of L1 structures to L2 structures (Spada & Lightbown, 1999). In effect the teacher can use oral translation of a text with the class as a kind of group think-aloud protocol where the strategies the students use to understand the text are elicited, shared, developed and evaluated. Teachers who never offer this type of group translation have to resort to L2 only comprehension tasks: true/false; multiple choice; find synonyms in the text. These tasks are essentially product focused. They tell the teacher what the learner knows or can do. By and large they fail to inform the teacher of what strategy-combinations, appropriate or inappropriate, the learner is using *during the process* of comprehension. Paradoxically, the avoidance of providing L1/L2 equivalents leads to an over-reliance on searching for cognates in text (Macaro, 2000b) to the detriment of other, equally important strategies. The strategies the learners deploy have the potential to make their learning faster, more personalised and more effective (Oxford, 1990). Banning codeswitching reduces this potential.

Teachers, deprived of codeswitching from their tool kit find it hard to offer students pre-listening activities which trigger appropriate combinations of listening strategies. Pre-listening activities set the context for the text which helps the learner to activate his/her schemata (Chung, 1999). Pre-listening activities elicit key words which activate schema connections in the learners' brains and also apply a filter to all the possible information they might be listening out for. If the language the students are going to hear in the listening activity contains considerable amounts of new language, it may be extremely difficult for the teacher to provide the contextual clues in the L2 as these will be 'as new' as the language the students are going to be listening to in the actual aural text. Pre-listening activities are also there to lower feelings of anxiety about a listening task. Learners are likely to react more positively to the imminent text if they are reassured, at least partly, in their L1. If codeswitching is allowed to develop over a period of time in the classroom as a teaching tool, there should be no reason why students should not be able to codeswitch receptively *immediately*—that is prepare their minds for the in-coming L2 even though the teacher has used some L1 in the pre-listening.

Teachers who avoid codeswitching tend to shy away from the kind of task-based learning promoted by certain authors (Prahbu, 1987; Di Pietro, 1987; Skehan, 1998). Both in the study of experienced teachers (Macaro, 1997) and in the study of novice teachers (Macaro, 2001b) there was strong evidence that practitioners were avoiding task based activities because of the difficulty of setting them up entirely in the L2. This contributes to a tendency for all classroom tasks to be highly standardised (therefore easily recognisable without complex L2), repetitive, of low cognitive challenge and often of the behaviourist presentation, practice, production type (PPP). PPP allows teachers to remain in the L2 by taking the learners in lock-step fashion from exposure to new language elements, to the use of them in authentic tasks. I am not arguing for the scrapping of PPP altogether as a learning sequence. However, it is not the only progression leading to use in authentic tasks. Groups of students can be given tasks to accomplish even without teacher input and practice. For example they can be given a situation in which they, as a group, have to produce a dialogue via: initial brainstorming of known words, consulting the dictionary, using the teacher as a resource etc. In order to set up this kind of collaborative activity, codeswitching by the teacher will promote the generation of higher order content. In turn, learners may have to codeswitch in order to use the teacher as a resource and to manage their task.

Again, I want to point out that the effects of not codeswitching are not detrimental to the learning process in themselves. The argument I am slowly constructing is that it narrows down the total range of classroom activities possible thus reducing learner strategy development in terms of range, combination and self-evaluation of strategy use. Rather than putting in place bad classroom practices (I actually doubt that there are more than a handful anyway!), avoidance of codeswitching inhibits the use of certain classroom activities which are highly useful.

Teachers deprived of the codeswitching tool will find it harder to trigger a range of strategies in their learners when asking them to carry out a writing task. We know from studies which have attempted to gauge the effectiveness or otherwise of thinking in L1 when writing (Kobayashi & Rinnert, 1992; Friedlander, 1990; Qi, 1998; Cohen & Brooks-Carson, 2001) that whether the advanced preparation for a writing task is carried out in L1 or L2 produces different results at the task formulation stage (when ideas are actually being put down on paper). Thinking in L1 produces more elaborate content and greater risk-taking than thinking in L2 although the latter produces greater accuracy. This would seem obvious as the L1 language store is much greater. If the teacher elicits ideas only in L2 (say in a brainstorming activity), and especially if the teacher encourages the learners to avoid mental translation, they are going to tap into a much more limited pool of language than if they codeswitched and allowed the learners to codeswitch (for example by asking 'how might you say *X* in L2'?). Lally (2000) obtained slightly different results in her study using a similar technique. Although there were no significant differences in vocabulary use, the students who prepared the task in L1 scored higher on 'organisation' and on 'global impression'. In the study by Cohen & Brooks-Carson (2001) the group reported almost always having a greater number of ideas and thinking through more clearly in L1 although holistically the group that was encouraged not to think in L1 produced more accurate writing.

The trick for the teacher is to encourage the learners to make evaluative strategies such as: 'when am I likely to be better off sticking with language I know already (*e.g.* formulaic expressions; whole sentences I have used in the past) rather than generate new sentences via translation. Balanced against this I must try to address the task as fully and as creatively as I can'.

We have been considering how learners can be deprived of certain learning strategies by bilingual teachers not codeswitching. Let us consider codeswitching and strategy development just once more but in greater depth, this time in an expository task. Let us take a hypothetical example. The teacher in a class of Italian learners of English wants to put across the following information formulated by a potential sentence such as:

> Ernesto Macaro was raised in the gutter but he managed to avoid a life of crime

Option 1: the teacher 'guesses' that the students do not know the meaning of 'raised in the gutter' and *pre-empts* with a codeswitch:

> Ernesto Macaro *è stato cresciuto nel fango*[1] but he managed to avoid a life of crime

In a naturalistic codeswitching situation this could happen and it would facilitate communication and might, indeed, be used to convey additional cultural meaning! Clearly, in a formal classroom situation, this option deprives the learners of the potential to learn 'raised in the gutter'. It also deprives the learners of the beneficial 'effort' of trying to infer from context.

Option 2 is to 'guess' that the learners will not understand 'raised in the gutter' and to *pre-empt* via a paraphrase such as 'was brought up badly by parents who were poor'. This too deprives the learners of learning the phrase 'raised in the gutter'.

Option 3: The teacher does not pre-empt either with a codeswitch or with a paraphrase. Instead, s/he uses the original phrase and then looks around for signs of incomprehension. The phrase 'raised in the gutter', if met with looks of incomprehension from the students, now gives the teacher the choice of *repeating* the sentence either with a codeswitch or with a paraphrase—the decision between a communication strategy or a potential learning strategy. Option 3a, then, the teacher decides to *repeat* with a paraphrase:

> Ernesto Macaro was 'brought up badly by parents who were poor' . . . but he managed to avoid a life of crime.

Option 3b, the teacher decides to *repeat* with a codeswitch perhaps with some sort of paralinguistic feature such as a smirk:

> Ernesto Macaro *è stato cresciuto nel fango* but he managed to avoid a life of crime

In favour of Option 3a are the inferencing strategies that the hearer will try to deploy in order to arrive at the exact meaning of 'raised in the gutter'.

The learner may activate a number of L2/L2 connections not all of which will be totally transparent: brought up = raised; gutter = parents who are poor. In order to make 'sensible' connections the learner will have to have plenty of undisturbed processing time and/or have the opportunity to ask for clarification (through interaction)—something that will not be possible if the teacher input has moved on. Option 3b requires little inferencing but learners will have a fairly heavy cognitive demand in having to trace back to the auditory loop first activated when the target phrase 'raised in the gutter' was first uttered.

Option 4 is *repeating* via a codeswitch *plus* the problematic phrase. Here the learners will be activating L1/L2 connections based on the cultural associations that the Italian students have built up over a period of many years:

> Ernesto Macaro was raised in the gutter, *e stato cresciuto nel fango*, but he managed to avoid a life of crime

These cultural connections we know to be very strongly imprinted in our brains as part of our schemata. Our access to this schemata is going to be much more rapid using an L1 stimulus because that is the way they have been stored and activated in the past. In addition, using L1/L2 direct connections will result in minimum processing load on working memory thus allowing future storage connection strategies to be activated for the phrase 'raised in the gutter'. The downside is that the inferencing strategies are not being developed.

The teacher does have a fifth option, of course, and that is to opt for repetition, paraphrase and codeswitch. Here the teacher will be activating the maximum number of connections and reinforcing them for future recall:

> Ernesto Macaro was raised in the gutter (initial processing time on learner's current mental model)....brought up badly by parents who are poor .... (secondary processing time on revised model)...*e stato cresciuto nel fango* (final processing time).. but managed to avoid a life of crime (storage through combination of strategies).

As we can see, a principled use of codeswitching in this circumstance imposes heavy demands on the bilingual teacher in terms of decision making, demands that the monolingual teacher does not have to contend with. All of these options will appear to the bilingual teacher to have their merits. Nevertheless, it would seem that there are pedagogical principles which need to be explored further and informed by research. The key to the (above) decision making resides in whether the problematic phrase is intended for message communication only or also for memorisation for later use. We do not know for sure whether new language elements are best remembered through inferencing or by direct L1/L2 connections. The likelihood is that it depend on a) the complexity of the language element b) the number of semantic and formal features that are shared between L1 and L2 and c) the circumstances (learning environment) in which the element is first introduced. Nevertheless a strand of research that points to the value in making L1/L2 connections does exist—the work on vocabulary memorisation strategies. Brown & Perry (1991) found that students were able to recall new vocabulary better if it was learnt through a combination of semantic association strategies (*e.g.* L2 gutter—drain pipe) and keyword techniques involving L1 visual imaging. Lotto & de Groot (1998) showed an advantage of L1-L2 word learning method over picture-L2 word learning method when it came to recall. On the other hand, Prince (1996) found that although vocabulary was learnt better by providing L1 equivalents, it was used in context better when it had been learnt in context via inferencing. These studies were all with written text, where learners had plenty of processing time. Future research needs to establish whether, in oral interaction, vocabulary and idiom are learnt better via inferencing or via L1 equivalents.

## 9.   CAN CODESWITCHING BE A SYSTEMATIC, PRINCIPLED AND PLANNED PART OF THE L2 CURRICULUM?

I will try to answer this question by way of conclusion, summarising what has gone before and proposing what work has to be done before the question can be more comprehensively answered.

Learners deprived of codeswitching in the discourse cannot develop an important communication strategy. Many 'future' conversations will, in fact, be undertaken by speakers who share the same two languages 'to some extent'. This is increasingly so in the commercial world as globalisation of work locations increases. Codeswitching, for this reason alone, should be an integral part of the L2 classroom. It should become one of the objectives when planning the curriculum.

There is nothing unnatural or 'psycholinguistically disturbing' about codeswitching in the L2 classroom. It just mirrors a natural process happening in naturalistic discourse. However, unlike that discourse, classroom interaction is designed to do other things as well: not just communicate information but also learn language and learn how to learn language. If codeswitching is, in effect, the bilingual teacher's compensation strategy for lack of L2 knowledge in the learners it must be made on the principled decision that the benefits of that switch are at least equal to, if not more than, the benefits of not codeswitching. Thus, to advocate complete freedom to 'codeswitch at will' is not acceptable. Furthermore, phrases such as 'use the L2 as much as possible' or 'judicious use of L1' are not sufficiently informative, especially for novice teachers. We have to arrive at a pedagogy of codeswitching which bases itself on a theory of optimality in L1 use—how and when does codeswitching best lead to language learning, learning how to learn, and to the development of communication skills?

Learners do increase their vocabulary store and the syntactic models through inferencing—that is through implicit processes. This can only be achieved through extensive exposure to the target language. On the other hand inferencing the correct meaning of a word in a given context does not necessarily mean that there is retention of the inferred meaning since the immediate communicative need will have been met. Learners may need to be guided to 'notice' features of vocabulary and syntax in the input. In the case of oral interaction, we do not know as yet whether noticing is more facilitated by a codeswitch or by maintaining the L2. Until we have more evidence teachers will want to continue to provide a balance of L2 inferencing and L1-L2 equivalents.

But what would the balance be? When and how often should teachers codeswitch? Both teachers and learners, as we have seen, have a 'gut feeling' codeswitching is related to moments in the lesson when the L1 seems more appropriate as a means to an end. There is thus some indication from the research that we could draw up systematic and principled guidelines based on *functional* use of L1. To do this we would have to reassert the principle that second language learning is best carried out through communicative interaction—that is, where teachers and learners use the L2 *predominantly* but switch to L1 in order to ensure communication. However, the switch does not just ensure communication. Its function is also to ensure that more learning will take place than if the switch had not taken place. Switches, if possible, should lead to some recognisable learning in L2 as well as lubricating the classroom discourse. Whilst the codeswitch may facilitate a task or an interaction in the immediate future, the user of the codeswitch should envisage that at some time in the longer term the codeswitch will not be necessary because the language store *will have increased.*

A functional approach to answering the last question of this chapter would have as a guiding principle that codeswitching is beneficial where the classroom interaction either facilitates that interaction or improves the learning of the L2 or both. However, if we just take the functional approach to answering the question we have no concept of exactly how much we are talking about, the reason being that the function that the language is being put to will vary according to the tasks planned by the teacher. If, on the other hand, we take a quantitative approach we simply go back to the notion of 'predominantly' in L2. What does predominantly in the L2 mean? Can we quantify this? At the moment it would be difficult for a codeswitching pedagogy to be based on quantitative measures. We cannot say 'oh about 10% L1 use is OK'. Insufficient studies on the amounts and the effects of codeswitching in formal classrooms have taken place. My own research evidence, in a limited context, is beginning to suggest that beyond 10-15% the nature of the codeswitching changes. That is to say, the teacher goes over the threshold described earlier. However, we will need much larger studies (both descriptive and interventionist), and in a variety of learning contexts, of the effect of codeswitching on interaction and in turn on language learning before we can give secure guidelines based on quantity.

The answer may therefore lie in a dynamic interaction between functionally based codeswitching ('I need to use the L1 as a means to a better end') and a quantitative one ('if I gradually and constantly increase my use of L1 it will eventually stop being a foreign language lesson'). This dynamic interaction, based on evidence and reflection, will eventually empower the bilingual teacher rather than make him or her a victim of historical language learning developments, a puppet of the latest methodological fashions, or the scapegoat of uninformed government policies.

## 10.    NOTES

[1] Literally: 'was brought up in mud'.

## 11.    REFERENCES

Asher, C. (1993). Using The target language as the medium of instruction in the communicative classroom: the influence of practice on principle. *Studies in Modern Languages Education, 1,* 53-71.

Baddeley, A.D., & Logie, R.H. (1999). Working memory: The multiple-component model. In A. Myake & P. Shah (Eds.), *Models of working memory: Mechanisms of active maintenance and executive control.* Cambridge: Cambridge University Press. 28-61.

Bailey, N., Madden, C. & Krashen, S. (1974). Is there a 'natural sequence' in adult second language learning? *Language Learning, 24* (2), 235-243.

Bishop, G. (2000). Dictionaries, examinations and stress. *Language Learning Journal, 21,* 57-65.

Brown, T.S. & Perry, F.L. (1991). A comparison of three learning strategies for ESL vocabulary acquisition. *TESOL Quarterly, 25* (4), 655-670.

Chaudron, C. (1988). *Second language classrooms: Research on teaching and learning.* Cambridge: Cambridge University Press.

Chung, J. M. (1999). The effects of using video texts supported with advance organizers and captions on Chinese college students' listening comprehension: An empirical study. *Foreign Language Annals, 32* (3), 295-308.

Clark, A., & Trafford, J. (1996). Return to gender: Boys' and girls' attitudes and achievements. *Language Learning Journal, 14,* 40-49.

Cohen, A.D. (1998). *Strategies in learning and using a second language.* London: Longman.

Cohen, A.D. & Brooks-Carson, A. (2001). Research on direct versus translated writing: Students' strategies and their results. *Modern Language Journal, 85* (2), 169-188.

Department of Education and Science (1990). *National curriculum modern foreign languages working group: Initial advice.* London: HMSO.

Department of Education for Northern Ireland (1985). Good practice in education. Paper 2. *Modern languages teaching in Northern Ireland.* Bangor, Northern Ireland: Department of Education for Northern Ireland.

Di Pietro, R.J. (1987). *Strategic interaction.* Cambridge: Cambridge University Press.

Dickson, P. (1992). *Using the target language in modern foreign language classrooms.* Slough: NFER.

Duff, P.A. & Polio, C.G. (1990). How much foreign language is there in the foreign language classroom? *Modern Language Journal, 74* (2), 154-166.

Dulay, H. & Burt, M. (1974). Natural sequences in child second language acquisition. *Language Learning, 24* (1), 37-53.

Friedlander, A. (1990). Composing in English: Effects of first language on writing in English as a second language. In B. Kroll (Ed.), *Second language writing: Research insights for the classroom.* Cambridge: Cambridge University Press. 109-125.

Harley, B. (2000). Listening strategies in ESL: Do age and L1 make a difference? *TESOL Quarterly, 34* (4), 769-777.

Hopkins, S. (1989). Use of the mother tongue in the teaching of English as a second language to adults. *TESOL Quarterly, 2* (1), 18-24.

Jones, B., Jones, G., Demetriou, H., Downes, P. & Ruddock J. (2001). *Boys' performance in modern foreign languages: Listening to the learners.* London: CILT.

Kern, R.G. (1994). The role of mental translation in second language reading. *Studies in Second Language Acquisition, 16* (4), 441-61.

Knight, S. (1996). Dictionary use while reading: The effects on comprehension and vocabulary acquisition for students of different verbal abilities. *Modern Language Journal, 78* (3), 285-299.

Kobayashi, H. & Rinnert, C. (1992). Effects of first language on second language writing: Translation versus direct composition. *Language Learning, 42* (2), 183-215.

Krashen, S.D. (1987). *Principles and practice in second language acquisition.* Hemel: Prentice Hall.

Krashen, S.D. & Terrell, T.D. (1988). *The Natural Approach.* London: Prentice Hall.

Lally, C.G. (2000). First language influences in second language composition: The effect of pre-writing. *Foreign Language Annals, 33* (4), 428-432.

Libben, G. (2000). Representation and processing in the second language lexicon: The homogeneity hypothesis. In J. Archibald (Ed.), *Second language acquisition and linguistic theory.* Oxford: Blackwell. 228-248.

Long, M. H. (1981). Input, interaction and second language acquisition. In H. Winitz (Ed.), *Native language and foreign language acquisition.* Annals of the New York Academy of Sciences, 379. 259-278.

Lotto, L. & de Groot, A. M. B. (1998). Effects of learning method and word type on acquiring vocabulary in an unfamiliar language. *Language Learning, 48* (1), 31-69.

Macaro, E. (1997). *Target language collaborative learning and autonomy.* Clevedon: Multilingual Matters.

Macaro, E. (2000a). Issues in target language teaching. In K. Field (Ed.), *Issues in modern foreign language teaching.* London: Routledge. 171-189.

Macaro, E. (2000b). Learner strategies in foreign language learning: cross-national factors. *Tuttitalia, 22,* 9-18.

Macaro, E. (2001a). *Learning strategies in foreign and second language classrooms.* London: Continuum.

Macaro, E. (2001b). Analysing student teachers' codeswitching in foreign language classrooms: Theories and decision making. *Modern Language Journal, 85* (4), 531-548.

Macaro, E. & Mutton, T. (2002). Developing language teachers through a co-researcher model. *Language Learning Journal, 25,* 27-39.

Myake, A. & Shah, P. (Eds.) (1999). *Models of working memory: Mechanisms of active maintenance and executive control.* Cambridge: Cambridge University Press.

Neather, T., Woods, C., Rodriguez, I., Davis, M. & Dunne, E. (1995). Target language testing in modern foreign languages. Report of a project commissioned by the School Curriculum and Assessment Authority. London: SCAA.

Office for Standards in Education - OFSTED (1993). *Handbook. Inspection schedule.* London: HMSO.

Office for Standards in Education - OFSTED (1995). *Modern foreign languages: A review of inspection findings 1993/94.* London: HMSO.

Oxford, R.L. (1990). *Language learning strategies: What every teacher should know.* Boston, MA: Heinle & Heinle.

Pica, T. (1994). Research on negotiation: What does it reveal about second-language learning conditions, processes and outcomes. *Language Learning, 44* (3), 493-527.

Prahbu, N.S. (1987). *Second language pedagogy.* Oxford: Oxford University Press.

Prince, P. (1996). Second language vocabulary learning: The role of context versus translations as a function of proficiency. *Modern Language Journal, 80* (4), 478-493.

Qi, D.S. (1998). An inquiry into language switching in second language composing processes. *Canadian Modern Language Review, 54* (3), 413-435.

Sinclair, J. & Brazil D. (1982). *Teacher talk.* Oxford: Oxford University Press.

Sinclair, J. & Coulthard, R.M. (1975). *Towards an analysis of discourse.* Oxford: Oxford University Press.

Skehan, P. (1998). *A Cognitive approach to language learning.* Oxford: Oxford University Press.

Spada, N. & Lightbown, P.M. (1999). Instruction, first language influence and developmental readiness in second language acquisition. *Modern Language Journal, 83* (1), 1-22.

Stables, A. & Wikeley, F. (1999). From bad to worse? Pupils' attitudes to modern foreign languages at ages 14 and 15. *Language Learning Journal, 20,* 27-31.

Tarone, E. & Swain, M. (1995). A sociolinguistic perspective on second language use in immersion classrooms. *Modern Language Journal, 79* (2), 166-78.

Weinreich, U. (1953) (cited in Libben). *Languages in contact: Findings and problems.* New York: Linguistic Circle of New York.

Chapter 6

# CONSTRUCTING SOCIAL RELATIONSHIPS AND LINGUISTIC KNOWLEDGE THROUGH NON-NATIVE-SPEAKING TEACHER TALK

JOSEP MARIA COTS - JOSEP MARIA DÍAZ
*Universitat de Lleida*

## 1. INTRODUCTION: THE STUDY OF TEACHER TALK

This study focuses on the role of non-native speaking (NNS) EFL teacher talk in the construction of social relationships and linguistic knowledge in the classroom. The aim of the study is, in the first place, to explore the extent to which it is possible to identify different interactional styles associated with the semantic notions of *modality* and *participant inscription* in the discourse. In the second place, the study is intended as a contribution to the relatively recent body of work on native speaking (NS) teachers vs. NNS teachers by adopting a microanalytical approach to NNS teacher talk, which is relatively absent from the literature.

Teacher talk, in general, has been approached from two main angles of research: speech modifications and teacher-student interaction. Modifications in teacher speech have often been described taking into account structural rather than pragmatic aspects. In a thorough review of research carried out until the late 1980s, Chaudron (1988) points out the main areas of research in connection with the teachers' verbal behaviour in the classroom: rate of speech, prosody, phonology, pauses, vocabulary and, especially, syntax. In this latter area, researchers' efforts have concentrated on length of utterances, subordination, markedness, grammaticality and sentence types.

E. Llurda (Ed.), *Non-Native Language Teachers. Perceptions, Challenges and Contributions to the Profession*,
85—105.

From the angle of teacher-student interaction, the focus has been placed on the two most characteristic types of move that teachers adopt in the foreign language classroom: questions and feedback. Johnson (1995), continuing a tradition initiated by Sinclair & Coulthard (1975), represents an alternative way of approaching teacher-student interaction by concentrating on the interactional patterns that are produced in the classroom and the degree to which these patterns contribute to optimising the process of language learning. Hall & Walsh (2002), for instance, show that there are two frequent versions of the triadic classroom exchange in teacher-whole group interaction, 'initiation > response > evaluation' and 'initiation > response > follow-up', and that they produce different language learning environments, from a process of transmission to a process of inquiry.

The emphasis on structural description that is represented by the two previous approaches to teacher talk has ignored the fact that human beings use talk to shape representations of reality and interpretations of experience. Language, in this sense, is not just an aseptic 'vehicle' for conveying information but rather one to act upon the world (Austin, 1962; Searle, 1969) and, as Mercer (1995: 15) puts it, 'a tool for transforming experience into cultural knowledge and understanding'. Our knowledge of the world, therefore, can be said to be socially constructed in the different communicative events in which we participate. This process of knowledge construction takes place amidst a complexity of social relationships with the other participants that are created and recreated simultaneously to the construction of knowledge (Habermas, 2001).

The lesson may be considered as one of the most representative types of speech event (Cazden, 1988) in our society with the explicit goal of making it possible for the participants to construct knowledge. However, the lesson is also a social site that we associate with specific frames (Minsky, 1975) and scripts (Schank & Abelson, 1977). As with any other type of familiar social practice, participants approach a lesson with certain expectations about setting, ends, norms of interaction, topics, etc. Some of these expectations are related to verbal behaviour; they are sometimes made explicit and on other occasions they are left implicit. In spite of these expectations, participants can always attempt to shape reality by means of language, proposing specific ways of establishing social relationships with others and representing the world in specific ways.

In the foreign language classroom, as in other social situations, knowledge and understanding exist to the extent that they are the result of an act of sharing (Mercer: 66). Teacher and students use language and communicate with others to transform their experience into linguistic knowledge and skills that will allow the students to learn about and communicate in the foreign language. The higher expertise of the teacher as well as the position of power s/he occupies create a situation of 'unbalanced sharing', one in which it is mainly the teacher, rather than the learners, who shares his/her experience of the language and the world and who defines through interaction the type of social relationship s/he wants to have with them. Since the teacher's is the dominant public discourse in the classroom, it should be possible to begin to grasp the nature of the knowledge that is constructed as well as the social roles and relationships that are created by concentrating on teacher talk.

The literature on detailed analyses of NNS teacher classroom behaviour is very scarce. As can be seen in Braine's historical review of the research on NNS teacher (this volume), the majority of studies have been based on teachers' and/or students' perceptions obtained through questionnaires. Medgyes (1994) calls for some caution in the use of questionnaires as representative of teacher's behaviour in the classroom. Árva & Medgyes (2000), represent an interesting exception to this tendency in that, besides employing a questionnaire, the authors base their study on the observation of the teachers' classroom behaviour. Although several studies mentioned by Braine (this volume; see, for instance, Samimy & Brutt-Griffler, 1999; Inbar-Lourie, 2001; and Cheung, 2002) make some reference to teacher-student relations, none of the studies on NNS teachers we know of has adopted a microanalytical approach that focuses on specific details of the teacher's verbal behaviour and its potential consequences both from a social and an epistemic point of view.

## 2.     ANALYTICAL FRAMEWORK

The present study is based on the assumption that one way of characterising teacher talk is by focusing on the speaker's expression of subjectivity through the introduction of modality devices and through the inscription of the participants in the discourse. The analytical framework we adopt is centred around the notion of 'subjectivity in discourse', from the *théorie de l'énonciation* (*e.g.* Benveniste, 1977; Ducrot, 1980; Kerbrat-Orecchioni, 1980). According to this theory, utterances contain linguistic clues strategically deployed by the addresser so that the addressee can interpret them in a specific way (Calsamiglia & Tusón, 1999: 135). We start from the premise that given a proposition such as 'Sue arrives today', the speaker can choose between stating it or denying it in a categorical way ('Sue arrives / does not arrive today') and introducing different types of relations of subjectivity between the interlocutors and the proposition stated: 'I/You know Sue arrives today', 'Sue must arrive today', 'I hope Sue will arrive today', 'You want Sue to arrive today', etc.

According to Fairclough (1989), modality has to do with the expression of a speaker's authority in relation to others and in relation to the truth or probability of a representation of reality. He defines the first type as *relational* modality and it clearly corresponds to the *deontic* type of modal logic. The second type of modality is defined as *expressive* and its counterpart in modal logic is known as *epistemic* modality. By means of relational modality speakers express relations of obligation between themselves or their listeners and the proposition(s) stated. It includes all those verbal acts that a speaker undertakes in order to define (or redefine) his/her social relation with an interlocutor and, in terms of systemic linguistics, it would correspond to the interpersonal function of language. Expressive modality has to do with the representation of reality and the status of the speaker's understanding or knowledge of it; this is what in systemic linguistics would be considered as the ideational function. This is the sense in which Fairclough (1992: 160) says that modality 'is a point of intersection in discourse between the signification of reality and the enactment of social relations—or in terms of systemic linguistics, between the ideational and interpersonal functions of language'.

Although the central aspect of modality is related to the meanings of obligation and certainty, Calsamiglia & Tusón (1999: 177) suggest that it is possible to consider in discourse other subjective meanings, which can be expressed in terms of scales which allow the speakers to position themselves in connection with the contents of the proposition stated:

1. Obligation (relational/deontic): obligatory, allowed, optional, forbidden,
2. Certainty (expressive/epistemic): certain, probable, dubious, improbable.
3. Frequency: always, never, sometimes.
4. Quantity: everything, nothing, something.
5. Space: everywhere, nowhere, somewhere.
6. Volition: want, refuse, wish, try.

Fairclough (1992) establishes a further distinction between *subjective* modality, where the speaker's presence is made explicit (*e.g.* I think he'll come tomorrow) and *objective* modality where it is not clear whose perspective is being represented, whether the speaker's or that of another individual (*e.g.* He may come tomorrow). The analysis of the different verbal contexts in which subjective modality is used gives us the possibility to discover how the teacher inscribes the participants involved in the classroom situation (teacher, represented by 'I' or inclusive 'we', and students, represented by 'you' or inclusive 'we') and the different processes, attributes and circumstances that s/he associates with them.

An important notion in the analysis of the data is that of *discourse strategy*. Following the work of Gumperz (1982) and Tannen (1989) we define discourse strategy as the speaker's and listener's systematic use of linguistic and general socio-cultural knowledge to achieve their intended goals when producing or interpreting a message in a given context. Discourse strategies may be realised at different levels of speech production (prosody, paralinguistic, code choice, lexis, syntax, etc.) and their inclusion by the speaker relies on the listener's linguistic and sociocultural knowledge to trigger a particular inferential process.

One last tool that is employed in the analysis of the data is Coulthard's (1985) concept of *act*, which can be defined as a segment of speech with a specific interactive function. According to the author, acts constitute the last level of five proposed ranks in the analysis of classroom interaction: lesson, transaction, exchange, move and act.

## 3.     ANALYSIS OF THE DATA

The analysis of the data is divided into two parts: modalisation (4.1) and participant inscription (4.2). For the first part, the analysis centres on the tapescripts of two intermediate-level EFL lessons taught by two NNS teachers in Catalonia (Spain): A (male in his late 20s) and B (female in her late 30s). These teachers, in our view, represent opposite poles in a teaching style continuum in terms of the way they define their social relationship with the students and the nature of linguistic knowledge.

The second part of the analysis introduces a quantitative point of view, focusing on participant inscription and the processes associated with the discourse participants. In this case, the data have been extended with two elementary-level EFL lessons taught by two NNS teachers (C, male in his early 20s, and D, female in his early 40s) and another two EFL lessons taught by NS teachers, corresponding to intermediate (E) and beginner level (F); both teachers were male in their early 30s.

## 3.1     Modalisation in teacher talk

The analysis of modalisation in teacher talk involves, in the first place, a classification of the different acts depending on whether their occurrence contributes to the construction of social relationships between teacher and pupils or to the construction of knowledge.

The second step in the analysis involves a specification of each type of act as realisation of a particular discourse strategy. Thus, for the acts included under **social relationships** we distinguish between 'power' and 'solidarity' strategies to discriminate between those acts through which the speaker's position of power upon the addressee is made explicit, and those acts in which the speaker presents himself as an equal of the addressee. The analysis of the acts included under **linguistic knowledge** is based on the degree of certainty with which the teacher conveys knowledge about the language and it is based on a classification into two types of strategies: 'categorical knowledge' and 'non-categorical knowledge'.

The first and second steps of our analysis are schematically represented in Figure 1:

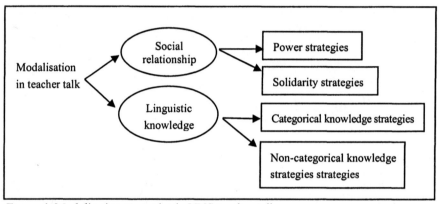

*Figure 1.* Modalisation strategies in NNS teacher talk.

The third step in the analysis involves a further sub-classification of the acts according to their pragmatic function (*e.g.* instructions, feedback), their content (*e.g.* patterns of usage, negative attribute) or a formal feature (*e.g.* verb of cognition in 1st person, modal verb/adverb). In this latter case we consider the following tokens as linguistic resources for modalising discourse:

- Modal verbs (including verbal periphrases such as *supposed to*).
- Personal pronouns: first and second person.
- Verbal mood and tense: imperative, 'future' (*going to, will*).
- Verbs of volition and cognition preceded by first person singular (*e.g. think, know, want, would like, guess, imagine, believe*).
- 'Modal' adverbs (*e.g. really, just, perhaps, maybe, probably, only, certainly*).
- Interactivity markers: tag questions, *you know.*
- Evaluative adjectives (*e.g. nasty, funny*)
- Irony.

## 3.1.1 Social relationships

The analysis of the construction of social relationships between teacher and students is based on the idea that through the inclusion of certain strategies it is possible to increase or diminish the social power differential between them.

The first set of strategies analysed are defined as *power strategies,* and they include those acts through which the teachers make explicit a relationship of role-dependency between them and the students. We distinguish two main types of act associated with a position of power: (a) class instructions and (b) direct confrontation with the interlocutor.

The different types of acts, together with their realisation, are summarised in Table 1. The numbers given in brackets correspond to the extracts exemplifying each realisation.

*Table 1.* Power strategies in NNS teacher talk

| |
| --- |
| A.  Class instructions |
|     (i)  Direct commands (1, 2). |
|     (ii)  Requests (3). |
|     (iii) Task announcements (4, 5). |
| B.  Direct confrontation |
|     (i)  Addressee's negative attribute (6). |
|     (ii)  Interrogation (7). |
|     (iii) Demeaning irony (8). |

All of the examples of power strategies were produced by Teacher A, since he represents a clearly authoritative style.

### A. Class instructions

Class instructions threaten the addressees' negative face (Brown & Levinson, 1987), in that they represent a limitation on the person's rights not to be imposed on by others. In our data these strategies adopt three different realisations:

(i) Direct commands expressed either through a proposition including 'I want...' (*e.g.* I want complete silence.) or a verb in the imperative mood.

*Extract 1*
T:    Wait , wait! shsh, silence, I want, I want complete silence, Judith, before
       you ask a question
*Extract 2*
T: Everybody shut up. Mireia speak up, speak clear
S: 'King Lear' opened last week at the London theatre

(ii) Indirect commands in the form of a request.

*Extract 3*
T:   Miquel are you ready? Boys and girls? Miquel, er can you start? Remember the first text is about_ yes, writing the_ it has to do with shows and stuff like that

(iii) A proposition announcing task procedures and including either a verb expressing futurity or a modal of obligation.

*Extract 4*
T:   Now, we are going to do a quiz, now, if you could... please turn to page 73
*Extract 5*
T:   Remember I told you. I told you to underline the connectors and the discourse markers, I see that somebody_ some people haven't done that. Who has written this?
S:   Jo. [me]
T:   Right. You're **supposed to** write your names at the top like that. You're supposed to underline the connectors, all right?

## B. Direct confrontation
We define an act as 'direct confrontation' when it represents a threat to the addressee's positive face (*i.e.* the desire to be accepted as a worthy respectable social member). In our data this type of act adopts the following realisations:
(i) A proposition in which the teacher explicitly assigns a negative attribute or action to the student.

*Extract 6.*
T:   The class is not over yet, so we have to do an exercise. **I told you to shut up. You haven't shut up. You haven't behaved properly**. Now we have one exercise left.

(ii) 'Interrogation' questions, in which the teacher adopts a threatening tone.

*Extract 7. Students had to ask questions about a text they had previously read.*
T:   No no no. Wait a minute, we will see
S:   *Què van fer?* [what did they do?]
T:   **If you don't know, you don't know. Do you know it or you don't?**

(iii) Use of demeaning irony assigning a negative attribute or action to the student.

*Extract 8. The teacher is scolding a student for not paying attention.*
L:    er
S:    Marc, **are you having a good time**? The more you speak_ Because of you
      everybody will finish the class later today

The second set of strategies that are taken into account in the analysis of social relationships are defined as *solidarity strategies*. Here we include acts produced by the teachers in order to diminish the impression of their social power upon the students. As represented in Table 2, this type of strategies are realised through (a) the introduction of downtoners (Quirk, Greenbaum, Leech & Svartvik,1985) in utterances through which the teacher exerts some imposition on the students, and (b) 'self-disclosure acts', through which the teacher shares with the students aspects of his/her inner self. All of the examples of solidarity strategies come from Teacher B's talk because she represents the opposite pole to A's authoritative style.

*Table 2.* Solidarity strategies in NNS teacher talk

| |
|---|
| C. Downtoning |
|    (i)    'We/us' to give instructions (9). |
|    (ii)   Interactivity markers (10) |
| D. Self disclosure |
|    (i)    Verbs of volition/cognition in the 1$^{st}$ person (11, 12). |
|    (ii)   Evaluative adjectives (12). |

**C. Downtoning**
Adapting the definition of downtoner given by Quirk, Greenbaum, Leech & Svartvik (1985), we define downtoning as the attempt to diminish the impression of power or imposition of an utterance through the inclusion of particular tokens within its structure. The tokens that appear in the data analysed are the following:

(i) Use of the first person plural pronoun, *we/us,* instead of the second, *you,* to give instructions addressed to the students. In this way, the teacher represents herself as just another member of the group.

*Extract 9*
T:    (...) Right, so **we'll** try to do this. **We** start doing it orally, one each, then
      I'll give you some time, about some minutes to finish and then, **we'll** do the
      same with the other one; so **let's** start with you Helen please

(ii) Interactivity markers requesting the cooperation of the addressee (*e.g.* tag questions, *you know, right?* etc.)

*Extract 10*
T:   Right. So I think the last one we did together was thirty eight, **wasn't it**?
S:   Yes

## D. Self-disclosure

This act can be characterised by the (i) inclusion of verbs of cognition / volition in the first person (*e.g.* think, like, hope, imagine) and (ii) evaluative adjectives (*e.g.* funny, strange, nasty, etc.), both of which contribute to reflecting the teacher's mental state and personal appreciation of his/her environment.

*Extract 11*
T:   So, if you do have the time, **I hope** you do, **I'd like** to have my
     compositions and... The other day we worked in class, we did the
     conditionals. I had an extra-copy but well, this extra-copy I gave to the
     people who are in there, and **I forgot** to make an extra-copy. So **I think**
     Helen, you can lend it to her
*Extract 12*
T:   (...) This is **funny** because **I'm imagining** myself if I would say that (...)

### 3.1.2   Linguistic knowledge

In the analysis of those acts through which the teacher constructs specific linguistic knowledge, we distinguish between categorical and non-categorical knowledge, depending on the degree of certainty with which the information is presented. In this case, the examples are from both Teacher A's and Teacher B's lessons.

We consider that categorical knowledge is constructed through adopting a view of language use as the result of strict application of invariable rules. As show in Table 3, in the data analysed categorical knowledge is constructed in the form of two types of act: (a) corrective feedback and (b) informative act declaring linguistic rules,

*Table 3.* Categorical knowledge in NNS teacher talk

| A. Corrective feedback |
|---|
|    Accept/evaluate act (13) |

| B. Informative act |
|---|
|    (i)    Objective facts (14). |
|    (ii)   Obligatory choices (15). |
|    (iii)  One-to-one relation between students' L1 and the target language forms. (16). |

## A. Corrective feedback

Following Coulthard's (1985) classification of 'acts' that are typically found in the analysis of classroom interaction, in our data categorical knowledge may appear as an 'accept' or 'evaluate' act in the follow-up move, after the student's 'reply' to an 'elicitation' from the teacher.

*Extract 13 (Teacher B)*
T:   It's past simple and we won't use the continuous type. Forty-five [referring to the sentence number in the exercise]
S:   She is an old friend, I have known her for years
T:   For years? **Good, that's right.** She's an old friend. I have known her for years. **Perfect, yeah, right.** Joan, the next one

## B. Informative act

Categorical knowledge is also constructed in the form of 'informative' acts through which the teacher presents language use as either (i) impersonal objective facts (extract 14), (ii) obligatory choices (extract 15) or as (iii) a one-to-one relation between the target language and the students' L1 forms (extract 16).

*Extract 14 (Teacher A)*
T:   (...) For those of you who don't, who are not very sure about it yet at this level you should know this. WH-interrogative pronoun, auxiliary subject, main verb, the main verb and the complements. The parenthesis means, as you know, that **if there's a WH write it. If there's not a Wh you start by the auxiliary, there is no complement. You leave it as it is, like this, question mark at the end**, right?
*Extract 15 (Teacher B)*
T:   Good, 'I don't have to work tomorrow', that's right. There's no need for me to work tomorrow. **I can't say 'must' because that would be a prohibition.** Somebody doesn't allow me to work. Good. Forty, Mar-, please.
*Extract 16 (Teacher A)*
S:   You need to dedicate
T    **Dedicate means *dedicar* in Catalan but_**
S:   Spend, spend
T:   No, but no_ because **spend means *passar temps***
S:   Devote

The construction of non-categorical linguistic knowledge by the teacher is consistent with a view of language use as variable and subject to the user's point of view or preference. Non-categorical knowledge appears in the form of informative acts through which, rather than presenting language as the result of strict application of rules, the teacher represents language use as (i) different patterns of usage, (ii) speaker's multiple choices and (iii) decisions based on the speaker's personal point of view (see Table 4).

*Table 4*. Non-categorical knowledge in NNS teacher talk
C. Informative act
  (i)    Patterns of usage (17)
  (ii)   Multiple choices (18)
  (iii)  Personal point of view (19)

(i) By presenting language use as patterns of usage, which can be characterised in terms of their frequency, the teacher is reinforcing the view of language as a variable phenomenon that needs to be analysed in terms of the actual use that speakers make of it.

*Extract 17 (Teacher B)*
T:    'Have' and 'been', that's right, so 'I have often been to America'. 'Often' would be in the same place as 'just' or 'already', but with the present perfect. **Maybe 'just' or 'already' are more common.**

(ii) Another realisation of non-categorical knowledge through an informative act involves the presentation of more than one option to express the same meaning.

*Extract 18 (Teacher B) The class is engaged in checking a fill-in-the-blank exercise; in this particular extract, T and S are discussing one of the sentences of the exercise in which the blank to be filled corresponded to the answer to question 'Who's there?'*
T:    And the next one, Alex please.
S:    Who's there? Me.
T:    Well, **you could say 'me', but we would say 'it's me'.** The person over there is me. So *I would say 'it's me', rather than just 'me'. It sounds good*

(iii) The third type of informative act that we associate with non-categorical knowledge is connected with the previous strategy of presenting the 'multiple-choice' relationship between meaning and form. Because of the different options available, it is ultimately the user who makes the choice. Extracts 18 (above, in bold and italics) and 19 (below), contain examples of this strategy.

*Extract 19 (Teacher B)*
T:    (...) Yeah, in this case 'may' and 'might' have that slight difference, but so slight; **'could' is maybe the one I would use in this sentence,** 'could' is **the one that sounds real to me,** that somebody would say. Well, the next one.

## 3.2        Participant inscription in teacher talk

The analysis of the inscription of teacher and students in teacher talk, as well as of the processes with which they are associated, is aimed at obtaining an idea of the degree of personalisation of the teacher's discourse and its anchoring to the participants in the communicative situation as a particular way of constructing both social relationships and knowledge.

In this second part of the analysis we have adopted a quantitative approach to the data, focusing on the frequency with which the first and second person pronouns are used by the teacher and the types of processes with which these pronouns are associated in the utterance. For the analysis of the processes, we adopt the approach of functional grammar (Halliday, 1985; Downing & Locke, 1992), according to which a clause represents a pattern of experience, conceptualised as a situation type. A situation type has a semantic framework consisting of the following components: process (realised by the Verb or Predicator), participants (realised by Subject, DO and IO), attributes ascribed to participants (realised by Complements), and circumstances associated with the process (realised by Adverbials). Functional grammar considers four main types of processes:

1. Material processes (or processes of 'doing'); *e.g.* kick, run, paint.
2. Mental processes (or processes of 'perception, cognition and of affection'); eg. see, know, think.
3. Relational processes (or processes of 'being' or 'becoming'); *e.g.* be, stand, turn.
4. Verbal processes (or processes of 'saying' and 'communicating'); *e.g.* tell, ask, suggest.

### 3.2.1        Participant inscription

The analysis of participant inscription in teacher talk involves, in the first place, a quantification of the occurrences of first and second person pronouns referring to the teacher ('I'), to one or more students ('you'), and to both teacher and students ('we'). For each of the pronouns we consider the absolute number of occurrences in the entire lesson and, in parenthesis, the ratio (expressed in percentage) between this number and the total number of words for the lesson. For this part of the study we have incorporated four other teachers (C, D, E and F). The results of the analysis are represented in Table 5:

*Table 5.* Participation inscription in teacher talk

| | Total number of words for the lesson | I | you | we |
|---|---|---|---|---|
| Teacher A. Male NNS (Intermediate level) | 5370 | 45 (0.83) | **225 (4.18)** | 30 (0.55) |
| Teacher B. Female NNS (Intermediate level) | 6736 | **103 (1.5)** | 120 (1.78) | 50 (0.74) |
| Teacher C. Male NNS (Elementary level) | 3382 | 4 (0.11) | 41 (1.21) | 15 (0.44) |
| Teacher D. Female NNS (Elementary level) | 4026 | 9 (0.22) | 125 (3.1) | 30 (0.74) |
| Teacher E. Male NS (Intermediate level) | 7046 | 32 (0.45) | **182 (2.58)** | **6 (0.08)** |
| Teacher F. Male NS (Elementary level) | 5622 | 6 (0.1) | 26 (0.46) | **2 (0.03)** |

From this chart we would like to make the following observations, which might be corroborated through the analysis of further data:

1. The highest number of occurrences of 'you' appear in the talk of teachers A and E. In the case of teacher A, this result is in accordance with the clearly authoritative and confrontational style shown in the analysis of the way he constructs his social relationships with the students (section 4.1.1). It is also interesting to point out that both these teachers are men. Thus, in this case the gender variable might be more relevant than the nativeness variable.
2. The teacher with the highest number of first person references (teacher B) is the one that favours most clearly the use of solidarity and non-categorical knowledge strategies. This result suggests that the inscription of the teacher in her talk can be interpreted as an attempt to construct a self which can be closer to students from the point of view of both her social role as well as the knowledge that she possesses.
3. The NS teachers (E and F) show a clearly lower tendency to use inclusive 'we' than the NNS teachers. In future studies it would be interesting to follow up on this observation to clarify whether it is possible to talk about cultural styles of teaching foreign languages, depending on whether the teacher shares or not the cultural background of the students.
4. With the exception of teacher B, the teachers inscribe the students in their talk (by means of the inclusion of 'you') in a clearly higher frequency than themselves (represented by the inclusion of 'I'), with a ratio of between 5/1 to 14/1. Although this is not very frequent in ordinary conversation, we hypothesise that it is typical of any socio-

communicative situation in which there is some kind of service to be supplied. In a teaching situation, the teacher, or service-provider, has as one of his/her goals to involve the pupils in the learning activities, and for this reason s/he needs to appeal to them by using the second person form. The balance that can be observed in the case of teacher B is indicative of her 'more personal' approach to the lesson encounter.

### 3.2.2    Types of processes

The analysis of the different types of processes associated with the discourse of the participants is intended as a qualitatively-oriented step into the description of the process of personalization. The examination of the type of action/state that the teacher associates with either him/herself or with one or more students gives us an idea of how the teacher defines the role of discourse participants in terms of what they are expected to do or be in the particular environment. For this analysis we focus on the sentential sequences Subject + Verb in which the Subject function (Agent) is realised by a first or second person pronoun. The verbs that we obtain are later classified according to their meaning into four main types of processes: material, mental, relational and verbal. We are interested not in the number of occurrences but rather in the variety of processes with which each of the participants is associated. In this case, the analysis focuses on the three teachers who teach at intermediate level (A, B and E) because they are the ones who include a greater variety of processes in their discourse.

#### A. Processes associated with the use of 'I'
If we consider the different types of processes that teachers A, B and E associate with the personal pronoun 'I', as listed in Table 6, it seems clear that the higher level of personalization of the discourse of Teacher B is not only based on the sheer accumulation of the first person singular pronoun, but it also has a qualitative side, since she is the one that reveals a greater variety of material and mental processes in which she takes parts as Agent. Furthermore, she is the only one of the three teachers whose talk includes an attributive (vs. locative) use of the relational process represented by the verb 'be'. The attributive use of 'be' with the first person pronoun functioning as subject implies that Teacher B's discourse is more personal than that of the other two teachers because she is the only one who talks about herself in terms of what she is or how she feels.

*Table 6.* Processed associated with the use of 'I'

|           | Material     | Mental   | Relational    | Verbal  |
|-----------|--------------|----------|---------------|---------|
| Teacher A |              | see      | be (locative) | tell    |
|           |              | want     |               | say     |
|           |              | know     |               | mean    |
|           |              | care     |               | ask     |
|           |              | suppose  |               | remind  |
|           |              | agree    |               |         |
| Teacher B | do / did     | forgot   | be            | explain |
|           | give / gave  | hope     |               | say     |
|           | get rid of   | know     |               | tell    |
|           | have         | like     |               | thank   |
|           | hand         | prefer   |               |         |
|           | hear         | remember |               |         |
|           | leave (time) | see      |               |         |
|           | make         | suppose  |               |         |
|           | prepared     | think    |               |         |
|           | use          | want     |               |         |
|           |              | wish     |               |         |
|           |              | wonder   |               |         |
| Teacher E | cut          | care     |               | say     |
|           | give         | like     |               | talk    |
|           | have         | want     |               |         |
|           | invent       |          |               |         |
|           | start        |          |               |         |
|           | take         |          |               |         |

## B. Processes associated with the use of 'you'

The results presented in Table 7 (below) lead us to conclude that teachers not only inscribe much more frequently their students than themselves in their talk (table 5), but also that they associate their students to a greater variety of material and verbal processes (tables 6 and 7).

We can also see that, with the exception of Teacher B, whose talk contains the highest number of self inscriptions (through the inclusion of the first person pronoun 'I'), the other two teachers associate with their pupils a lesser variety of mental and relational than material processes. One reason for this might be that this type of processes refer to more intimate / personal aspects (thinking, feeling, being) and since this is precisely an aspect about themselves that is very rare in the discourse of the two male teachers (A and E), they may not feel legitimated to ask their pupils to talk about it. Here, again, we need to call attention upon the fact that the gender variable might be a more powerful explanation for the difference in the degree of personalisation than the nativeness variable.

*Table 7.* Processes associated with the use of 'you'

| | Material | | Mental | Relational | Verbal | |
|---|---|---|---|---|---|---|
| Teacher A | do | use | see | be (locative) | tell | listen |
| | have | get | know | be | shut up | insult |
| | match | design | understand | | read | call |
| | start | get | guess | | pronounce | talk |
| | play | leave | want | | write | complain |
| | look up | go | remember | | answer | spell |
| | make | work | pay attention | | refer | mean |
| | turn | finish | | | translate | speak |
| | give | | | | say | swear |
| Teacher B | give | | think | be | tell | |
| | put | | make sure | get | repeat | |
| | use | | confuse | | say | |
| | turn | | hesitate | | | |
| | lend | | prefer | | | |
| | have | | want | | | |
| | hand | | know | | | |
| | get | | understand | | | |
| | choose | | see | | | |
| | jump | | remember | | | |
| | | | find | | | |
| | | | like | | | |
| Teacher E | arrive | look | know | be | read | |
| | buy | meet | like | | repeat | |
| | come | move | prefer | | say | |
| | do | put | want | | tell | |
| | find | skate | | | understand | |
| | finish | see | | | | |
| | go | sit | | | | |
| | have | start | | | | |
| | hide | stop | | | | |
| | invent | study | | | | |
| | know | swim | | | | |
| | listen | use | | | | |
| | live | | | | | |

The relatively high number of different material processes that appear in the case of Teacher E is due to the fact that they were introduced as part of an activity in which the pupils were practising a grammatical structure through responding to personal questions that the teacher was asking them. The following is an example:

*Extract 20*
T:   Ok. And when did you start playing basketball?
S:   I started playing basketball the last year.

Finally, we may remark that whereas the relational process represented by 'be' (attributive) was only associated with the first person singular pronoun in the case of Teacher B, we find it associated with the second person pronoun in the discourse of the three teachers. In other words, whereas only Teacher B assigns attributes to her own person (*i.e.* she talks about what she is like or how she feels), the three teachers feel legitimated to assign attributes to their students (*i.e.* say what they are or feel like).

### C. Processes associated with the use of 'we'

From the low number of occurrences of the first person plural pronoun (we), as show in Table 8, we can see that teachers and students are not constituted in the teachers' discourse as forming part of a homogeneous group. This interpretation is corroborated by the absence of relational and mental processes. It is also noticeable that many of the material processes mentioned refer to classroom actions or events (*e.g.* do, start, correct, make, play, work, put...).

*Table 8.* Processes associated with the use of 'we'

|  | Material | Mental | Relational | Verbal |
|---|---|---|---|---|
| Teacher A | start | | | talk |
| | correct | | | say |
| | leave | | | read |
| | do | | | |
| | go forward | | | |
| | divide | | | |
| | get | | | |
| | have | | | |
| Teacher B | do | want | be (locative) | say |
| | start | | | call |
| | worked | | | write |
| | put | | | |
| | use | | | |
| | correct | | | |
| | have | | | |
| | make | | | |
| Teacher E | do | imagine | | listen |
| | meet | | | |
| | play | | | |

## 4.      FINAL REMARKS

This paper reports on a study intended to explore the role of particular classroom discourse strategies deployed by NNS EFL teachers in the discursive construction of social relationships and linguistic knowledge. The main goal of the analysis was to test whether by means of the semantic notions of *modality* and *participant inscription* it was possible to identify particular discourse strategies. Although we do not ignore that a thorough analysis of classroom discourse requires taking into consideration the discourse of both teacher and students, it seems undeniable that the voice of the teacher is vested with an authority that the latter do not have; therefore, it is justifiable to assign to teacher talk a primary focus in the analysis.

The qualitative approach we have adopted for the analysis of discourse modalisation has allowed us to identify particular strategies distributed alongside two continuums. The first of these continuums is connected with the representation of social relationships; in this case teacher talk moves between a discourse of power and a discourse of solidarity. The second axis concerns the representation of knowledge; here the choices go from a categorical to a non-categorical discourse. Bearing in mind the four discourse spaces created by the two continuums, we could tentatively characterise the talk of teachers A and B as shown in Figure 2:

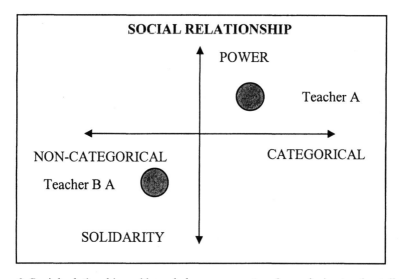

*Figure 2.* Social relationship and knowledge as parameters for analysing teacher talk.

The more quantitatively oriented analysis of participant inscription, together with the types of process associated with them, has proved to be a promising analytical tool in the analysis of teacher talk. From the results obtained it is possible to derive some initial hypotheses in connection with the issue of native versus non-native teachers. One of these hypotheses is that gender could be a more relevant variable than nativeness to account for the degree of personalisation of the teacher's discourse. Another hypothesis we can advance from the data is connected with the presence of inclusive *we* in the discourse of the teacher and its relationship with whether the teacher shares or not the cultural background of the students.

The micro-analysis of the discourse we have carried out brings primary sources to the study of NNS teachers and offers an alternative empirical basis that can be used to complement the existing literature on the topic, mostly based on the use of questionnaires on the perceptions of teachers and their students. Furthermore, the analysis offers a tool for the promotion of teacher reflection through the observation of their own and other's classroom behaviour. As Stubbs (1986) points out, although to many good teachers the analysis of discourse tells them, in different words, something they know already, the systematic study of classroom discourse can, in the first place, provide many ideas concerning the effectiveness of certain activities or techniques. In the second place, the analysis of discourse in the classroom can help to relate the work that teachers do to a coherent theory, which will subsequently illuminate both their own practice and that of other teachers. In this paper we have attempted to relate the work of the teachers studied to a theory of teaching/learning which sees the classroom not only as an instructional setting but also as a social one, in which linguistic knowledge and social relationships are discursively constructed and negotiated through the speakers' adoption of specific strategies.

## 5.     TRANSCRIPTION CONVENTIONS

T:    Teacher turn
S:    Student turn
int_  Interruption
[]    Transcriber's comments
er    Hesitation
(...)  Segment of speech omitted from the extract
*Italics   Catalan*
`Courier [English translation]`

## 6.     REFERENCES

Árva, V. & Medgyes, P. (2000). Native and non-native teachers in the classroom. *System, 28* (3), 355-372.
Austin, J. (1962). *How to do things with words.* Oxford: Clarendon Press.
Benveniste, E. (1977). El aparato formal de la enunciación. In *Problemas de lingüística general.* Vol. 2. México: Siglo XXI. 82-91.
Brown, P. & Levinson, S. (1987). *Politeness: Some universals in language use.* Cambridge: Cambridge University Press.

Calsamiglia, H. & Tusón, A. (1999). *Las cosas del decir. Manual de análisis del discurso.* Barcelona: Ariel.

Cazden, C. (1988). *Classroom discourse: The language of teaching and learning.* Portsmouth, NH: Heinemann.

Chaudron, C. (1988). *Second language classrooms: Research on teaching and learning.* Cambridge: Cambridge University Press.

Cheung, Y. L. (2002). The attitude of university students in Honk Kong towards native and non-native teachers of English. Unpublished M. Phil. Thesis. Hong Kong: The Chinese University of Hong Kong.

Coulthard, M. (1985). *An introduction to discourse analysis.* London & New York: Longman.

Downing, A. & Locke, P. (1992). *A university course in English grammar.* London: Prentice Hall.

Ducrot, O. (1980). *Les mots du discours.* Paris: Minuit.

Fairclough, N. (1989). *Language and power.* London & New York: Longman.

Fairclough, N. (1992). *Discourse and social change.* Cambridge: Polity Press.

Gumperz, John J. (1982). *Discourse strategies.* Cambridge: Cambridge University Press.

Habermas, J. (2001). *Acción comunicativa y razón sin transcendencia.* Barcelona & Buenos Aires: Ediciones Paidós.

Hall, J. & Walsh, M. (2002). Teacher-student interaction and language learning. *Annual Review of Applied Linguistics, 22,* 186-203.

Halliday, M. (1985). *An introduction to functional grammar.* London: Edward Arnold.

Inbar-Lourie, O. (1999). The native speaker construct: Investigation by perceptions. Unpublished doctoral dissertation. Tel-Aviv University, Tel-Aviv, Israel.

Johnson, K. (1995). *Understanding communication in second language classrooms.* Cambridge: Cambridge University Press.

Kerbrat-Orecchioni, C. (1980). *La enunciación. De la subjetividad en el lenguaje.* Buenos Aires: Hachette.

Medgyes, P. (1994). *The non-native teacher.* London: Macmillan. (1999) 2nd edition. Ismaning: Max Hueber Verlag.

Mercer, N. (1995). *The guided construction of knowledge.* Clevedon: Multilingual Matters.

Minsky, M. (1975). A framework for representing knowledge. In P. Winston (Ed.), *The psychology of computer vision.* New York: McGraw-Hill. 211-277.

Quirk, R., Greenbaum, S., Leech, G. & Svartvik, J. (1985). *A comprehensive grammar of the English language.* London & New York: Longman.

Samimy, K. & Brutt-Griffler, J. (1999). To be a native or non-native speaker: perception of 'non-native' students in a graduate TESOL program. In G. Braine (Ed.), *Non-native educators in English language teaching.* Mahwah, NJ: Lawrence Erlbaum Associates. 127-144.

Schank, R. & Abelson, R. (1977). *Scripts, plans, goals, and understanding.* Hillsdale, NJ: Lawrence Erlbaum Associates.

Searle, J. (1969). *Speech acts.* Cambridge: Cambridge University Press.

Sinclair, J. & Coulthard, M. (1975). *Towards an analysis of discourse.* Oxford: Oxford University Press.

Stubbs, M. (1986). *Educational linguistics.* Oxford: Blackwell.

Tannen, D. (1989). *Talking voices. Repetition, dialogue and imagery in conversational discourse.* Cambridge: Cambridge University Press.

# Chapter 7

# NON-NATIVE SPEAKER TEACHERS AND AWARENESS OF LEXICAL DIFFICULTY IN PEDAGOGICAL TEXTS

ARTHUR MCNEILL
*The Chinese University of Hong Kong*

## 1.      INTRODUCTION

It is often assumed that language teachers who teach their mother tongue have a number of advantages over teachers who are not native speakers (NSs) of the language they teach. Native speaker intuitions about language are supposed to result in the production of correct, idiomatic utterances, as well as providing the ability to recognise acceptable and unacceptable versions of the language. Non-native speaker teachers (NNSTs) often believe that their command of the language they teach is inadequate and that their lack of NS insights can make it difficult for them to perform their jobs as well as they would like. The communicative approach to language teaching, with its emphasis on oral interaction in the classroom, has presented particular challenges to NNSTs. However, a possible disadvantage faced by the NSTs, especially teachers of English as a foreign language, whose careers typically take them to different parts of the world, is the linguistic distance between teacher and learner. Are NSTs likely to be less sensitive to their students' language needs because they have less access to their L1 and, by extension, to the way in which students process L2? This chapter examines an aspect of language teaching whi-ch has received relatively little attention in language education research: native and non-native speaker teachers' sensitivity to language difficulty from a learner's perspective.

E. Llurda (Ed.), *Non-Native Language Teachers. Perceptions, Challenges and Contributions to the Profession*, 107—128.

The difficulties involved in defining what constitutes a NS have long been of interest to applied linguists. Davies (1991), for example, argues that the differences are far from clear-cut and that there is the possibility of mobility from non-native speaker to native-speaker status. Medgyes (1994) and Paikeday (1985) have argued that the ways in which native and non-native speakers are perceived, in particular, the ways in which both types of teacher are regarded by students and colleagues are, in many respects, more important than attempts to define the characteristics of each. This chapter will not attempt any additional analysis of the notion of the NS, because the research it reports is based on groups of teachers for whom the status of NS/NNS is not an issue. Fascinating as definitions and descriptions of NS are, it is important to recognise that the majority of language learners receive their language tuition from NNSTs who would not make a claim to be considered as NSs. There can be no doubt that the recent spread of global English has increased the demand for native English speakers in schools and universities around the world. However, the same global English phenomenon has also led to expansion in the number of NNSs being trained to become English language teachers in their own countries. While NSTs will continue to be 'imported' to work alongside local teachers, in most educational systems the bulk of English language teaching will remain in the hands of NNSs.

This chapter reports some empirical work based on a comparative study of native and non-native speaker teachers of English. The research is based on an experiment in which four groups of teachers took part in a decision-making task, where they were asked to identify sources of difficulty in a pedagogical text. The actual difficulty level of the language content was established by means of an objective vocabulary test administered to 200 language learners. The main focus of interest is a comparison between native and non-native speaker teachers. A secondary focus is the role of 'expertise' in developing teachers' sensitivity to language difficulty. Half of the teachers in the sample were experienced graduate teachers with postgraduate qualifications in education, while the other half were newcomers to teaching. The motivation for undertaking research in this area is the assumption that teachers who are aware of the language which their students find difficult are more likely to be effective in teaching because they can focus their attention on learners' actual needs. Conversely, it is assumed that teachers who are less aware of their students' language problems will be less effective because they devote teaching time to language which may not be required by students and neglect areas where a teacher's help would be beneficial. It is argued that sensitivity to difficulty in language learning is an important aspect of professionalism and ought to be included in any description or model of teacher language awareness.

## 2.     LITERATURE REVIEW

### 2.1     Language teachers and language awareness

Before turning to the details of the study, it will be useful to consider briefly the ways in which language awareness has been conceptualized. The range of interests and domains which tend to fall within the scope of language awareness are described and distinguished by James & Garrett (1991). Within the British language awareness movement, at least as far as English mother tongue is concerned, the thrust of language awareness activity appears to be the relationship between implicit and explicit knowledge about English. It is assumed that all L1 users have an implicit knowledge of their mother tongue because they have mastered it successfully. A question which has preoccupied research in L1 is whether explicit knowledge is a useful indicator of an individual's language awareness. Figure 1 provides an illustration of the language awareness (LA) focus of most L1 studies.

| *Participant:* | language learner | | language teacher | |
| --- | --- | --- | --- | --- |
| *Language:* | L1 | | L1 | |
| *LA Focus:* | implicit $\rightarrow$ | explicit | implicit $\rightarrow$ | explicit |
| | knowledge | knowledge | knowledge | knowledge |

*Figure 1.* Operationalisation of language awareness (LA) in L1 studies.

For learners and teachers of a second or foreign language, the approach to language awareness obviously requires a different focus, because L2 learners do not generally possess an implicit knowledge of the language being studied. The few studies which have been reported (*e.g.* Andrews, 1994; Berry, 1995) rely on the following indicators of teacher and student language awareness: knowledge of metalinguistic terminology and the ability to correct grammar errors (Figure 2).

| *Participant:* | language learner | language teacher |
| --- | --- | --- |
| *Language:* | L2 | L2 |
| *Typical LA Focus:* | error correction | metalinguistic knowledge |

*Figure 2.* Operationalisation of language awareness (LA) in L2 studies.

The above models basically consist of only two elements: (a) a language user or learner, and (b) language. For teachers concerned with facilitating the language learning of students, awareness of language acquisition and processing is also important, in addition to an understanding of the language being studied. One of the ideas being explored in the present research is that language awareness for teachers might encompass not only the ability to analyse and explain language, but also awareness of the relationship between the language being taught and particular groups of learners. Such a broadening of the definition of language awareness involves a shift from a static type knowledge of language to a more dynamic knowledge which relates language as a subject of study to particular teaching contexts. Figure 3 proposes a framework for L2 teachers' language awareness which goes beyond metalinguistic knowledge and includes an awareness of the difficulty level represented by different language items and of the previous knowledge and abilities of students.

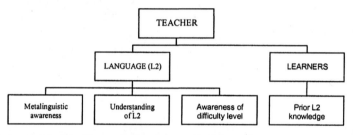

*Figure 3.* Model of language awareness for L2 teachers.

The above model assumes that the greater a teacher's knowledge of the lower levels of the figure (*i.e.* both the difficulty level of the language items and students' prior L2 knowledge), the more effective they will be in identifying appropriate language content for their courses. The model also assumes, possibly as a statement of the obvious, that teachers' understanding of the language they have to teach (*i.e.* the so-called target language) is an important component of their language awareness.

## 2.2     Expertise in teaching

A reasonable assumption to make is that teaching expertise is influenced by such factors as teaching experience, knowledge of the subject matter being taught and the amount and type of specialist training received. A number of scholars have attempted to identify and describe the characteristics of teachers who are deemed by their colleagues to be 'expert' teachers. According to Berliner's (1992) theory of the development of teaching expertise, teachers' performance and attitudes develop across a number of levels, which Berliner has identified as 'novice', 'advanced', 'beginner', 'competent', 'proficient' and 'expert'. Each level is associated with a particular quality of decision-making. Berliner defines novice teachers as those who have some knowledge of teaching theory, but have not had much opportunity to put the theory into practice. The pedagogical decision-making of this type of teacher, according to Berliner, relies almost entirely on theory. He assumes that teachers' competence is influenced by their experience of actual teaching. 'Expert' teachers have to make decisions not just in their own classrooms, but also concerning beyond their own classrooms, for example, about the school curriculum, student progression from level to level, choice of textbooks, etc. The decision-making of this type of teacher, according to Berliner, is influenced both by extensive experience in the field and by a high level of pedagogical subject knowledge, derived from their formal training in education and master's degrees in related fields.

## 2.3     Teachers' intuitions about difficulty

Relatively little is known about how well teachers anticipate students' language problems. One of the first studies to examine teachers' ability to identify vocabulary difficulty in L2 texts was carried out by Brutten (1981) with NS ESL teachers in the US. Brutten asked groups of teachers and students to preview the same text and to underline the difficult words. A comparison of the selections revealed high commonality between the teachers and students. When a similar study was conducted with NNSTs in Hong Kong (McNeill, 1992), it was found that although there was a high level of consensus between teachers and students about word difficulty, huge differences were found among the individual teachers. Research with European ESL teachers has also concluded that groups of teachers are unlikely to agree with one another on the sources of vocabulary difficulty in pedagogical texts (Bulteel, 1992; Goethals, 1994).

## 3.     RESEARCH QUESTIONS

The study attempts to answer four questions:

1. What similarities and differences can be detected in the way NS and NNS teachers predict learners' vocabulary difficulties in reading texts?
2. To what extent does the ability to predict learners' vocabulary difficulties vary among individual teachers?
3. What similarities and differences can be detected in the way 'novice' and 'expert' teachers predict vocabulary problems in reading texts?
4. To what extent does expertise improve the judgements of NNS teachers?

## 4.       DESIGN OF THE STUDY

The participants were four groups of English teachers (n=65) and 200 Cantonese-speaking secondary school students in Hong Kong whose level of English was upper-intermediate. The teachers were asked to make predictions about lexical difficulty in a reading text intended for upper-intermediate level students and to justify their decisions. The students were tested on their understanding of the lexical content of the text and the teachers' predictions were compared with the students' actual difficulties with the same material. Although studies of teacher decision-making are not uncommon in the literature, in most cases there is no objective measure for assessing the quality of the teachers' decisions.

### 4.1      Teachers

Two of the teacher groups were NNSs of English (all of them spoke Cantonese as their first language) and the other two were native English speakers. It is estimated that about 98% of the population of Hong Kong are native speakers of Cantonese. All of the NNSTs in the study were local Hong Kong teachers who learned English as a foreign language at school and university. Although most of them had been educated at English medium institutions, they used Cantonese for most of their everyday communication. None of the teachers would wish to claim they were NSs of English. The teachers in the NS groups all grew up in the English-speaking world (UK, Australia, Canada or US) and had come as adults to work in Hong Kong. Two of the groups consisted of experienced, trained graduate teachers, while the other two groups consisted of inexperienced teachers who were still attending initial training to become English teachers. The composition of the four teacher groups is summarised in Table 1.

*Table 1.* Details of teacher subjects

|                   | Non-native Speakers | Native Speakers |
|-------------------|---------------------|-----------------|
| 'Expert' Teachers | 20 (NNE)            | 15 (NSE)        |
| 'Novice' Teachers | 15 (NNN)            | 15 (NSN)        |

Members of the NNE ('non-native speaker expert') group had a postgraduate teaching qualification and a master's degree in applied linguistics/TESOL or equivalent. All had been teaching English in Hong Kong for at least two years. Group NNN ('non-native speaker novice') were all English subject specialists in the first year of a full-time bachelor's degree in education (B.Ed.) at the University of Hong Kong. They had all received at least part of their secondary education at schools in Hong Kong.

Their only experience of teaching English was giving occasional private tuition to school pupils. None of the NNS participants would wish to be considered as NSs. Although all of them grew up in Hong Kong and received most of their education there through the medium of English, their dominant language is Cantonese. Their use of English tends to be restricted to school and university, with Cantonese being used almost exclusively at home and on social occasions.

Group NSE ('native speaker expert') were all graduates who had completed postgraduate qualifications in teaching English as a second language. They had also completed (or were about to complete) a master's degree in applied linguistics/TESOL or equivalent. While all of the NSE teachers had taught in Hong Kong for at least two years and were familiar with the Hong Kong secondary schools syllabus, none had studied Cantonese formally and none had more than basic competence in Cantonese. Group NSN ('native speaker novice') were all attending the UCLES/Royal Society of Arts Certificate in Teaching English as a Foreign Language at the British Council in Hong Kong. This is a pre-service course intended for teachers interested in embarking on a career in TEFL. None of the NSN teachers had more than a very elementary command of Cantonese. However, they had all lived in Hong Kong for at least two years and had limited experience of teaching English, mostly restricted to one-to-one tutorials.

## 4.2    Students

Two-hundred secondary school students (approximately 60% of whom were female and 40% male) from ten different schools took the vocabulary tests. The students were all aged between fifteen and sixteen and were in Form 6 of the 'arts' stream of the secondary school system.

## 4.3    Materials

The reading text was a 600-word general science passage about laser surgery, entitled 'The sword that can heal' (reproduced in Appendix A). The text is typical of the reading passages used in the upper forms of the secondary school system in Hong Kong. With the co-operation of two experienced secondary school teachers, the vocabulary content of the text was scrutinised and 40 words were identified as being the most difficult from a typical student's point of view. These words were then used to construct a simple 40-item vocabulary test (Appendix B). The 40 English words were simply arranged in a list, with a space next to each where students had to give the meaning in Chinese.

## 4.4     Procedure

The students were first given the test (Test 1) and allowed 20 minutes to give the L1 equivalents. The completed test papers were collected and the students then received a copy of the reading, together with a clean copy of the vocabulary test (Test 2). They were then given 20 minutes to re-take the vocabulary test, referring as often as they wished to the text from which the words were taken. Test 1, then, gave an indication of the students' knowledge of the 40 words in isolation (*i.e.* static vocabulary), while Test 2 measured knowledge of words in context (*i.e.* dynamic vocabulary).

The teachers were asked to read through the text and to imagine they would be using it in a reading lesson with Form 6 students. They were asked to select twelve words which were unfamiliar to the students and which, in their view, were essential for an understanding of the general sense of the text. The teachers were also asked to explain their reasons for believing that the selected words would represent a source of difficulty for the learners.

## 5.      DATA ANALYSIS

For each of the 40 words a score was calculated, based on the number of times it was selected by the teachers group. Using the scores on the students' vocabulary tests, two further scores were awarded to each word, based on the number of students who got the item right in each of the two tests. A Spearman rank order correlation was calculated to determine the strength of the relationship between the teachers' selections of words and the actual difficulty levels of the words, as determined by the vocabulary tests.

When the students' vocabulary tests were analysed, it was found that eight of the 40 words were particularly difficult and were known by less than 15% of the student sample. At the other extreme, there were another eight words which had been proved to be rather easy; their meanings were known by at least 85% of the students. Each teacher was given a score out of eight for the number of 'hard' words identified and a score out of eight for the number of 'easy' words identified. These scores were used to prepare a series of barcharts to illustrate individual teachers' performance on the task. Ideally, a teacher should aim for the highest possible score (maximum=8) on the 'hard' words and the lowest possible score (maximum=8) on the 'easy' words.

The scores of the four groups of teachers on the word difficulty task were then compared by means of a oneway ANOVA and a posthoc Tukey's Multiple Range Test. Finally, an informal analysis was carried out, based on the reasons given by the teachers in support of their decisions.

# 6.      RESULTS AND DISCUSSION

## 6.1      Correlations

The correlations between the teachers' selections of words for explanation and the difficulty level of the words, as established by the two students' vocabulary tests are shown in Table 2.

*Table 2.* Correlations between teachers' selections (NSN, NNN, NSE, NNE) and actual word difficulty

| Group | Test 1 (words in isolation) | Test 2 (words in context) |
|---|---|---|
| NSN | .0487 (ns) | .0796 (ns) |
| NNN | .5889 ($p<.001$) | .5199 ($p<.001$) |
| NSE | .2002 (ns) | .2298 (ns) |
| NNE | .5061 ($p<.001$) | .4564 ($p<.01$) |

The two native speaker groups, NSE and NSN, performed less well than their non-native speaker counterparts. The correlation between their selections of vocabulary items words and the actual difficulty level of the words failed to reach significance level. By contrast, the two non-native groups demonstrated a significant correlation with the difficulty level of the words. The NSTs generally failed to identify the words which students found difficult. By contrast, the NNSTs were much more in tune with the learners' problems. To return to the first research question, the correlation results certainly suggest that NNSTs, as a group, are more successful than NSTs at predicting learners' vocabulary difficulties in reading texts.

When the performances of the groups are compared by Expertise, we find that both non-native groups, *i.e.* both experts and novices, produced significant correlations with the student data. This result suggests that Expertise for NNSTs does not lead to increased sensitivity to vocabulary difficulty. Among the native speakers, the expert group (NSE) produced a higher correlation coefficient than the novice group (NSN). However, both failed to reach significance level. As a partial answer to the third research question, the correlation results suggest that Expertise does not necessarily improve awareness of language difficulty. However, a more detailed picture is provided in the following section, which examines individual teachers' performances.

Interestingly, the most successful of the four groups are the novice non-native speakers, *i.e.* a group of teachers with no real background in education or applied linguistics. However, their closeness in age and experience to the students no doubt allowed them to empathise more with their students' difficulties. In this study, the NNN teachers all spoke the same L1 as the students.

A fairly obvious conclusion from the results (Table 2) is that teachers who speak their students' L1 have a distinct advantage in knowing where their students' language difficulties lie. Even the expert native speaker teachers (NSE) did not perform well on the task of identifying the difficulties, which suggests that their experience and training had not had a major effect on their ability to focus on learners' difficulties with the text. In fact, it might be argued that the NNN group were at an advantage over their NNE colleagues inasmuch as they had not been influenced by any linguistic or educational theory which might have interfered with their selections and possibly clouded their intuitive judgement. Both NNS groups found it more difficult to identify unknown contextualised vocabulary than isolated words, while both NS groups performed slightly better with the contextualised vocabulary. Although neither of the NS groups was particularly successful in the word identification task, the experts performed better than the novices, which suggests that their experience and training had made some contribution to their expertise in this respect.

## 6.2     Individual teachers' performances

In order to chart the performances of the members of each group, four barcharts were prepared, based on each teacher's selection of 'hard' and 'easy' words. The four groups' performances are illustrated in Figures 4 to 7.

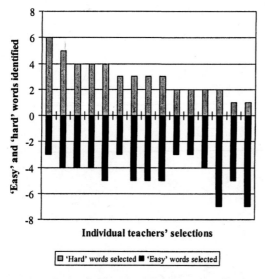

*Figure 4.* NNE teachers' selections of 'hard' and 'easy' words.

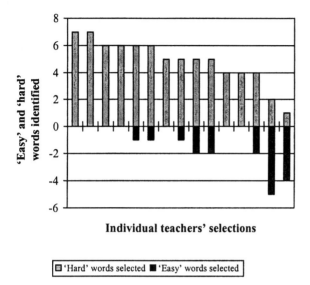

*Figure 5*. NSE teachers' selections of 'hard' and 'casy' words.

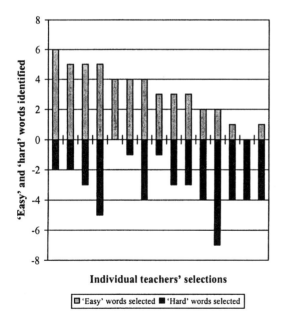

*Figure 6*. NNN teachers' selections of 'hard' and 'easy' words.

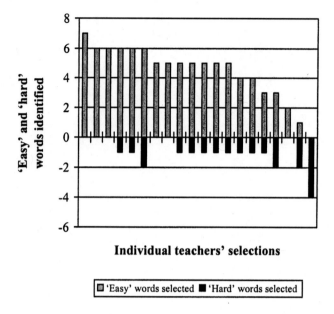

*Figure 7.* NSN teachers' selections of 'hard' and 'easy' words.

The barcharts provide a visual impression of how the individual members of each group performed. The pictures suggest that both non-native speaker groups, NNE and NNN, tended to perform consistently well on the task, with the exception of two individuals in each group. Although the majority made good selections, two members of each group failed to identify more than two 'hard' words and included 'easy' words in their selections (Research Questions 1 and 2).

As far as the native speakers are concerned, the pattern of choice was less systematic among the experts (NSE), with some teachers focusing successfully on 'hard' words and ignoring most of the 'easy' ones, while others failed to identify more than a couple of 'hard' words and included several 'easy' words in their selection. The range in this group was very wide indeed, with a number of teachers having little success in tuning in to the students' difficulties (Research Questions 1 and 2).

As for the 'novices' among the native speakers (NSN), a more systematic pattern can be detected. It is systematic in its preference for 'easy' over 'hard' words (Research Question 3). The reasons why this group gravitated, more or less *en masse*, in the wrong direction are not immediately apparent. However, the reasons which the NSN teachers gave in support of their selections suggest that they were generally influenced by their own reactions to particular words rather than an awareness of how the students would perceive them. A word-centred rather than student-centred approach to pre-viewing reading texts for classroom use might well be a characteristic of novice ESL teachers. In terms of Berliner's (1992) theory of teacher development, expert teachers are able to anticipate students' difficulties since they are aware of the interaction of the learners with the learning material. By contrast, novice teachers take a more static view of the learning process and tend to judge learners and materials in isolation, rather than considering how the two might interact with each other. While the NSN group's difficulties with the prediction task might appear to support this view, the NNN group's strong performance would appear to contradict it. However, it is quite possible that the NNNs were too close in experience and language proficiency to the student group and that their good prediction was largely a result of estimating their own vocabulary difficulties, rather than any real awareness of the students' needs.

When comparing the groups, it appears that good and poor predictors can be found in each language group. A further difference emerges when we examine the amount of attention which the 'easy' items attracted. While the majority of the NNE teachers ignored the 'easy' words, the NSE were much more likely to assume that these words might constitute a problem for the students. One possible explanation for this is that the NSE group did not know what the Chinese equivalents were and the extent to which they were readily available within the Chinese lexical system. The NNE group, on the other hand, were able to judge whether, for example, a literal translation existed in Chinese and might be in a better position to judge whether the students could work out the meaning. The last section of this chapter examines some linguistic issues which appear to have caused confusion in the teachers' minds. A general point from the informal analysis worth reporting here is that the NSE teachers were generally more eloquent than the others in providing justifications for their decisions, including—ironically—cases in which their judgements were incorrect.

## 6.3    Differences between groups (ANOVA)

The four groups' scores on the 'hard' words and on overall vocabulary judgment (calculated by subtracting each teacher's 'easy' word score from the 'hard' word score) were then compared by means of a one-way ANOVA. The results are shown in Tables 3 and 4.

*Table 3.* Oneway ANOVA of scores on 'hard' word identification task (NNN, NNE, NSN, NSE groups)

| Source | df | SS | MS | F | *p<* |
|---|---|---|---|---|---|
| Between groups | 3 | 128.3795 | 42.7932 | 19.6171 | .001 |
| Within groups | 61 | 133.0667 | 2.1814 | | |

*Table 4.* Oneway ANOVA of Overall Vocabulary Judgement scores (NNN, NNE, NSN, NSE groups)

| Source | df | SS | MS | F | *p<* |
|---|---|---|---|---|---|
| Between groups | 3 | 293.6449 | 97.8816 | 12.3768 | .001 |
| Within groups | 61 | 482.4167 | 7.9085 | | |

Significant F-values were obtained in both measures, suggesting that there are real differences in the four groups' performances. In order to establish whether significant differences exist between particular pairs of groups, Tukey's Multiple Range Test was run using the Overall Vocabulary Judgement scores. The results are shown in Table 5.

Significant differences emerge between all groups when compared by language, regardless of teaching expertise. By contrast, no significant differences were found when comparing teachers by expertise within the same language (Research Question 4).

*Table 5.* Tukey's Multiple Range Test for Overall Vocabulary Judgement (NNN, NNE, NSN, NSE groups)

| Differences between groups by Language | | Result |
|---|---|---|
| Native Speaker | Non-Native Speaker | |
| Expert | Expert | |
| Novice | Novice | |
| Expert | Novice | all significant (*p<*.05) |
| Novice | Expert | |
| Differences between groups by Expertise | | Result |
| Expert | Novice | |
| Native speaker | Native speaker | |
| Non-native speaker | Non-native speaker | no significant difference (*p<*.05) |

## 6.4    An informal analysis of the teachers' misjudgements

When the teachers made their selections, they were asked explain why they considered the words to represent a source of difficulty for the learners. The reasons given by the teachers in support of selecting what turned out to be easy words were analysed in order to gain some insights into how their decision-making was influenced. The three most frequently cited reasons in this category were that (a) derived words were difficult for learners to recognise, (b) polysemous words were likely to cause confusion and (c) 'transparency' was a source of problems for students. Examples of these three issues are discussed below.

A number of teachers believed that when a word occurs in a text in a derived form, students who are familiar with the root form of the word might not be able to cope with other morphological realisations. For example, it was considered that students who knew the word 'solid' would not be able to understand 'solidify'. In fact, 'solidify' was known by over 85% of the students. Other examples of derived words identified as difficult by teachers, but known to most of the students, are given in Table 6. The problems which learners face with different forms of L2 words has been recognised by a number of researchers (*e.g.* Meara & Ingle, 1986, Zimmerman, 1987). A possible explanation for the teachers' concern with regard to derived forms might relate to the attention given to derived forms in TESL methodology courses, where teachers are made aware of the different morphological realisations of words and may assume that derived forms represent a general problem for learners. Yet, it would appear from the results of the present study that students may well be able to decode the meaning of derived words, contrary to the expectations of their teachers. It has been established that students in Hong Kong tend to experience problems with the production of derived words, particularly in the final syllable, where inflections occur most frequently in English (McNeill, 1990). However, learners appear to have far fewer problems with reception, *i.e.* with the decoding of derived words.

*Table 6.* Examples of derived forms wrongly believed to be problematical

| Root known to the students | Derived form believed to be too difficult for the students |
| --- | --- |
| Microscope | microscopic |
| Prefer | preferential |
| Vapor | vaporise |
| Surgeon | surgical, surgery |

Another group of words erroneously singled out as a source of difficulty were polysemous words. For example, a number of teachers believed that a student who knew the word 'tissue' in the meaning of paper handkerchief would be unable to understand it to refer to body tissue. In fact, 'tissue' in the sense of 'body tissue' was known to over 85% of the students, according to the results of Test 2. A number of applied linguists (*e.g.* Carter, 1987a, 1987b; Visser 1990) stress the importance of core vocabulary and promote the notion that words have a core meaning which can be extended to cover uses which may appear far removed from the core meaning. It is often assumed that the further removed a particular instance of word use is from its core meaning, the less accessible it is to an L2 learner. It is possible that the teachers who took part in the study over-reacted to those words which were not used in their core meaning and under-estimated students' ability to cope with extensions of meaning by themselves. Further examples of items identified as representing this kind of difficulty in the present study are listed in Table 7.

*Table 7*. Examples of misjudged polysemous words

| Basic meaning known to students | Meaning considered to be too difficult for students to deduce on their own |
| --- | --- |
| Laser | A laser beam used in surgery |
| Cells | Body cells |
| Fibre | Optical fibres |
| Application | The application of a technique |

Another aspect of vocabulary study which appeared to confuse many teachers was transparency and the related notion 'deceptive transparency' (Laufer, 1988, 1989). While it is widely assumed that words with an obviously transparent structure (T) are easy for learners to understand (for example, 'door' + 'mat' = 'doormat'; 'car' + 'park' = 'carpark'), other compounds may be misleading. For example, words such as 'discourse' and 'outline' are not easily understood by analysing their component parts and may be regarded as deceptively transparent (DT) from a learner's point of view. In the present study, transparency of meaning and deceptive transparency both appeared to trigger off warning signals in many teachers' minds, possibly because the two concepts were not always clearly distinguished in the teachers' minds. Examples of 'easy' words from the text assumed by many teachers to be potentially difficult include: *birthmark* (T); *pin-point* (T); *invaluable* (DT). Possibly influenced by Laufer's (1988, 1989) work, teacher education courses on vocabulary learning appear to have attached importance to similar lexical forms ('synforms') and transparency in recent years. Whether teachers' heightened awareness of phenomena such as transparent and deceptively transparent words leads to more effective language teaching remains to be established.

A striking feature of the reasons given by the teachers for their selection of words was the fluency and conviction with which they were formulated, particularly within the two expert groups. Since all of these teachers had been educated to master's level and held senior teaching posts, they were familiar with the major issues in reading pedagogy and vocabulary teaching. Ironically, much of the expert knowledge was associated with inaccurate judgements. It is probably fair to say that, according to the reasons supplied by the teachers in support of their decisions, those who emerged as good judges of lexical difficulty tended to relate their decisions to their students' prior knowledge and their students' reading habits. By contrast, the poor judges tended to justify their selections with reference to properties of individual words. The difficulty level of a word depends not only on language variables, such as transparency and polysemy, but involves learner variables, such as the previous language knowledge, content knowledge, academic skills, interests, etc. In the literature on teaching expertise, there is increasing evidence that expert teachers rely heavily on what they have learned through the experience of interacting with their students (*e.g.* Bereiter & Scardamalia, 1993), whereas less competent teachers are believed to rely more heavily on their subject content knowledge. To relate the discussion to the wider issue of teachers' language awareness, it would appear from the teachers who emerged as successful in the task used in the present study that awareness of students' previous learning and their abilities is an important component of being able to identify vocabulary problems. This evidence adds support to the view that our notion of language awareness for language teachers should include awareness of learners, in addition to knowledge of and competence in L2, as proposed in the model of teacher language awareness shown in Figure 3.

When the teachers provided reasons in support of their selections, it is possible that many of the reasons given by the poor judges apply to vocabulary learning and productive vocabulary use, but are less relevant to word recognition in a reading task in which students are only required to understand the main ideas. It may be the case that the poor judges made over-generalisations about certain language features and assumed that these represented difficulty in some absolute sense.

## 7.     CONCLUSION

The results of the study suggest that ESL teachers who speak the same L1 as their students are generally more accurate in identifying sources of lexical difficulty in reading texts than teachers whose mother tongue is English and who are not familiar with the students' L1. In practice, most non-native speaker ESL teachers share their students' L1 and therefore are more likely to be successful at focusing on areas of potential difficulty from their students' perspective. However, the research also showed that within each of the four groups of teachers, large individual differences exist in the ability to identify lexical difficulty. Some possible explanations for poor decision-making were provided by the teachers themselves in the reasons they gave to support their word selections. These appear to be based on possible over-generalisation of findings from research in second language vocabulary learning.

The four groups of teachers in the study allowed us to examine the ways in which teacher variables such as language (L1/L2) and expertise contribute to awareness of lexical difficulty. However, novice teachers are not always young (and therefore close to their students in experience) and NNSTs do not always teach students who speak the same language as they do. Further research with older novice teachers might well show that they do not tune into learners difficulties as well as younger novices do and that the closeness in age between the novices in the present study and the students accounted for the teachers' impressive ability to identify lexical problems. While native English speakers teach ESL all over the world, non-native speaker ESL teachers tend to work in their own countries, teaching students from the same language background. Interesting follow-up work might usefully be carried out with NNSTs who teach students whose mother tongue they (the teachers) do not know or who teach multi-lingual groups.

At a more theoretical level, the results of the study invite speculation about the relationship between teaching expertise and language awareness. A question which was posed at the outset was whether language awareness is a necessary component of teaching expertise. Currently, expertise in the professions is not objectively measured, but tends to rely on peer judgements and other *ad hoc* indicators. In the present study, it was found that many novice teachers (NNN) demonstrated a very high level of awareness of learners' vocabulary difficulties, which suggests that any relationship we can establish between language awareness and expertise is unlikely to be a linear one. Yet it seems reasonable to assume that language awareness might be measured objectively, provided an acceptable description or definition of language awareness for language teachers can be arrived at. It should also be acknowledged that notions of expertise in teaching are also still evolving and the possibility of producing more objective measures of teaching expertise is not inconceivable.

## 8.    REFERENCES

Andrews, S. (1994). The grammatical awareness and knowledge of Hong Kong teachers of English. In N. Bird, P. Falvey, A.B.M. Tsui, D.A. Allison & A. McNeill (Eds.), *Language and learning*. Hong Kong: Education Department. 508-520.
Bereiter, C. & Scardamalia, M. (1993). *Surpassing ourselves*. Chicago, IL: Open Court.
Berliner, D.C. (1992). The nature of expertise in teaching. In F.K. Oser, A. Dick & J.L. Patry (Eds.), *Effective and responsible teaching: The new synthesis*. CA: Jossey-Bass. 227-248.

Berry, R. (1995). Grammatical terminology: Is there a student/teacher gap? In D. Nunan, R. Berry & V. Berry (Eds.), *Language awareness in language education* (Vol 2). Hong Kong: Department of Curriculum Studies, The University of Hong Kong. 51-68.

Brutten, S.R. (1981). An analysis of student and teacher indications of vocabulary difficulty. *RELC Journal, 12* (1), 66-71.

Bulteel, J. (1992). Criteria for vocabulary selection for teaching purposes. Principles, lists and teaching practice. Licentiate thesis, Applied Linguistics. KU Leuven.

Carter, R. (1987a). Is there a core vocabulary? Some implications for language teaching. *Applied Linguistics, 8* (2), 178-193.

Carter, R. (1987b). *Vocabulary: Applied linguistic perspectives.* London: Allen & Unwin.

Davies, A. (1991). *The native speaker in applied linguistics.* Edinburgh: University of Edinburgh Press.

Goethals, M. (1994). Vocabulary management in foreign language teaching and learning. In K. Carlon, K. Davidse & B. Rudzka-Ostyn (Eds.) *Orbis/Supplementa 2 (Perspectives on English).* Leuven: Peeters. 484-506.

James, C. & Garrett, P. (Eds.) (1991). *Language awareness in the classroom.* London: Longman.

Laufer, B. (1988). The concept of 'synforms' (similar lexical forms) in L2 learning. *Language and Education, 2* (2), 113-132.

Laufer, B. (1989). A factor of difficulty in vocabulary learning: Deceptive transparency. *AILA Review, 6*, 10-20.

McNeill, A. (1990). Vocabulary learning and teaching: Evidence from lexical errors in the spontaneous speech of ESL learners. *Institute of Language in Education Journal, 7*, 141-153.

McNeill, A. (1992). Helping ESL learners to read: Teacher and student perceptions of vocabulary difficulties. In N. Bird & J. Harris (Eds.), *Quilt and quill: Achieving and maintaining quality in language teaching and learning.* Hong Kong: Education Department. 150-165.

Meara, P. & Ingle, S. (1986). The formal representation of words in an L2 speaker's lexicon. *Second Language Research, 2* (2), 160-171.

Medgyes, P. (1994). *The non-native teacher.* London: Macmillan. (1999) 2nd edition. Ismaning: Max Hueber Verlag.

Paikeday, T.M. (1985). *The native speaker is dead!* Toronto: Paikeday Publishing Inc.

Visser, A. (1990). Learning vocabulary through underlying meanings: An investigation of an interactive technique. *RELC Journal, 21* (1), 11-28.

Zimmerman, R. (1987). Form-oriented and content-oriented lexical errors in L2 learners. *International Review of Applied Linguistics, 25* (1), 55-67.

# APPENDIX A: READING TEXT USED IN THE STUDY

### The Sword that can Heal

While military scientists test lasers against satellites, surgeons use them as miraculously accurate scalpels. They can even be used to detonate hydrogen bombs. The beam can be focused to spot one fiftieth the size of a human hair, yet its intensity is enough to kill cancer cells or drill through the most delicate bones.

More than a decade ago, eye surgeons realised that they could use the laser's beam to seal individually the microscopic blood vessels in the retina. The beam is so fine that only the target is heated. Now its pin-head blasting power has been turned to destroying cancer cells and reducing birthmarks. For cancer treatment, the diseased cells must be killed while their healthy neighbours are left unharmed. Where the cancer can be directly and accurately attacked, laser treatment does well: early cancer of the cervix and skin cancers have been widely and successfully treated. This type of cancer is not very easy to reach. For cancers that are less accessible, there is a new and potentially valuable technique in which the patient is injected with a chemical that then attaches itself preferentially to cancer cells. When the laser strikes the chemical, it releases a form of oxygen that kills these cells.

The marvellous accuracy of the surgical laser can be increased by sending the beam along fibres of glass far finer than the human hair. The 'optical fibres' carry it around corners and direct it precisely at a tiny area; so little of the beam spills from the glass that there is no risk of damaging healthy cells. This technique is particularly useful in ear surgery.

Furthermore, the laser beam can also remove bone, and so it is valuable in ear surgery. The sounds we hear are carried from the eardrum to the nerves of the ear by a delicate set of pivoting bones which sometimes solidify, causing deafness. A laser beam vaporises the bone without touching any of the surrounding tissue. A beam is diffused to avoid scarring and the mark becomes inconspicuous. This accuracy in targeting makes the laser a useful tool for the dentist also; a nerve can be reached through a hole drilled in the enamel.

Birthmarks, once almost untreatable, are a mass of blood vessels and, being red, they absorb the laser beam strongly. It seals them so that the mark becomes less conspicuous. The normal cells of the skin's surface, which don't absorb much of the laser beam, act in the healing and help to conceal the mark. The beam can cut with a precision that no scalpel could achieve. The operation can transform the lives of people who were previously doomed to a lifetime of cosmetic surgery.

Though this application is widely used in America, there are in Britain only two hospitals offering the treatment, and one feels bound to warn patients that success is not certain. However, some ten new centres will soon be opened. Britain, though, is one of the leaders in laser treatment of bleeding peptic ulcers and this, combined with new medicines can mean ulcer treatment without conventional surgery. The laser is now being used to treat all kinds of illnesses in this country.

(Tony Osman in the Sunday Times Colour Magazine; reproduced by Greenall, S. & Swan, M. in Effective Reading, Cambridge: Cambridge University Press, 1986)

## APPENDIX B: ITEMS IN THE VOCABULARY TEST USED IN THE STUDY (TEST 1 AND TEST 2)

1. Laser
2. Surgeon
3. Beam
4. Intensity
5. Seal
6. Pin-Point
7. Miraculously
8. Scalpel
9. Detonate
10. Drill
11. Accessible
12. Cells
13. Microscopic
14. Preferential
15. Retina
16. Fine
17. Spill
18. Blasting
19. Birthmark
20. Solidify
21. Cervix
22. Surgery
23. Tissue
24. Optical Fibre
25. Pivoting
26. Scarring
27. Diffused
28. Inconspicuous
29. Doomed
30. Precision
31. Enamel
32. Delicate
33. Bound
34. Healing
35. Conventional
36. Transform
37. Concealment
38. Application
39. Ulcer
40. Absorb

PART III

# PERSPECTIVES ON NNS TEACHERS-IN-TRAINING

Chapter 8

# NON-NATIVE TESOL STUDENTS AS SEEN BY PRACTICUM SUPERVISORS

ENRIC LLURDA
*Universitat de Lleida*

## 1.     INTRODUCTION

Research on NNS teachers is fairly recent and has mostly centered on teachers' self-perceptions of their non-nativeness, with a particular emphasis on the specific contributions they could make to their students, and some reference to the problems associated with their non-native condition. Relevant studies have provided powerful insights into NNS teachers' minds by surveying their opinions and attitudes (*e.g.*, Medgyes, 1994), sometimes complemented by direct observation of their classes (Árva & Medgyes, 2000), or interviewing them face-to-face and by email over a period of time (*e.g.*, Liu, J., 1999a, b). In the present volume, the range of studies is widened in several directions, including studies on students' views (Inbar-Lourie; Lasagabaster & Sierra; Benke & Medgyes; Pacek), classroom observation (Cots & Díaz), ethnographic case studies on NNS teaching assistants (Liu), teachers' self-ascription of NS/NNS identity (Inbar-Lourie), teachers' intuitions regarding difficulty of new lexical items (McNeill), and the present study on practicum supervisors' views on NNS student teachers, which looks at the expanding group of NNS students in TESOL programs across North American universities. This group had already been considered in Samimy & Brutt-Griffler's (1999) study of NNS students' self-perceptions during their participation in a specific course designed to cover the topic of NNS professionals. The novelty about the present research lies in the fact that the questions were not responded by the subjects under study

E. Llurda (Ed.), *Non-Native Language Teachers. Perceptions, Challenges and Contributions to the Profession*, 131—154.

(*i.e.*, NNS teachers or TESOL students). Instead, the questionnaire was aimed at NNS students' practicum supervisors. These enjoy a privileged position that allows them to observe classes conducted by NSs and NNSs alike. In consequence, practicum supervisors can provide very informative *external* assessments of NNS students' practice teaching and skills as compared to NSs'. This externality constitutes one of the primary values of the study.

## 2.    METHOD

The present study is about the skills needed by NNSs to become successful language teachers. The hypothesis that inspired and guided the research could be phrased as follows:

> H: High-level language skills are essential for NNS language teachers' successful teaching. Pedagogical skills are also important, provided an acceptable level of the former has been achieved.

I decided to look into this issue by conducting a survey among TESOL practicum supervisors, experienced in observing NNS student teachers in their practica. The survey involved a written questionnaire, in which supervisors were asked to respond to several questions regarding their students' practice teaching. Although there were some open questions, a great deal of them were closed, asking informants to choose one option, with the particularity that they had to estimate the percentage of NNS students that fell within each of the given categories.

A preliminary version of the questionnaire was sent to two experienced practicum supervisors for piloting. Some changes were suggested, and they were incorporated into the final version. The questionnaire was designed on the assumption that good language skills are fundamental for language teachers, and therefore several questions dealt with this issue, as well as the effects of language and teaching skills in successful language teaching. In addition, the questionnaire was also planned to be a source of information on the actual typology of NNS students in North-American TESOL programs.

The questionnaire (see Appendix A) enquired about the general characteristics of the NNS students (questions 1-7), their language skills (questions 9-14), as well as the respondents' opinions regarding NNS performance in the practicum and likelihood of professional opportunities after graduation (questions 15-20). There were mostly closed questions, in which respondents had to provide a numerical answer that reflected the percentage of their students that would fit in each category, and a few open questions, in which supervisors were expected to open up their minds and give details that could make their ideas more easily appreciated.

Questions 9-14 centred around some language proficiency components that have been mentioned in the literature as being important in determining the characteristics of NNS teachers (Medgyes, 1994; Tang, 1997; Kamhi-Stein, 2000a, 2000b). Some of those components, namely language awareness and grammar, have been cited as constituting NNSs' strengths, in comparison to NSs. Other components corresponded to alleged NNSs' weaknesses or disadvantages (*e.g.*, fluency, listening comprehension, and pronunciation).

Questions addressing the likelihood of professional opportunities (17-20) were based on the premise that not all NNSs may be suited for teaching language at all levels in all possible settings, but that some may be more gifted than NSs in some specific situations. Supervisors were therefore asked to indicate how many of their NNS student teachers would feel comfortable teaching English in North America, in their country of origin, at which levels, and whether there were NNS teachers who they could not recommend to do any teaching at all.

Questions 15-16 and 21-24 provided some space for personal comments. Thus, respondents could include a more personal perspective in their answers. Question 15 allowed them to complement their answers to previous closed questions, whereas question 16 was itself a closed question with some space for comment. In questions 21 and 22, respondents could further comment on their particular NNS students and how representative they thought they were of the whole NNS teacher community, whereas questions 23 and 24 dealt with the influence of language proficiency and teaching skills on successful language teaching. Responses to these open-ended questions were later grouped by type of argument and are discussed below.

The selection of participants was based on the graduate TESOL programs listed in Garshick's (1998) Directory of Professional Preparation Programs in the United States and Canada, 1999-2001. As there was likely to be a large number of unreturned questionnaires, the survey was sent to all the programs listed in the book that mentioned a Practicum course as part of the program requirements. A cover letter was sent with the questionnaire to 178 universities. Forty-one questionnaires were returned from individuals at a variety of universities. Twenty-eight of the institutions were state schools and the remaining thirteen private institutions, all distributed across most North American geographical regions.

One problem that was evident only after several completed questionnaires had already been received was that three of the responses came from Quebec, a Canadian province where English is not the dominant language. Although the programs were run exclusively in English, the context and the students were clearly different from other participating institutions. The fact that the programs were run in a French-speaking area was thought to alter the homogeneity of the sample, which was the main reason why only North American programs had been selected for the study. Eventually, it was decided that the three responses from non-English settings would not be included in the analysis.

In addition to the three questionnaires from Quebec, six other questionnaires could not be taken into account as the respondents indicated that their programs did not have any NNS student during the previous academic year. That limits to thirty-two the total number of responses on which results will be reported.

## 3.    RESULTS

The thirty-two departments or schools in which the surveyed TESOL programs were offered were quite varied and appeared to be representative of the different areas that are academically involved in the preparation of ESL/EFL teachers in North America: English, ESL, Linguistics, Applied Linguistics, Education, and International Studies.

Twenty-seven universities offered a Masters program in ESL/TESOL and the remaining five offered other kinds of certification in ESL/TESOL at the undergraduate level. Looking at the geographical location of those thirty-two universities, twelve were located in US states or Canadian provinces on the Atlantic coast, six were in states or provinces along the west coast, and the remaining fourteen were scattered all around North America, including Hawai'i.

The number of students who were enrolled in the practicum in these programs during the previous semester ranged from 5 to 50, a wide range of program size that reflects the variety found across North American institutions offering degrees in TESOL. The mean number of students was 21.3 and the median 22. The number of non-native students ranged from 1 to 30. The mean was 7.7 and the median 8. As it can be observed, NNSs amounted to 36% of the total number of students in the programs.

If we look at the characteristics of the NNSs who took part in the programs, almost all were in their late twenties and about three out of four students were female. It should be noted, too, that in 10 programs 100% of the NNS students were female. The students' first language background was quite varied, although there was a predominance of Asian languages (Chinese, Japanese, and Korean), with a lesser incidence of Spanish and Arabic, and to a much lesser extent French, German, Italian, Portuguese, Greek, Swahili, and Russian. As shown by responses to question 7, a majority (around 78%) had recently arrived from their home country and were likely to return home in order to pursue a language teaching career. The remaining 22% were presumably NNSs who had already been living in North America for quite a number of years by the time they enrolled in the TESOL program.

## 3.1    Language skills of NNS students in the programs

Language awareness was the only skill in which most NNS were reported to do better or equal to NSs: 50% equal; 34% higher, and 17% lower (see Table 1). The only other skill in which NNSs were thought to be equal to NSs was listening comprehension. Almost half of the NNS students (48%) were reported to have a 'Similar to NS' listening comprehension, whereas 38% fell into the category of 'Good but not equivalent to NSs'. Only 14% had 'Weak' listening skills, according to the supervisors (Table 2).

Results to fluency and grammar questions were fairly similar. The fluency of 49% of the NNSs was labeled as 'Good but Foreign' (Table 3). The remaining half was distributed between 'Similar to NSs' (23%) and 'Weak' (28%). As for grammar assessments, a majority of students (53%) were in the 'Good but Foreign' category. 'Similar to NS' was the label chosen for 32% of NNS students, and the remaining 15% were reported to have 'Weak' grammar (Table 4).

The results to the question on speaking rate show that almost half of the students (48%) had a rate 'Similar to NSs', 44% spoke 'Slower than NSs', and 8% of NNSs spoke 'faster than NSs' (Table 5).

A majority of NNSs (60%) were assessed as having 'Fully intelligible but noticeable' foreign accent. The other two accent options—'Similar to NSs' and 'Problematic'—were respectively applied to 24% and 16% of the NNS students (Table 6).

*Table 1.* NNS students' language awareness

| | | |
|---|---|---|
| Higher than most NSs | 80 | 34% |
| Equal to most NSs | 118 | 50% |
| Lower than most NSs | 40 | 17% |
| | (n=238) | 100% |

$\chi^2 = 38.36$     df = 2     $p < .01$

*Table 2.* NNS students' listening comprehension

| | | |
|---|---|---|
| Similar to a NS | 112 | 48% |
| Good but foreign | 90 | 38% |
| Weak | 34 | 14% |
| | (n=236) | 100% |

$\chi^2 = 41.12$    df = 2    $p < .01$

*Table 3.* NNS students' fluency

| | | |
|---|---|---|
| Similar to a NS | 57 | 23% |
| Good but foreign | 118 | 49% |
| Weak | 68 | 28% |
| | (n=243) | 100% |

$\chi^2 = 26.10$    df = 2    $p < .01$

*Table 4.* NNS students' grammar

| | | |
|---|---|---|
| Similar to a NS | 77 | 32% |
| Good but foreign | 127 | 53% |
| Weak | 36 | 15% |
| | (n=240) | 100% |

$\chi^2 = 51.92$    df = 2    $p < .01$

*Table 5.* NNS students' speaking rate

| | | |
|---|---|---|
| Similar to a NS | 113 | 48% |
| Faster than a NS | 19 | 8% |
| Slower than a NS | 104 | 44% |
| | (n=236) | 100% |

$\chi^2 = 68.40$    df = 2    $p < .01$

*Table 6.* NNS students' accent

| | | |
|---|---|---|
| Similar to a NS | 57 | 24% |
| Intelligible but noticeable | 145 | 60% |
| Problematic | 40 | 16% |
| | (n=242) | 100% |

$\chi^2 = 78.76$    df = 2    $p < .01$

All the $\chi^2$ values were significant at the 0.01 level, indicating that the distribution of NNSs in each category (*i.e.*, higher than NSs; equal to NSs; lower than NSs) is not random in any of the six language aspects included in the questionnaire: language awareness, fluency, grammar, listening comprehension, speaking rate, and accent. Therefore, it appears that respondents were actually assessing NNSs' language skills—relative to those of NSs—in a principled, significant way.

## 3.2 Teaching performance of NNS students

There was no specific question in the questionnaire that enquired about NNSs' pedagogical skills. However, questions 16-20 asked practicum supervisors to compare NNSs' teaching performance to NSs', as well as how many of the NNSs taking part in their programs they would be willing to recommend to teach at different levels (*i.e.*, advanced, high-intermediate, low-intermediate, and beginner) and in different settings (*i.e.*, ESL and EFL).

According to responses to question 16—'How would you rate NNSs' teaching performance overall in the Practicum compared to that of NSs enrolled in the same program?'—a great majority of NNSs' (72%) teaching performance was equal to NSs', but 22% of the NNSs were weaker than most NSs, and only 6% did better than NSs.

Another interesting insight was provided by the responses to question 19 — 'How many of your NNS students would you recommend to teach at any of the following levels?': Most NNSs would be recommended to teach at beginner and low-intermediate levels (89% and 90%, respectively); 77% would be recommended to teach at high-intermediate level; and only 62% were considered ready to teach at advanced levels.

Question 17—'What percentage of your NNS students would feel comfortable teaching ESL speakers in North America?'—had an average response of 59%, whereas question 18—'What percentage of your NNS students would feel comfortable teaching EFL students in their country of origin?'—had a significantly higher percentage, 97%. According to responses given to question 20—'How many of your NNS students would you never recommend to do any teaching at all?'—, only 6% of the NNS students would never be recommended to do any teaching.

It must be noted that the percentages obtained by the different options in questions 17-20 are not exclusive of each other. For instance, one respondent argued that she would not recommend two of her three NNSs to teach at all (question 20) but she thought the three students would feel comfortable teaching in an EFL context (question 18).

## 3.3 Relationship between language proficiency and teaching skills

Question 15—'To what extent do you think the factors in questions 9-14 (language awareness, fluency, grammar, listening comprehension skills, speaking rate, foreign accent) affect your NNS students' English language teaching ability?'—allowed open responses and was consequently quite diversely responded to. Answers ranged from 'Negligible' to 'Very important'. Six responses included the word 'some' (*e.g.*, 'Somewhat'; 'To some extent'). Another six preferred a more limiting adjective (*e.g.*, 'To a minor extent'; 'A little'; 'Not much'). Two did not see much effect at all of language skills on teaching (*e.g.*, 'Negligible'; 'For the most part, not at all'). Another two placed a greater importance on language skills (*e.g.*, 'Very important'; 'To a great extent'). Finally, some respondents gave an indirect answer to the question, which nonetheless suggested that they viewed language skills as important in language teaching performance. (*e.g.*, R-12: 'I'm quite concerned about the TESOL student with low speaking and grammatical ability'; R-17: 'Weak students often have more trouble communicating with students').

Question 23 of the survey addressed the relative importance of language proficiency and teaching skills in teaching success. Fourteen respondents (44%) considered that both teaching skills and language proficiency strongly affect success. Nine respondents (28%) thought that language skills are primary, and eight (25%) thought that teaching skills are more important. The remaining respondent did not answer this question.

## 3.4     Open-ended questions

Respondents were given some room in the questionnaire to write some additional comments on the NNSs in the programs (questions 16 and 21, especially). Those comments have been grouped into the following six distinct categories (some sample responses corresponding to each category are included):

a) NNSs enrolled in the programs are already selected students

- Many of our NNSs are Fulbright scholarship recipients—'The cream of the crop'.
- We have highly competitive admission and so we have excellent NNS and NS graduate students.

b) They enrich the program as they bring diversity into it

- They enhance the program for NSs because they bring in different perspectives
- Our NSs benefit from their presence.

c) They are questioned for being NNSs

- One problem I sometimes encounter is resistance from NS practicum students who are reluctant to work with NNSs.
- They do face some resistance on the part of certain teachers.

d) Language problems (NNSs)

- NNS teachers' problems are not essentially in the areas of grammar and vocabulary. Their major problem is in the communication in L2 (spoken or written) and mostly in the area of pragmatics.
- The NNSs who have failed have generally had both language and skills problems.

e) Variability among NNSs

- Some come from countries with VERY traditional language training (as students and teachers). Others come from more progressive places. Some are young—with little experience and very open minds; some are older and more set in their ways. Just like our NSs. Difficult to generalize.
- NNS tend to be more heterogenous than NSs in their reaction to supervision. The most flexible and the most rigid teachers tend to be NNS.

f) They act as role models

- Many students have no resistance to being taught by a capable NNS; in fact, the NNS intern serves as a model for how much the students may accomplish.
- My NNS student teachers have frequently been called upon to work with students of their own language groups or contact/act as liaison with parents. It has only been an advantage and never a disadvantage.

g) Comparable to NSs with foreign language experience

- Their grammar knowledge, cross-cultural sensitivity and awareness to student needs is NOT superior to our NS students who have lived abroad and have fair competency in some L2. However, in these areas they probably do have some advantages over NSs lacking foreign language competence or cross-cultural experience.

- Good teaching skill and language proficiency are both necessary, and for any teacher who possesses the two qualities, L1 background is inconsequential.

## 4.    DISCUSSION

First, it seems quite reasonable to consider that NNS graduate TESOL students in North American TESOL programs are well represented in the present sample, especially if we observe the similarity between the figures obtained here with regard to the number of NNS students taking part in the programs and those reported in previous studies (Polio, 1994; Liu, D., 1999).

A considerable number of international students travel every year to North America to obtain a degree in TESOL that will allow them to return to their countries of origin with training, expertise, improved language proficiency, and higher expectations of getting a highly qualified job (Govardhan, Nayar & Sheorey, 1999). Liu, D. (1999) states that NNSs enrolled yearly at TESOL programs in North American universities amount to 37% of the total number of students. In our study, 36% of students in the participating programs were NNSs. There seems to be evidence, then, that approximately one out of three TESOL graduates in North American institutions is a NNS of English. Therefore, in spite of Greis' (1985: 317) description of such students as 'a small minority', the figure appears high enough as to deserve examination of the training of such students, as well as their needs and challenges in TESOL education.

Another interesting comparison to be made is between our data and the results of a survey conducted by Polio (1994) among 43 international students enrolled in the MA TESOL programs of 7 large US universities. Polio's survey—in spite of having different goals from this one—yields very similar results in terms of who the international students are, where they come from and what their plans are regarding the future. According to Polio, over 90% planned to return to teach after obtaining their degree. Most of these students (72%) came from Asian countries (Japan 33%, Taiwan 30%, and Korea 9%). The NNS students involved in the present survey are not very different from Polio's, as 78% had recently arrived in North America and would presumably go home after graduation, and Chinese, Japanese and Korean were the most frequently cited first languages.

The high percentage of international students who attend TESOL programs in North America with the aim of going back to their home country to teach EFL reinforces the argument for the need of more attention to be paid to NNS teacher trainees and to their needs as future EFL teachers, as opposed to standard ESL teacher education. However, it has been claimed that North American TESOL programs do not adequately prepare their students for the task of teaching in an EFL setting (Brinton & Holten, 1989; Govardhan, Nayar & Sheorey, 1999), in spite of the high percentage of prospective EFL teachers-in-training that take part in such programs. As Govardhan, Nayar & Sheorey (1999) point out, MA TESOL programs in North America need to pay more attention to the likelihood of their students ending up working in an EFL setting. However, money and staff limitations prevent those programs from introducing EFL-related aspects. Besides, the practicum in North American programs will have necessarily to be in an ESL setting, rather than an EFL one. Still, some attempts have been made to introduce elements related to NNS needs and EFL teaching in those programs (Kamhi-Stein, 2000b; Carrier, 2003). Yet, the disregard for the needs of NNS TESOL students is evident.

## 4.1    NNSs' language skills

Looking at the results obtained in questions 9-14, it becomes clear that most NNSs participating in MA programs in the US and Canada are highly competent second language speakers who nonetheless have some limitations in their command of English, especially if we compare them to their NS counterparts. Their fluency and grammar are mostly considered to be 'good but foreign' (fluency 49%; grammar 53%), and their foreign accent is mostly considered to be 'fully intelligible but noticeable' (60%). Nonetheless, there is a relatively important proportion (ranging from 14% and 28%) of international students in the programs who can be labeled as either weak or problematic in fluency, grammar, listening comprehension, language awareness, and accent.

There is also a considerable number of highly proficient NNSs who fall within the category of near-native (ranging from 23% to 32% in fluency, grammar, and accent, to reach a peak of 48% in listening comprehension). However, we must be careful when dealing with such a concept as 'near-native', as it is shown by Valdés' (1998) discussion on near-nativeness, and by Koike & Liskin-Gasparro (1999), who conducted a study in which graduate students and experienced faculty of Spanish departments across the US were asked to define what it meant to be near-native. The authors claim that there is a lot of variation on how different people interpret this term, and call for a more precise description of the proficiency levels of NNSs, especially when it comes to the point of selecting a NNS language teacher.

It must be noted that most programs in the current survey required a minimum entrance TOEFL score of 550, and some required even higher scores for admission, which clearly acted as a filter to prevent low competence second language speakers from entering the programs, and therefore to increase the average level of proficiency of NNS graduate students in North America as compared to those who stayed in their countries, a fact that is supported by the reference to the exceptionality of students in the programs that can be found in some of the responses to the open-ended questions in the questionnaire. However, based on the existence of the substantial proportion of international students in the surveyed MA TESOL programs who fall short of being equivalent to NSs (*i.e.*, in most aspects, over a half of the total do not fit into the category of 'Similar to NS'), and the relatively high number of NNSs with 'weak' skills, it seems reasonable to give support to overt recommendations for a language component in such programs in North America and elsewhere (Berry, 1990; Cullen, 1994; Murdoch, 1994), or to back specific proposals of activities aimed at improving language skills (Kamhi-Stein, 2000b). Recommending higher amounts of target language teaching in teacher training programs is not a very popular practice, as has been acknowledged by Medgyes (1994), and as a review of the courses offered in North American programs makes clear (see Garshick, 1998, for this purpose). It is also my personal experience, and that of many colleagues of mine in different Spanish universities offering English degrees, that most of the language courses are offered by the latest arrived recruits, who often do not hold full-time permanent positions, which indicates the low status such courses have among English professors, in spite of the great importance students tend to assign to them. The issue is important, but before making any claims or recommendations regarding the need for more language teaching in teacher training programs, one may have to consider whether higher language proficiency will lead prospective English language teachers to perform better in their classes.

If we now focus more closely on the language awareness component as reflected by answers to question 9, we must refer to the increased level of language awareness that has been repeatedly mentioned in the literature as one of the strengths of NNSs over NSs (Medgyes, 1994; Canagarajah, 1999). The responses to the questionnaire appear to support such a claim, as an overall 84% of NNSs are believed to have an equal or higher level of language awareness than NSs. Thus, many NNS students who are not among the group that could tentatively be labeled as near-native speakers, possess a highly sophisticated knowledge about how English works. This result is congruent with the common perception that NNSs tend to give greater importance to grammatical analysis than NSs, and can provide insights into the language in spite of more limited communicative skills.

Fluency scores indicate that about half of students can be placed within the group of 'highly proficient but distinctively non-native', as the 49% obtained by the 'good but foreign' option seems to indicate. This group fairly corresponds to the image of non-native speaker teachers that most people (especially in EFL contexts) have in mind, as opposed to the much smaller group of extremely fluent speakers that one might compare to NSs (23% in our data).

If we look at grammar assessments, we may see that a majority of NNSs were included in the 'good but foreign' category, which can be interpreted as meaning that their grammar is good enough for most communicative purposes, and even teaching purposes, although it is clearly unlike a native speaker's grammar. This leads us into the question of what is the minimum mastery of the target language grammar that a good language teacher should have. Should teachers be required to have native-like grammar intuitions? Following Cook's argumentation (this volume), the answer should be 'no', as NNS teachers cannot be like native L1 users. Still, it is not infrequent for language teachers to be asked about the accuracy and adequacy of certain lexical items or grammatical constructions. Besides, language teachers are often confronted with the task of correcting learners' language output, and the errors that may certainly appear. Medgyes (1999) argues that only a teacher with a total command of grammatical intuitions (*i.e.*, a native or native-like teacher) can truly perform such a task. If that was the case, according to the results in section 3.2 fewer than one third of teachers pursuing MA TESOL degrees in North America would be up to such a level. This figure is in contrast with the results to questions 17 and 18 (*i.e.*, how many of their NS students they would recommend to teach in ESL and EFL settings). There are approximately twice as many students who would be recommended to teach in an ESL setting than students considered to have English grammar similar to NSs, which suggests that practicum supervisors, after having observed NNS teachers whose speaking is not native-like do some practice teaching, do not see any problem in having them teach in an ESL setting.

Listening comprehension and speaking rate are the aspects of the NNS practicum students' that are closest to native-like ratings (48% in both cases). Although practicum supervisors do not test their student teachers' listening comprehension skills, their everyday one-to-one interaction with them is probably enough for obtaining a good idea of their listening skills. Taking this into account, it is quite significant that they think that roughly 50% of the student teachers have similar listening skills to NSs, and therefore they can understand any sample of language that may be addressed to them in the academic context. The setback can be found in those student teachers who seem to have weak listening skills (14%), as their capacity to teach English, especially in an ESL setting, may be questioned.

With regard to speaking rate, 48% of NNS students seem to have a similar rate to NSs, and 8% are perceived to speak faster than NSs. The present data do not allow us to associate faster or slower rate to either better or worse speaking ability, however, Munro & Derwing (1998) found that the most intelligible NNSs are those who speak at a rate which is slightly slower than regular NS rate. It follows, then, that more than half of the NNS teachers probably speak faster than desirable.

If any foreign language feature is widely recognized as the most difficult for NNSs to get rid of completely, this is foreign accent (Lippi-Green, 1997). A remarkable one quarter of the NNSs are considered to have an accent similar to NSs, a figure that is certainly high considering that many researchers have claimed that it is almost impossible to reach native-like pronunciation in adulthood (Long, 1990; Scovel, 1988). One possible interpretation is that the 22% NNS students who had not recently arrived to North America had actually moved to North America when they were fairly young and were raised in an English-speaking environment. Most likely, those students were the ones who were labeled as having a native-like accent. Following this assumption, the majority of those who have arrived in North America in their adulthood (78%) are those who still retain a foreign accent, which is 'fully intelligible but noticeable' (60%). The more troublesome figure, though, is the 16% of NSS prospective teachers who are reported to have a 'problematic accent', which, given the wording of the three options in this question ('similar to NS'—'fully intelligible but noticeable—'problematic') seems to indicate serious difficulties in being clearly understood. And not being understood is definitely not a a desirable thing for a language teacher.

Overall, one must acknowledge the great variability that can be found among NNSs in terms of language proficiency, even though those NNSs had all obtained high enough TOEFL scores as to be accepted in their programmes. Quite possibly, most of these individuals will eventually get a degree in TESOL, which will qualify them to teach English as a second or foreign language. Their language skills, however, will be quite diverse, and it is this difference among NNS TESOL graduates that is likely to be the key factor in predicting their professional success in language teaching. This is, in my opinion, one of the reasons why NNSs constantly have to assert their credibility as language teachers (Tang, 1997; Kamhi-Stein, 2000b). Being a NS implies having a good command of the language. Mastery of the language has nothing to do with pedagogical skills, teacher training, or the willingness to devote the time and effort necessary to become an accomplished teacher. Both NS and NNS speakers working as English language teachers may or may not be sufficiently trained, may or may not have good teaching skills, may or may not be willing to spend the time and effort. In addition, a NNS cannot guarantee his/her employer or students that s/he has total command of the language. The fact that there exists variability in linguistic proficiency probably explains some of the discrimination and negative *a priori* attitudes experienced by many NNS teachers. Once the students or the administrators are aware of the high proficiency level of a particular NNS teacher, such attitudes tend to disappear, as it is acknowledged by Kamhi-Stein's (2000a) anecdotal report of how often parents and administrators may question NNSs as English teachers, only to support them after realizing they are very good at their job.

The picture we obtain shows a majority of competent—albeit clearly non-native—speakers of English, with a few cases of not so competent individuals, who presumably need to work further on their language skills in order to be able to satisfactorily perform their teaching duties. It is a fact that variability among NNSs in language proficiency is bound to be encountered anywhere (see Bley-Vroman's, 1989, discussion on the logical problem of foreign language learning). However, the question of what proficiency level is adequate for language teaching is open to discussion. First, near-nativeness is a concept that has not been successfully defined (Valdés, 1998; Koike & Liskin-Gasparro, 1999). Second, as Canagarajah (1999) points out, a good teacher may not need a full command of the language in order to teach, as long as s/he knows the language better than the students and s/he conveys the curiosity and desire to learn the language.

It is also true, however, that millions of ELT learners have failed and still fail to go past the very first stages of the second language. One respondent to the current survey said: 'I have observed NNSs make systemic errors in their ESL teaching which misled/confused their learners. I have seen them having problems answering questions about English due to a lack of native-speaker intuition' (R-18). Another respondent distinguished between knowledge of grammar and vocabulary on the one hand, and communicative ability, on the other: 'NNS teachers' problems are not essentially in the areas of grammar and vocabulary. Their major problem is in the communication in L2 (spoken or written) and mostly in the area of pragmatics' (R-24). These cases should also be used as examples of how some non-native teachers (*i.e.*, those with very limited language skills) may not contribute to (or even impair) their students' potential for foreign language learning.

Péter Medgyes' contribution to Braine's volume (Medgyes, 1999) is built around the idea that NNS language teachers should aim at native-like competence. It may actually be inferred from his words that anything short of that level may eventually result in a poor performance as teachers. Greis (1985), in discussing the training of NNS English language teachers, cites their lack of self-confidence and the need to evaluate level of proficiency on arrival at the program. Cullen (2001) expressed a similar thought when he wrote: 'A teacher without the requisite language skills will crucially lack authority and self-confidence in the classroom, and this will affect all aspects of his or her performance' (p. 29). Berry (1990) agreed on the importance of the teacher's language level in language teaching, and called for greater attention to language improvement in teacher training programs:

> Language improvement is a valid aim of teacher training since it:
> a) increases teacher confidence
> b) facilitates the use of the target language in the classroom
> c) widens the choice of methodology
>
> (Berry, 1990: 99)

Respondents to our questionnaire on NNS teachers acknowledged the importance of language proficiency, as well as teaching skills, in language teaching. A virtual tie was the outcome of question 23, which inquired the extent to which language skills and teaching skills affect success in language teaching. The most popular position with regard to this issue consisted in valuing the importance of both types of skills (44%), with a very little difference found between those who mentioned language skills as the relevant factor in language teaching (28%), and those who opted for teaching skills (25%).

The point I am making here is that NNS teachers who experience a (real or perceived) language deficit will have language teaching problems, as they are likely to experience difficulty in: 1) conveying messages to their students in the target language; 2) addressing their questions on language use; and 3) providing a good language model. Such difficulty may in turn contribute to having a low level of self-confidence. Therefore, low-proficiency teachers may eventually feel much more comfortable in a teacher-fronted textbook-oriented class, than in one where students get involved in the management of their classes and participate in a free and spontaneous environment. In sum, a high level of proficiency must be regarded as an essential condition for language teaching, but one which alone does not guarantee successful language teaching.

## 4.2    NNSs' teaching performance

Comparison of the percentage of students who would be recommended to teach ESL (59%), vs. those who would be recommended for EFL (97%), suggests that supervisors view these settings as requiring different conditions on the part of the NNS teacher. Thus, teaching in an ESL (*e.g.*, North America) or in a EFL (*e.g.*, Spain, China) setting would pose different demands on the students. At a point when some authors question the *raison d'etre* of the ESL/EFL distinction (Nunan, 1999/2000), it can be argued that such a distinction is still valid, and that there may be arguments to claim that

NNSs are better suited to teach in EFL contexts. In contrast with this view, Canagarajah (1999) suggests that NSs should ideally teach in EFL settings, whereas ESL settings should be left to NNSs. His point is that NSs can contribute a lot of cultural knowledge in EFL settings, and NNSs can add their multicultural perspective to ESL settings. However, the responses given by practicum supervisors indicate that they think that 97% of their students are suited to teach in their country of origin, but only 59% are suited to teach in an ESL setting. Two tentative explanations may be given for this. First of all, the language factor is key in determining how prepared a NNS is to teach ESL to immigrant students who are usually highly motivated to improve their communicative skills in the new society. A second factor may be that NNS knowledge of the target culture is not complete enough to teach in an ESL context, whereas culture is considered an integral element in ESL teaching, but only a complementary component of EFL teaching.

Given the premise that ESL teaching aims to help integrate immigrant NNSs into a particular local community, people who have lived a long time in that context can best provide the familiarity with the target culture needed. They will have an advantage over non-residents, as the former will be informed about the language, culture (and subcultures), etiquette, non-standard forms of the language, and other language and communicative conventions needed in an ESL environment. Thus, a distinction between NSs and NNSs may not be as relevant as one between acculturated and non-acculturated people. In ESL contexts, this may be a key choice in deciding who is fit to teach English as a second language.

EFL settings, in contrast, are not aimed at integrating learners into any particular culture, as they are more likely designed to prepare students to cope with the general demands of English as an International Language (EIL), or to help them get past a required national test in English. This does not mean that EFL teaching does not need to incorporate any cultural information, but rather as McKay (2000) has pointed out, culture can be integrated within an EIL course. In her view, teaching culture will not entail teaching the culture of any of the particular nations who speak the language natively, but rather letting learners know about different target cultures and enabling them to speak about their own culture. McKay (2000) advocates the use of 'international target language materials that use a great variety of cultures in English—and non-English-speaking countries around the world' (p. 9). Such materials 'demonstrate that English today is being used globally by bilingual speakers, who have chosen not to internalize the norms of native English-speaking countries' (p. 10).

## 5.     CONCLUSIONS

One of the reasons why the present study was carried out was the need for more research in the area of non-native speaker teaching and, more particularly, research concerned with NNSs who are in the process of becoming ELT professionals. As the introductory review of the literature revealed, there is an important shortage of empirical research on NNS teachers, especially if we consider the interest this area has aroused in the last years. My main interest when designing the study was to provide insights into the role played by the language and teaching skills of NNSs in their teaching behaviour, especially focusing on those teachers-in-training who were being trained vis-à-vis NSs. I intended to quantify views on NNS teachers in an unprecedented way, by means of asking qualified observers of both NS and NNS teachers about NNSs' skills and performance. This was done by means of a questionnaire that emphasized language issues, with some—but little—space for open responses in which supervisors could qualify their responses with more detailed personal views on the topics. The methodology was effective, as it provided rather objective data, and facilitated clarifying insights into the respondents' perceptions on the nature of NNS TESOL graduate students.

The study has some important limitations, as the data are mostly based on supervisors' perceptions of the qualities of their NNS students, but no details are conveyed on each individual NNS. Most respondents were NSs and the extent to which their NS/NNNS condition affected their responses is unknown. Still, the results have brought some light onto the combined importance of language skills and teaching skills in language teaching. Data have been presented that show the variability in NNS teachers' language skills. There is also evidence that not all student teachers are equally qualified to teach in different contexts and at different levels. There is some ground to believe that NNS teachers with a high language proficiency level will be far better prepared to teach in an ESL context than NNSs with so-called 'weak' or 'problematic' language skills. Similarly, estimations of chances of success in teaching advanced or high-intermediate students seem to be determined by the language proficiency level of the NNS teacher. Therefore, the above results appear to respond affirmatively to the question that inspired this study. Language proficiency is a necessary condition for NNS language teachers, and a high level of proficiency and communicative skills are necessary for those who plan to teach in ESL contexts or at advanced levels. Once this condition is met, there will be no need to look differently at NS and NNS teachers, as both will still need a set of pedagogical skills, as well as a fair amount of energy, will, and resources, in order to become effective language teachers.

# 6.     REFERENCES

Árva, V. & P. Medgyes (2000). Native and non-native teachers in the classroom. *System, 28* (3), 355-372.

Berry, R. (1990). The role of language improvement in teacher training: Killing two birds with one stone. *System, 18* (1), 97-105

Bley-Vroman, R. (1989). What is the logical problem of foreign language learning? In S. M. Gass & J. Schachter (Eds.), *Linguistic perspectives on second language acquisition*. Cambridge: Cambridge University Press. 41-68.

Brinton, D. & Holten, C. (1989). What novice teachers focus on: The practicum in TESL. *TESOL Quarterly, 23*, 343-350.

Canagarajah, A.S. (1999). Interrogating the 'native speaker fallacy': Non-linguistic roots, non-pedagogical results. In G. Braine (Ed.), *Non-native educators in English language teaching*. Mahwah, NJ: Lawrence Erlbaum Associates. 77-92.

Carrier, K.A. (2003). NNS teacher trainees in Western-based TESOL programs. *ELT Journal, 57* (3), 242-250.

Cullen, R. (1994). Incorporating a language component in teacher training programmes. *ELT Journal, 48* (2), 162-172.

Cullen, R. (2001). The use of lesson transcripts for developing teachers' classroom language. *System, 29* (1), 27-43.

Garshick, E. (Ed.) (1998). *Directory of professional preparation programs in the United States and Canada, 1999-2001*. Alexandria, VA: TESOL.

Govardhan, A.K., Nayar, B. & Sheorey, R. (1999). Do US MATESOL programs prepare students to teach abroad? *TESOL Quarterly, 33* (1), 114-125.

Greis, N. (1985). Toward a better preparation of the non-native ESOL teacher. In P. Larson, E.L. Judd & D.S. Meserschmitt (Eds.), *On TESOL '84. A brave new world for TESOL. Selected papers from the Eighteenth Annual Convention of TESOL*. Washington, DC: TESOL. 317-324.

Kamhi-Stein, L. (2000a). Non-native English speaking professionals: A new agenda for a new millennium. *MEXTESOL Journal, 23* (3), 11-20.

Kamhi-Stein, L.D. (2000b). Adapting U.S.-based TESOL education to meet the needs of non-native English speakers. *TESOL Journal, 9* (3), 10-14.

Koike, D.A. & Liskin-Gasparro, J.E. (1999). What is a near-native speaker? Perspectives of job seekers and search committees in Spanish. *ADFL Bulletin, 30* (3), 54-62.

Lippi-Green, R. (1997). *English with an accent*. New York: Routledge.

Liu, D. (1999). Training non-native TESOL students: Challenges for TESOL teacher education in the west. In G. Braine (Ed.), *Non-native educators in English language teaching*. Mahwah, NJ: Lawrence Erlbaum Associates. 197-210.

Liu, J. (1999a). From their own perspectives: The impact of non-native ESL professionals on their students. In G. Braine (Ed.), *Non-native educators in English language teaching*. Mahwah, NJ: Lawrence Erlbaum Associates. 159-176.

Liu, J. (1999b). Non-native-English-speaking professionals in TESOL. *TESOL Quarterly, 33* (1), 85-102.

Long, M. (1990). Maturational constraints on language development. *Studies in Second Language Acquisition, 12* (3), 251-285.

McKay, S.L. (2000). Teaching English as an international language: Implications for cultural materials in the classroom. *TESOL Journal, 9* (4), 7-11.

Medgyes, P. (1994). *The non-native teacher*. London: Macmillan. (1999) 2$^{nd}$ edition. Ismaning: Max Hueber Verlag.

Medgyes, P. (1999). Language training: A neglected area in teacher education. In G. Braine (Ed.), *Non-native educators in English language teaching*. Mahwah, NJ: Lawrence Erlbaum Associates. 177-195.

Munro, M.J. & Derwing, T.M. (1998). The effects of speaking rate on listener evaluations of native and foreign-accented speech. *Language Learning, 48* (2), 159-182.

Murdoch, G. (1994). Language development provision in teacher training curricula. *ELT Journal, 48* (3), 253-265.

Nunan, D. (1999/2000). Yes, but is it English? *TESOL Matters, 9,* 6.

Polio, C. (1994). International students in North American MA TESOL programs. Paper presented at the 28th Annual Convention of TESOL. Baltimore, MD. March.

Samimy, K.K. & Brutt-Griffler, J. (1999). To be a native or non-native speaker: Perceptions of 'non-native' students in a graduate TESOL program. In G. Braine (Ed.), *Non-native educators in English language teaching*. Mahwah, NJ: Lawrence Erlbaum Associates. 127-144.

Scovel, T. (1988). *A time to speak. A psycholinguistic inquiry into the critical period for human speech*. Rowley, MA: Newbury House.

Tang, C. (1997). On the power and status of non-native ESL teachers. *TESOL Quarterly, 31* (3), 577-580.

Valdés, G. (1998). The construct of near-native speaker in the foreign language profession: Perspectives on ideologies about language. *ADFL Bulletin, 29* (3), 4-8.

## APPENDIX A. NON-NATIVE SPEAKERS (NNSS) IN NORTH AMERICAN CREDIT TESOL PROGRAMS – QUESTIONNAIRE TO PRACTICUM SUPERVISORS

Based on your records of last year's graduates in TESOL, especially your observations of their performances in the practicum, please complete the following questionnaire:

**a) The program**

Name of program: Masters ......... Bachelors ............ Other ........
Entrance Requirements:
Language Requirements:

**b) The practicum**

i.   How long does it take?
Required number of supervised hours of teaching (responsibility for whole class): .............
Required number of hours of observation (could include small group work): .............

ii.  On average, how many times during the practicum are students officially observed teaching?

iii. Do you think the observations provide you with a fairly good assessment of the students' teaching skills?
☐ Yes
☐ Only partly (Please elaborate. Use back page if necessary)

iv.  Are there any aspects of your program that focus specifically on issues for NNS teachers? (Yes/No)

**c) The students** (In order to avoid terminological confusion, we will refer to NNS as those people who were born in a non-English speaking region, and whose L1 is not English)

1.   What is the total number of students (NSs and NNSs) that participated in a supervised practicum in TESOL last year at your university?

2.   How many of them were NNSs?

3.   What percentage of the NNSs students were female?

4.   Roughly speaking, what was the average age of the NNSs?

5.   Please list the most common L1s of your NNSs (no more than 5).

6.   Roughly what percentage of your NNSs had already taught ESL or EFL?

7.   What percentage of them had 'just' arrived from elsewhere in order to obtain the TESOL degree and presumably to go back to their home country after graduation?

8.   Looking at both NSs and NNSs, indicate the students' performance in the practicum. What percentage of NS/NNS students would you put into each of these categories? (Note that all the figures added should total 100%).

| Performance | % NSs | % NNSs | Total | |
|---|---|---|---|---|
| Top 25 % | | | = | 25 % |
| Between 25 and 50 % | | | = | 25 % |
| Between 50 and 75 % | | | = | 25 % |
| Bottom 25 % | | | = | 25 % |
| Total | % | % | = | 100 % |

9.   Did NNSs show a remarkable high/low level of 'language awareness', here defined as the capacity to understand and to help L2 students understand the complexities and the generalizable aspects of language, at all levels (grammar, phonology, lexis, discourse)? Please, indicate roughly what % of your NNS students fell into each of these categories.

     ... % Higher than most NSs
     ... % Less than most NSs
     ... %  No better or worse than average NSs

10.  How would you characterize your NNS students' fluency?

     ... % very similar to a NS
     ... % good, but clearly foreign
     ... % weak

11. How would you characterize your NNS students' grammar?

    ... % very similar to a NS
    ... % good, but clearly foreign
    ... % weak

12. How would you characterize your NNS students' listening comprehension skills?

    ... % very similar to a NS
    ... % good, but not equivalent to a NS
    ... % weak

13. How would you characterize your NNS students' speaking rate?

    ... % very similar to a NS
    ... % faster than a NS
    ... % slower than a NS

14. How would you characterize your NNS students' degree of foreign accent?

    ... % very similar to a NS
    ... % fully intelligible, but noticeable
    ... % problematic in some teaching settings

15. To what extent do you think the factors in 9-14 affect your NNS students' English language teaching ability?

16. How would you rate NNSs' teaching performance overall in the Practicum compared to that of NSs enrolled in the same program?

    ... % better than most NSs
    ... % weaker than most NSs
    ... % no better, no worse than the average NS

Please elaborate:

17. What percentage of your NNS students would feel comfortable teaching ESL speakers in North America?

18. What percentage of your NNS students would feel comfortable teaching English as a Foreign Language students in their country of origin?

19. How many of your NNS students (including those who failed the Practicum) would you recommend to teach at any of the following levels? Each level should be completed with a % figure out of 100, as it might be the case that you would recommend all your students to all levels of teaching; in that case, the answer would be 100% in each box.

    ... % TOEFL
    ... % advanced
    ... % high intermediate
    ... % low intermediate
    ... % beginner

20. How many of your NNS tudents would you never recommend to do any teaching at all?

    ... %

21. Do you have any additional comments on the NNSs in your program?

22. Are the responses here representative of NNS teachers in general?

23. To what extent do you think language proficiency affects success in teaching and to what extent teaching skills affect success?

24. Can you provide actual examples out of your own experience?

25. Could you please specify if you are a NS or a NNS?

Chapter 9

# CHINESE GRADUATE TEACHING ASSISTANTS TEACHING FRESHMAN COMPOSITION TO NATIVE ENGLISH SPEAKING STUDENTS

JUN LIU
*University of Arizona*

> As I was packing up to leave after teaching my Freshman English Composition class, I began to talk with some of the students who were already arriving for the next section. I asked a student whom I had taught the semester before how class was and he sheepishly replied it was... different. Another student, overhearing our conversation screwed up enough courage to ask if I wouldn't mind sticking around to teach their class. Thinking back to my own distaste for my most boring Freshman Composition course, I chuckled and asked who their instructor was. When they told me their instructor was, 'not even American', I stopped laughing. This exchange sparked off a weeklong running debate between this class and myself about the predicament they found themselves in: being taught English by a non-native speaker. Whereas I viewed their situation as a non-issue, the students seemed to fear for their compositional skills and felt they had in some way been cheated by the University.

> A quote from an American Graduate Teaching Assistant teaching freshman composition classes in a southwestern university in spring, 2001

## 1.     INTRODUCTION

A phenomenon that deserves attention in first-year composition classes in North America is the fact that a growing number of non-native English speaking teachers (NNESTs) teach composition to native English speaking students (NESs). While an increasing amount of research in the area of

E. Llurda (Ed.), *Non-Native Language Teachers. Perceptions, Challenges and Contributions to the Profession*, 155—177.

teaching first-year composition has focused on the special needs and identities of, and adjusted teaching approaches to, immigrants and US residents born abroad, as well as indigenous Language minority groups whose characteristics resemble neither mainstream English-speaking students nor international students (*e.g.*, Silva, 1993; Reid, 1993; Nayar, 1997; Harklau, Losey & Siegal, 1999), little research to date has touched on the issue of NNESTs teaching first-year composition to NESs.

Although labeling one person as a native speaker and another as a non-native speaker of a particular language has become more and more complicated and thus has been seriously debated based on a number of variables, such as one's language proficiency, social identity, birth place, length of stay in the target culture, and physical traits (Kamhi-Stein, 2000; Liu, 1999; Medgyes, 1994, 1996; Phillipson, 1992, 1996; Thomas, 1999), it is less controversial to consider someone a non-native English speaker (NNES) if this person is born and raised in a foreign country where English does not have a functional role in the society, and the person has received education up to the college level in that country. No one would argue, for example, that those who are born in China, learned English in China, and now teach English in China are not NNESs.

In fact, more than 80% of the English teachers worldwide are NNESs (Canagarajah, 1999). As a result, studying English under these instructors in an English as a Foreign Language (EFL) setting (*e.g.*, Japan, Korea, or China) has been well accepted. However, learning English under these instructors in an English as a Second Language (ESL) setting (*e.g.*, US, Canada, or the UK) tends to cause concern on the part of ESL students who come to an English speaking country with the expectation of being taught by native English speaking teachers (NESTs), and on the part of school/program administrators who might have to hire more NESTs because of their ESL students' concerns and because of the pressure by what is called 'native speaker fallacy' (Phillipson, 1992). In order to meet the high expectation of ESL students, NNESTs have to work harder than NESTs in order to prove themselves worthy of being in the profession (Thomas, 1999). Medgyes (1994) posits that NNESTs are usually known for having suffered from two unfair and undesirable conditions. The first is called an *inferiority complex* as these NNESTs will never be able to measure up to the linguistic standards that are so valued in their profession, such as a native accent from the US or UK. They will be led to believe that their interlanguage, or the knowledge of the L2 they possess, is always inadequate (Cook, 1999). The second condition is called a type of *schizophrenia* because of the pressure to lose their own identity while assimilating into the target culture.

However, NNESTs have been identified with unique strengths in teaching the English language. Medgyes (1994) summarizes six characteristics that help establish the credibility of NNESTs. He acknowledges that NNESTs can (1) provide a good learner model for imitation, (2) teach language learning strategies more effectively, (3) supply learners with more information about the English language, (4) anticipate and prevent language difficulties better, (5) be more empathetic to the needs and problems of learners, and (6) make use of the learners' mother tongue. In addition, Tang (1997) posits that NNESTs can be in a favorable position by being able to predict potential difficulties for the students, and to know how to help them learn based on their own language learning experiences. But these potentially good traits of NNESTs might not be present or evident when the very learners they teach are NESs. The challenge NNESTs face is how well they can establish credibility in front of the NESs. It will pose even a greater challenge if the NNESTs are graduate teaching assistants (GTAs) who might not have an adequate amount of teaching experience in their own countries, without mentioning the possible lack of teaching experiences in the English speaking countries they find themselves in. As Williams (1992) posits, an increasing number of universities in North America have to hire NNES GTAs to teach introductory undergraduate courses, and because of possible lack of comprehensibility of the speech of these GTAs, a number of complaints have been filed by NESs and their parents. According to a few recent studies, some NNES GTAs have the tendency to experience miscommunication with their NESs (Plakans, 1997) though sources for such miscommunication are complex as it could be linguistic, cultural, pedagogical, contextual or a combination of them all. One way to help NNES GTAs to compensate for comprehensibility problems such as pronunciation is to help them gain strategic competence by using more discourse marking devices. In her qualitative analysis of differences between native and non-native-speaker discourse patterns, Tyler (1992) suggests that it is vital to use teaching materials and techniques to train NNES GTAs to recognize and thus use as many of the discourse structuring devices as their NES counterparts.

## 2. THE STUDY

The purpose of the study reported in this chapter is to understand the major issues concerning a sub-group of NNESTs, namely, NNES GTAs teaching freshman composition to NESs in an English speaking country, and the coping strategies useful for these GTAs in teaching these courses. To be more specific, this ethnographic case study focused on four Chinese graduate teaching assistants (CGTAs) teaching freshman composition to NESs at a major southwestern university in the US. Because two of the participants started teaching in the fall of 2000 and two in the fall of 2001, the data collection lasted about two years.

While there were altogether 8 international graduate teaching assistants (1 Turkish, 1 Romanian, 1 Albanian, 1 German, and 4 Chinese) teaching first-year composition at the time period when the study was conducted, I purposefully focused my study on the 4 Chinese GTAs for two reasons. One is that the shared linguistic and cultural backgrounds of the participants would give me a better basis for comparison and cultural interpretation. The other is due to my own status as an insider in this cultural group. I believe that my shared linguistic and cultural backgrounds with the participants would not only enhance the rapport and trust between me as the researcher and the participants, but also facilitate my data collection in allowing me and my participants to use both L1 (Chinese) and L2 (English) through voluntary codeswitching in order to maximize the input, insights, and reflection free from linguistic constraints (Liu, 2001).

The main source of the data for the study was collected via both email and face to face interviews (see Appendix A). The interview data were then synthesized according to the following themes: 1) The participants' perceptions towards their teaching assignments and their NESs; 2) Challenges and difficulties the participants encountered; 3) Getting accepted: Establishing credibility as NNESTs; and 4) The participants' strategies for and benefits from teaching writing to NESs. In order to gain students' perspectives towards their teaching, I obtained the participants' permission, and reviewed their students' teaching evaluations, which are incorporated in the synthesis as 5) NESs' perspectives towards these CGTAs in freshman composition classes.

## 2.1    The participants

The 4 CGTAs: Lee, Hong, Bai and Xie (pseudonyms) are all from Mainland China and all obtained a BA in English in their respective universities in China.

Lee graduated from one of the top universities in Shanghai and was assigned to work in the Foreign Affairs Office in that university upon graduation. She had only 6 months of teaching experience before she was accepted to the English as a Second Language

Program (pseudonym) in a southwest American university. Hong, graduated from a provincial university majoring in English, taught English in a number of universities including a well-known cram school for TOEFL and GRE in China for three years. She also worked as a sales manager in a sino-American company in China for a year. When she enrolled in the same MA program as Lee, she felt it hard to readjust to an 'academic environment'. Bai obtained her BA in English in a Chinese university and had 4 years of teaching experience in another Chinese university. She was accepted as a Ph.D. student to a writing program. Xie graduated from a prominent university in Beijing, and worked at a language school in Shanghai before she came to US for an MA in the same degree program as Lee and Hong. However, she had more teaching experience than Lee while in China. Except for Hong who is considered extraverted, sociable, and extremely outgoing by her classmates and colleagues in the graduate program, the three other Chinese female teachers seem to be very introverted and shy, but attentive.

## 3. SYNTHESIS OF FINDINGS

### 3.1 The participants' perceptions towards their teaching assignment and their NES students

The initial reactions of the 4 CGTAs assigned to teach freshman composition to NESs were full of surprises, uncertainty, and self-doubt. This is mainly due to their lack of expectation to teach NESs. As Lee confessed:

> One year ago, when I received the letter of admission and a letter from the university telling me that I have got a Teaching Assistant (TA) position there, I thought what I would need to do was just grading papers or do some research for a professor. I got panicked when I learned that I actually needed to teach a section of English 101--freshman composition course to native English speakers. I wrote to my friends in Shanghai: 'This is incredible! How can I teach Americans how to write in English while I myself is a Chinese who have never been to an English speaking country before!' I was afraid the students will throw me out of the classroom.

Lee's intimidation was echoed by her former officemate, Xie, who was 'shocked to learn' that she would teach composition to American college. Although Xie considered herself 'a very good writer in both Chinese and English', she was not sure whether she could handle NESs in class. The mere fact that she could not speak as fluently as her students 'horrified' her. The other two CGTAs, Bai and Hong also expressed their 'surprise' when they learned the news, and they were delighted for a while until they hit the reality.

It was obvious that the major source of intimidation came from the NNES 'inferiority complex' (Medgyes, 1994). Having never lived in

English-speaking countries before, these CGTAs had no clue what their American college students would think of them teaching writing skills in a second language in front of first language speakers.

Such worries were aggravated when the subject matter—English composition—they had to teach appeared to be something different from what they are familiar with in their L1 in terms of format, idiomatic expressions, and genres. As Bai revealed in an interview:

> I was shocked to learn that I would teach English composition to American college students. Although I consider myself a very good writer in Chinese, I was not sure whether my experiences in writing in Chinese would ever be useful to teach writing in English, which I had to learn almost simultaneously.

While all 4 CGTAs were excited to be given this opportunity as they badly needed financial assistance in order to work on their graduate degrees in their respective areas, they all felt very nervous when they started teaching their NESs in the first few weeks. The majority of the students were initially curious to have a non-native English speaking instructor teach them how to write in English. As Lee recalls,

> I guess they were a little bit curious, a little bit amazed in general. Different groups of students have different attitudes. Fortunately, the class that I taught last semester was great. They understood that it was a very difficult situation for me and they were very supportive and encouraging, and very co-operative. In the first few classes, since we were not very familiar with each other, they mainly used non-verbal behavior like smiling, nodding, and looking at me with full attention to show their support. For this semester, I got a group of 'rebellious tough guys'-they don't like to speak in class, and they had no facial expression when they sat there. According to my supervisor's point of view, the class is just normal. She said the guys are usually like that. They are expected to show indifference in class, so people will think they are cool. However, as time goes on, I found they could have a lot to say if the topic was something they are interested in.

Before they started teaching their NES classes, the four participants were all under the impression that they would expect very noisy classes and their NESs would be very outspoken in class. But, out of their expectation, they were greeted by very 'obedient, curious, and conformed students' at the beginning of their first semester of teaching because the NESs were simply 'surprised' to be taught by someone who is from a different country. Sometimes this quietness 'was a bit intimidating' as confessed by Xie. The four participants all felt that their students seemed to have the understanding that teaching writing as a second language to first language speakers was not an easy task. According to Bai, 'my students accepted me as their English teacher. Most of them were kind to me. They seemed to know how difficult it would be to teach composition in a foreign language'. Hong also confessed that, unlike what she had expected, her students were 'pretty cooperative and respectful, not wild at all'.

Nevertheless, three out of the four CGTAs in the study acknowledged that they had been criticized or had their ability to effectively teach the course challenged by their students. What was even more intriguing was that they indicated that some of these confrontations were initiated by a specific subdivision of the class: young freshman males. Most of these challenges were discrete such as in the case of grade disputes. What really surprised these CGTAs was that some students challenged their ability to teach and ability to write in English in front of the whole class, which they had never experienced in China. They took such a challenge as a personal attack or insult, and they felt quite perplexed as to what to do. As Lee said in an interview:

> One day a student came to my office hour, and demanded that I change his grade. When I showed him the paper and pointed out the weaknesses of the paper, he interrupted me and said right to my face that I should not teach freshman composition. He then added as he walked away: 'I spent money for the course and I deserve an English teacher, not someone from China to teach me English writing'.

Lee assured me that she at least received such unfair comments three times within a year, and I noticed tears dropping out of her eyes when she asked me what she could do to stop her students from making such derogatory comments. She then switched in Chinese: [translated into English by the author]:

> If I can support myself financially, I won't even consider taking this TAship. I do not deserve such ill treatment from my students. Back in China, I was well respected by my students, and I feel that some American freshman students do not make any effort to learn. Why should I reward them with a higher grade if they didn't even try to work hard?

## 3.2    Challenges and difficulties the participants encountered

What seems to be most challenging to these CGTAs is the gap between their understanding about American culture and expectations about American undergraduates and the expectations of their teachers by American students. Since none of the four CGTAs had any experience as an undergraduate in an American university, whatever was contradictory to their expectation always seemed to be a shock to them. For instance, Bai expected her students to be quiet in class to show respect for the instructor. But when she found out that one of her students constantly talked with others while she was teaching, she was offended but did not know what to do. In China, she said, 'I would call the student's name and force this student to keep quiet'. But in US, she was afraid of offending this student if she called his name. On another occasion, Hong had a student complaining in front of the class that the grade he received as unfair, and even demanded that Hong change his grade right away. Although Hong avoided the confrontation in class by ignoring this student's demand, she felt that she could have dealt this issue more positively had she known more about American culture.

Apart from some cultural misunderstandings and differences in expectations, the second biggest challenge seems to be linguistic in nature, which can be referred to as the non-native speaker syndrome. The four participants all felt, to various degrees, that they were unable to show a linguistic advantage over their NESs in vocabulary, idioms, accuracy, and fluency in speaking. The feeling of being inferior to their students in speaking sometimes affected their self-confidence. For instance, Xie felt that she usually had great ideas for teaching, but 'it is not easy for me to ask appropriate and thought-provoking questions'. They felt that they were disadvantaged by the lack of native speaker intuition. Sometimes it took a while for them to formulate questions and communicate with their students. For Bai, the most demanding thing was to make herself understood. As she confessed:

> When I began to teach freshman composition, I felt intimidated by my NES students who speak English much more fluently than I do. I wrote down the things that I would talk about in class. Of course, it was impossible for me to write everything down before each class. Sometimes, when I tried to describe something, I could not find the right word, or sometimes when I could find a word, I chose not to use it because I was afraid of mispronouncing it. My accent and my mistakes in speaking made me frustrated.

The linguistic difficulties and uncertainties sometimes made the participants feel more intimidated coupled with their concern about losing face in front of their students (Liu, 2001, Saville-Troike, 2002). In China, the teacher is the authority, and if the teacher reveals any mistakes in front of the students, it would make the teacher look bad, and thus could damage the 'authoritative role' of the teacher. Operating under this Confucian doctrine, the participants felt that they should be extremely cautious in speaking and teaching to avoid mistakes that would make them look bad and thus cause their loss of face in class. Bai shared with me her moment of 'embarrassment':

> Once in a small group conference, I used 'he' to refer to a female student. The moment I uttered the wrong pronoun, I realized the terrible mistake. This happens to me occasionally because of my mother tongue although we have different words for 'he', 'she', and 'it', these three pronouns have the same pronunciation. I remember that after I made this mistake, one of my students laughed and I felt very embarrassed. I became less and less confident in front of my young students who uttered every syllable effortlessly and with admirable precision.

Bai felt that incidents like this undermined her authority in front of her students. Although speaking is different from writing, Bai felt the urgency to improve her speaking ability in order to establish her authority in class and to win the trust from her students. Bai was not alone expressing concerns about her speaking ability. Lee, on several occasions, shared with me her deepest fear in teaching composition to NESs:

> I do not seem to have the ability to deliver a lecture eloquently. It is hard for me to make the lecture really interesting to my students, even make some changes in them. These require a lot of background information and understanding of the American culture.

## 3.3 Getting accepted: Establishing credibility as NNESTs

Having realized the challenges and difficulties they were facing, the participants tried various means to improve their teaching, to gain their students' trust and respect, and to establish their own identity as authorities as NNESTs in front of their NESs.

All the four participants came to realize that being non-native English speakers was a given which could not be altered, and did not need to be altered. Rather than feeling inferior to native English speakers, they gradually realized that their experience of learning English as a foreign language itself to the level of teaching native English speakers writing was something that was remarkable and they should feel proud of. Therefore, they accepted who they are as non-native English speakers, and tried to take advantage of their successful English learning experience and L1 writing skills in teaching English writing to NESs. As Bai stated:

I think that if we (as NNESTs) can share with our students the good things in our own culture, then we can bring our resources into full play. I also find that if you can write well in your native language, you can also write well in your second language. So we do have things to offer to our students. If students can trust us, we can do better in helping them with their writing.

Like Bai, Lee tried to demonstrate not only her knowledge about how to write a paper, but also what to write about by using concrete topics and examples drawing from readings. The nature of writing and close reading enabled her to integrate some personal 'views' into teaching, which immediately shortened the distance between her and her students. Also by using her personal stories as a way to engage her students in discussion and reflection, Lee's students realized that their teacher had more experience than most of them did, and so was knowledgeable and had much to offer.

Changing the teaching style to cater to the students' needs seemed to work effectively as well. In China, classes are usually very big, and therefore, the class size is not conducive to group discussion. But this is not true for composition classes in the US. Usually there are about 20 to 25 students in these classes, and the CGTAs found that the group discussion format was extremely effective as this allowed every student a chance to talk.

Part of the tension in some of these composition classes, agreed on by all the participants, was due to the lack of communication between the teacher and the students. The lack of communication could slowly lead to indifference on the part of the students, and frustration on the part of the instructor. As Bai mentioned, once she took advantage of student-teacher conferencing, her students seemed to be more cooperative and collegial:

There was a change in their attitude towards me as the course progressed. They cooperated with me better than they did at the beginning of the semester. I think maybe the personal conference helped them change their attitude because I could talk freely with them and point out their strengths and weaknesses in these conferences individually.

Another way of gaining students' respect is 'rigid grading' and 'detailed comments'. As Xie recalled, when she provided concrete comments why a paper deserves an A and another deserves a B, her students seemed convinced and showed more respect to her. Xie believed that the process of working with NES students in discussing their writing is always rewarding. She felt that student-teacher conferencing was a great opportunity to clarify some misunderstanding that might not be easy to explain on paper. Given the different linguistic and cultural backgrounds of the CGTAs from their students, such interaction seems necessary and beneficial. As Hong recalls:

I worked really closely with one student when she was writing her argumentative paper on abortion. We read together, and I let her know where the logic was not working or the order could have been reversed. Her essay went from B- to A+, which was so rewarding for both of us: now I know I do have something to offer my NS students as a critical reader.

While meaning negotiation between the instructor and the students over their papers is a viable way to establish CGTAs' credibility as a teacher, it sometimes also gives them the opportunity to serve as a cultural informant as reflected in the following example.

Once Lee asked her students to write a rhetorical analysis paper as one of the three major papers of the course in a beginning-level composition class. When she received a student's paper on Chinese culture as a self-selected topic, she was shocked. She immediately emailed me for advice and shared the student's draft with me. The draft was about two pages long with 664 words. Throughout the essay, I noticed many sentences were marked with red pen together with her comments. For example:

Excerpt One:
Student: 'Their [Chinese] constant looking down on Americans as being foolish, lazy, and nothing more than a gun totting cowboy or other likeliness of your typical macho man as is apparent in many aspects of their society'.
Lee's comments: How do you know? I mean, this concept is quite new to me.

Excerpt Two:
Student: 'The [Chinese] adults, upon moving to a new place, do not ever bother to learn the language of the country they preside in. The people are either too lazy or lack the motivation to learn a new language, or feel they should not have to for they already know the greatest language on the planet'.
Lee's comments: Biased! I know a lot of Americans living in China who do not speak Chinese.

Excerpt Three
Student: 'If China were so great, why would anyone leave it? With that it is hard to see how the Chinese culture could be that dominant over American society.
Lee's comments: This is a counter proof of your argument.
In the end comments, Lee wrote the following:
This is a very surprising essay to read. The opinions expressed in this essay is quite radical and the biased. In academic writing, we usually expect the essay to establish credibility by showing respect to people who might have opposite opinions. We will come to that in our argumentative essay.

After explaining the differences between a rhetorical essay and an argumentative essay, Lee concludes her comments with the following:

I am also very interested in knowing where the idea that the Chinese people are pride come from. I agree that Chinese people are proud of their culture and I believe every nation is proud of its own culture, too. This is a positive thing. So could you share with me your sources based on which you have formed your opinion towards China and Chinese people?

Lee decided to talk with the student about his essay and challenge him about his concept and biased comments, which she did. I was later informed that the idea and prejudice that student wrote in this draft came from a negative traveling experience his mother had many years before. The student was later introduced to more references about Chinese culture, and avoided ungrounded comments in his revised draft, which eventually received a B. Through this experience, Lee realized how much her cultural background helped her educate the student beyond the writing skill, and she feels strongly that teaching is education at the same time.

## 3.4    The participants' strategies and benefits for teaching writing to NESs

The four participating CGTAs all benefited from teaching composition to NESs. They see their benefits from four distinctive perspectives. First of all, they all felt that they learned a great deal linguistically and socio-linguistically. When asked what benefits they have derived from this teaching experience, Xie said, concurred with by others, that it was the language such as idiomatic expressions and slang learned from her students through talking and grading. Along with the language, they also learned a great deal about American culture (what young people are like and what they are thinking about, what their concern is, what their values are). Understanding American culture meanwhile helped them in seeking pedagogical means to cater to the needs of their students, such as group discussion, peer response, student-teacher conferencing, and the like. Affectively, these NNES teachers learned how to build up their confidence in teaching NESs as NNES. As Hong said in an interview:

I have learned that writing is a hard process for everyone, whether NS or NNS. As an ESL learner, sometimes I tend to think that I could never master the English writing because English is a foreign language for me; in fact, writing is very different from speaking as I see from my freshman students. Therefore, this teaching experience strengthened my belief that L2 writer could create truly great works.

The participants also realize that it is of ultimate importance for them to build rapport with their NESs. Because of cultural and linguistic differences, one strategy is to find a common ground or more connections between the teacher and the students and to find topics of relevant interest and concern of the students. As Lee puts,

> I find that discussing the assignment sheet and the grading rubric with them together is very effective as I usually take advantage of this to know my students and also for them to know me. I will also try to relate their topic with something they are truly concerned about.

Xie sometimes deliberately chose the differences in writing styles between Chinese and English to alert students in their writing. This greatly enhanced students' interest in reflecting on their own way of writing and what alternative writings styles are outside their own language. As Xie put it,

> My students are always fascinated by what I had to say about Chinese writing and how Chinese people arranged their arguments differently and why. Although my students do not understand Chinese, they like the alternative ways of thinking and composing, which, in effect, helped them thinking and writing.

Getting students interested in the instructor's culture seemed to work very effectively for these CGTAs. The instructor's cultural background made the students become more aware of cross-cultural differences and other social-political issues. By bringing to their students perspectives from a different culture, like the way Chinese students learn writing, it can help American students look at the process of learning writing from different cultural perspectives. As Hong cleverly put it:

> We know what they don't know, and we do not know what they know, so we are more ready to listen to our students (which is really important) and share with the students about what they do not know.

To take advantage of the cultural differences, the participants have found it useful to use movies, stories, and novels from China or about China to engage their students in discussion while they serve as cultural informants. For example, using movie clips from 'Crouching Tiger Hidden Dragon' enabled NESs to understand the Chinese philosophy of Gongfu training for will, perseverance, and endurance. Likewise, reading chapters from the novel 'The Dream of Red Mansion' inspired NESs' interests in ancient Chinese history. All these cultural materials served as the link between reading and writing. In her self-assessment of teaching, Hong wrote:

It used to be language that concerns me as I am not a native English speaker, but now I am more concerned with teaching itself and how I could use my bilingual and bicultural background to help the students become more open-minded thinkers and writers.

Bai also finds it important to relate the students to her own Chinese cultural background. In this way they could 'know me better and cooperate with me better'.

Another strategy they have adopted successfully is to give students their sense of ownership through group discussion, class debate, and presentations, which were usually missing in Chinese classrooms where the teacher does the majority of the talking simply because of the large number of students enrolled in each class. The participants in the study were initially skeptical about this strategy, as Lee puts it:

At first I used all my class time to lecture because I think a well-organized lecture will give students more information and knowledge about writing than discussion. I was surprised to see my students staring at me without much facial expressions. After I had a chance to observe some experienced teachers in their composition classes, I realized that those teachers did not talk too much. I followed their teaching style in my class in the next few weeks, and to my surprise, all of my students seemed to be great talkers. The class atmosphere is lively, relaxed, and harmonious—totally different than before.

Lee was perceived by her students as someone who was very strict and rule-governed. Once a student told her that it was not necessary to abide strictly by the syllabus and talk about writing all the time. That student later on suggested that they can just talk, for example, about whatever they like because she enjoyed talking with Lee about Chinese culture rather than rhetorical strategies. This comment led Lee to believe that it was all right to integrate cultural discussion into talking about writing, and into something her students could relate to themselves, instead of transition of 'knowledge'. Lee revealed her thoughts in an interview after talking with this student:

Talking with this student made me think that my composition class should have more variety. There are many ways to make the students realize a concept. As NNES teachers, we should be more creative than we used to be. Teaching freshman comp makes it possible to communicate with students in a very personal level. Sometimes they tell you what they worry about and ask for your advice, which make me feel like their mentor. Sometimes I was wondering whether I was overacting when I asked one of my students to quit smoking and go to recreation center in order to get rid of her chest pain-which she had doubted to be lung cancer.

## 3.5　　NESs' perspectives towards these CGTAs in freshman composition classes

Overall, NESs' evaluations towards the participants were mixed. There were a few recurring positive themes of these NNES CGTAs by the NESs, who seem to be impressed by the CGTAs highly developed literacy skills in the L1s, and their successful experiences of learning to write in English as their L2. The NESs believe that these qualities enabled their CGTAs to contribute to teaching from unique perspectives. The NESs felt strongly that their NNES CGTAs have tried very hard to teach, and were usually well prepared. A student from nursing wrote the following in her evaluation:

> I think my teacher is a hard worker. I can tell that she must have spent a lot of time preparing the lesson before each class. Although sometimes I do not understand all her comments on my paper, I am impressed by the detailed comments, and sometimes even with suggested references for further reading. I think my teacher is responsible, and has tried her best.

Another student from MIS made similar comments praising her teacher's effectiveness:

> My teacher had a lot of valuable lessons to teach our class about our writing and understanding of others. She was very intelligent and her personal background influenced the class. She will definitely excel into the excellent category with more experience.

Secondly, the NES perceived that the CGTAs showed respect to their students as evidenced by their willingness to spend time on grading their assignments, and explaining their comments when students have questions. As commented by a student majoring in music:

> I think the teacher really respects the students, and definitely notices when students are trying their best and trying to raise their grade. The types of essays we worked on really expanded my comprehension of new ideas.

But most important of all, the majority of NESs felt that they learned about different cultures (*e.g.*, Chinese) through readings and assignments, which they did not expect before. For instance, a student majoring in computer engineering comments:

> This class is very much cultural learning. I had the opportunity to learn about a different culture and different experiences I think this class was very cultural related which is good because I didn't just learn how to write, but how other cultures develop.

The use of cultural materials for reading and writing proved to be an effective teaching technique employed by the CGTAs. Their students seemed to enjoy it very much. As a student from architecture commented:

> I loved this class. I had a great experience because I was able to read different types of text than I normally would have. I've always wanted to be able to write sophisticated and intelligent essays. I'm glad I was introduced to the novel 'The Joy Luck Club' because it has given me a better appreciation for being an American. It also gave me am understanding of the treatment of women in China.

However, about half of the students had reservations and negative comments about their CGTAs. While learning about different cultures seemed to be rewarding, some students felt that using cultural materials for a writing class was not suitable, especially when readings are heavily focused on one particular culture—Chinese. A student whose major is undecided expresses his dissatisfaction as follows:

> I felt my teacher could have been a little more encouraging and understanding. All of our texts were based on Chinese culture. It would have been nice to have some variety. I felt that some of the things we went into were sort of useless. We could have spent more time on our essays and not as much time on Chinese culture and women.

Another student in nursing commented on this in a more directly manner:

> At times I felt like I was taking a course about Chinese culture and not English. It would be helpful if my teacher would state and explain her expectations more clearly. I also felt that she was prejudiced toward us because we are Americans.

The major source of frustration came from the doubt and dissatisfaction with the fact that their teachers are not native English speakers who 'do not even speak English fluently' as revealed by a student in biology major:

> It's hard to teach English if you don't speak it. I think my teacher lacks verbal skills to communicate fully. It was sometimes hard to understand the point she was making. And hard to see how things are related to our writing. It was, however, very frustrating having an English teacher who could not speak English fluently. Her grammar is very poor. While she has come a far way, I'm sure, it is not fair for the students that suffer.

Student's frustration sometimes is also related to their expectation of being taught by a professor being unmet, coupled by the fact that these

GTAs are 'not even American'. A student majoring accounting wrote the following in his evaluation:

> I paid an obscene amount of money for this course and this depresses me. I have not learned very much about my writing skills. I have heard all kinds of bad comments from others who have also had Chinese English teachers. I think we deserve to have a professor in the classroom, or at least someone who is fluent in English.

Some students went as far as blaming their bad grade or the experience of lack of learning to their CGTAs as revealed in the following comment by a student who has not yet declared his major:

> My teacher really sucks. She was not effective for me at all. I feel that because of her, I have lost interest in writing all together. Her comments on essays never made any sense and when she would try to explain, it would make me even more confused. I couldn't understand her either. If English is not someone's first Language, then that person should not be able to teach English until they can fully understand English and be able to speak English fluently and be able to write in English to where it makes sense.

Needless to say, there is sometimes a problem of miscommunication between the teacher and the students. The negative comments by the students pinpoint the fact that these students' dissatisfaction is closely related to who their teacher is not. Their teacher is not a professor, not a native English speaker, which could mean, according to some NESs, less competent in English. Whenever there is a communication breakdown, the NESs' disappointment occurs. Their disappointment is likely to lead to frustration as expressed by a student in nursing:

> My teacher meant well, but was hard to understand because she had a hard time explaining things. Sometimes questions had to be asked multiple times by different people, and we all got different answers to the same question.

It needs to be pointed out that the dissatisfaction and disappointment among the NESs are not evenly applicable to all the CGTAs, nor do these dissatisfactions and disappointments come from the same students. Certain CGTAs received a higher proportion of favorable comments while other CGTAs received a higher proportion of unfavorable comments. This indicates that teaching evaluations are not based on non-native English speaking status only. It is the quality of teaching and the individual factors such as teaching methods, rapport with the students, and the communication styles that count. In fact, the CGTA who had the most teaching experience in China received the most favorable teaching evaluations while the CGTA who had the least teaching experience in China received the least favorable ones.

## 4.      DISCUSSION

Does being a NEST or a NNEST make a difference in teaching English composition to NESs? Yes, and the differences are obvious, but they are perceived differently by the CGTAs and by their NESs. According to the participants, they are still trapped by the NNES 'inferiority complex' (Medgyes, 1994) and they see themselves as being inferior to their NESs as they lack intuition of the target language. At times, they felt intimidated when they were challenged by their NESs, and felt insecure in front of their NESs as they could not speak as fluently and idiomatically as these students. Because of this intimidation and insecurity, they found it more difficult to establish credibility in front of their NESs as compared to their NES counterparts due to their lack of familiarity with American culture and their lack of experience with American college life. They felt obligated to do a good job in teaching, but meanwhile felt stressed to perform well in the graduate courses they were taking since these courses required more time for processing information in reading and writing for them as compared with their NES colleagues. Hong expresses the difficulty she experienced in establishing her credibility in her self-assessment:

> Being a native speaker of Chinese myself, how could I establish my authority teaching freshman composition to native English speakers? After all, these American kids acquired English as their native language, whereas I learned English as a foreign language in China—the language barrier is just unconquerable. To compensate for that disadvantage, I wrote down every single sentence before my first class, spent three hours on the diagnostic essay prompt just to get every word right, etc. But of course, I could still hear myself making mistakes in my speech, and I still had doubt about my wording in my assignment sheet, which bothered me a lot.

There is no doubt that these CGTAs are well aware of the reality they are facing. Apart from the fact that they were 'shocked' to learn that the students they were to teach were native English speakers, and the subject matter they were going to teach is not knowledge about writing per se, but a skill which they themselves were concurrently developing. Meanwhile, they had to keep up with their own studies—three required courses per semester—as graduate students. 'It was nightmare!' as Lee confessed:

Once I had to sit up the whole night reading and writing comments on sixteen first drafts to get ready for the group conferences the next morning—it was a miracle that I made it in the end, but ten days later, I was struck with a fever and a bad cold which resulted my staying in bed for the next three days.

The matter of fact is that these CGTAs, like Hong and Lee, had to spend extra time preparing their lessons and grading the students' papers to meet the demands of their students. No matter how hard they tried, their efforts sometimes fell short because of the tremendous amount of academic pressure coupled with cultural adjustment as international graduate students.

The differences between being taught English composition by NNESTs as opposed to NESTs are perceived by NESs as 'surprising', if not 'odd'. Based on the students' evaluation of teaching by the CGTAs, it seems that some of these NESs tend to have low tolerance for speech or English that deviates from the norm as the quote at the very beginning of this chapter reveals—'They are not even American'. On the other hand, some NESs tend to view this difference as an opportunity to learn about another culture, which is manifested in the reading and the writing assignments. Furthermore, some NESs see being taught by CGTAs as 'amazing' simply because of the fact that their teachers can speak and teach writing in a second language.

It is clear from this study that the differences affecting both CGTAs and their NESs are not solely derived from the non-native English speaker status of the CGTAs. The differences are, in fact, due to such factors as different sets of cultural expectations for teachers and learners, intercultural miscommunication and misunderstanding, and disjuncture in teaching and learning styles, and lack of exposure to speakers of other background, for which both the teacher and the students share responsibility.

Having NNES GTAs teaching NESs is in many composition or writing programs in North America is encouraging as it creates opportunities for intercultural communication, and enhancement of the globalization of English. But the issue of concern is how well a teacher is qualified to teach regardless whether the teacher is a NES or a NNES (Medgyes, 1994, 1996; Liu, 1999). Given the difficulties the CGTAs experienced and the concerns their NESs expressed, it is important for composition program directors and coordinators to consider the sources of support to help these GTAs become more confident and competent in teaching freshman composition.

## 5.    RECOMMENDATION AND CONCLUSION

The analysis of the interview data, combined with data from documents (*e.g.*, students' teaching evaluations), reveal several salient challenges that NNESTs face in teaching first-year composition to NES students: the lack of cultural background knowledge of the language, their lack of prior exposure to fluent colloquia and spoken English, the uncertainty of the extent to which instructional materials are used in class, the initial negative attitudes of the students, and the high demand for explicit and direct instructions expected from NNESTs. The results of the study also reveal several characteristics that make NNESTs extremely popular and welcome: their L1 linguistic and cultural backgrounds, their English learning experiences, the anecdotes they can share to highlight rhetorical structures/styles through contrastive rhetoric, and their willingness to invite their NES students to contribute to class discussion and serve as cultural informants.

Based on the results of the study, a number of recommendations can be made for composition program directors, course coordinators, and NES teachers in supporting collaboration between NNES and NES teachers to meet the diverse needs of their learners.

An important source of support for GTAs is a systematic training program that will not only prepare these GTAs for the courses they are going to teach, but also provide an ongoing supporting network that will discuss issues of concern as they occur. The participants benefited from a seminar required for all GTAs by the composition program, but they felt that the training in this seminar had not taken into consideration their special needs. They wished that they had been given opportunities to observe the classes they were going to teach before they were put on spot. Given this concern, it might be a good idea to arrange the training program well in advance or make it a component of teacher training. Instead of teaching while being trained, these GTAs will have to spend the first semester taking a hands-on training seminar so that they will be ready to teach in the second semester and onwards. This could greatly reduce anxiety and boost their confidence. If this is impossible, at least the teaching load for GTAs in the first semester should be reduced to a minimum. As revealed in the data, all the GTAs felt 'stressed' to teach in their first semester while adjusting to a totally new environment and coping with a different system of learning and teaching. It was in their first semester that these CGTAS received most negative comments from their NESs as compared to their subsequent semesters. It is unfair for students in a writing program to have teachers who are coping with pressures, figuring out what to do, and doing while learning at the same time.

A peer support group is another viable strategy that will help novice GTAs gain confidence and the specific course-related help they need. Each CGTA expressed her desire to have an experienced TA to serve as her peer buddy and someone whose classes she can observe on regular basis, and whose teaching notes can be shared. Although having supervisors provides support, the level of support by peer buddies is different. Due to the social distance and concept of face operating in Chinese culture (Liu, 2001), the CGTAs in the study did not feel comfortable asking their supervisors questions they could ask from their peers. Xie, for instance, felt intimidated and even humiliated by her supervisor after she was repeatedly requested to provide different answers to the same question in a supervising session where others were present.

CGTAs should view their L1 linguistic and cultural backgrounds as an asset rather than a deficit in teaching. As revealed in the study, some participants successfully used materials from Chinese literature for reading and writing assignments in the composition classes, and their NESs enjoyed the opportunity to understand another culture, which, in return, strengthened their understanding of their own. However, dissatisfaction also arises when such materials were overused as in Bai's class. Had the participants been told what materials seemed to work well in the previous years, they would have had an easier time in choosing these materials. Therefore, the training session should also include the component of materials selection and development.

In sum, this study suggests the need to understand the special difficulties of NNES GTAs in teaching first-year composition classes, and also to understand the unique contributions this group is making and can make to our profession. We must be sensitive to the needs of NNESTs and make them feel appreciated and supported as part of our discourse community.

## 6. REFERENCES

Canagarajah, A. S. (1999). Interrogating the 'native speaker fallacy': Non-linguistic roots, non-pedagogical results. In G. Braine (Ed.), *Non-native educators in English language teaching*. Mahwah, NJ: Lawrence Erlbaum Associates. 77-92.

Cook, V.J. (1999). Going beyond the native speaker in Language teaching. *TESOL Quarterly, 33* (2), 185-210.

Harklau, L., Losey, K.M. & Siegal, M. (1999). *Generation 1.5 meets college composition: Issues in the teaching of writing to U.S. - Educated learners of ESL*. Mahwah, NJ: Lawrence Erlbaum Associates.

Kamhi-Stein, L.D. (2000). Non-native English-speaking professionals: A new agenda for a new millennium. *MEXTESOL Journal, 23* (3), 11-20.

Liu, J. (1999). Non-native-english-speaking professionals in TESOL. *TESOL Quarterly, 33* (1), 85-102.

Liu, J. (2001). *Asian students' classroom communication patterns in US universities: An emic perspective*. Norwood, NJ: Ablex Publishing.

Medgyes, P. (1994). *The non-native teacher*. London: Macmillan. (1999) 2nd edition. Ismaning: Max Hueber Verlag.

Medgyes, P. (1996). Native or non-native: Who's worth more? In T. Hedge & N. Whitney (Eds.), *Power, pedagogy & practice*. Oxford: Oxford University Press. 31-42.

Nayar, P.B. (1997). ESL/EFL dichotomy today: Language politics or pragmatics. *TESOL Quarterly, 31* (1), 9-37.

Phillipson, R. (1992). *Linguistic imperialism*. Oxford: Oxford University Press.

Phillipson, R. (1996). ELT: The native speaker's burden. In T. Hedge & N. Whitney (Eds.), *Power, pedagogy & practice*. Oxford: Oxford University Press. 23-30.

Plakans, B.S. (1997). Undergraduates' experiences with the attitudes toward international teaching assistants. *TESOL Quarterly, 31* (1), 95-119.

Reid. J. (1993). *Teaching ESL writing*. Englewood Cliffs, NJ: Prentice-Hall.

Saville-Troike, M. (2002). (3rd ed.) *The ethnography of communication*. Malden, MA: Blackwell.

Silva, T. (1993). Towards an understanding of the distinct nature of L2 writing: The ESL research and its implications. *TESOL Quarterly, 27* (4), 657-677.

Tang, C. (1997). On the power and status of non-native ESL teachers. *TESOL Quarterly, 31* (3), 577-580.

Thomas, J. (1999). Voices from the periphery: Non-Native teachers and issues of credibility. In G. Braine (Ed.), *Non-native educators in English language teaching*. Mahwah, NJ: Lawrence Erlbaum Associates. 5-14.

Tyler, A. (1992). Discourse structure and the perception of incoherence in international teaching assistants' spoken discourse. *TESOL Quarterly, 26* (4), 713-729.

Williams, J. (1992). Learning, discourse marking, and the comprehensibility of international teaching assistants. *TESOL Quarterly, 26* (4), 693-711.

# APPENDIX A

Guided questions for interviews:

1. Could you describe briefly your background and experiences in learning and teaching English (*e.g.*, when and where, how long, in what context, etc.)
2. What was your first reaction when you were assigned to teach freshmen composition to Native English Speaking (NES) students?
3. How were you perceived as and treated by your NES students in general, and in the first few classes in particular?
4. What are the major challenges and/or difficulties you have encountered in teaching English Composition to NES students as a NNES teacher?
5. Was there any attitudinal change among your students towards you as the course progressed, and what accounted for such attitudinal changes?
6. What are the major issues you are concerned about in teaching NES English as a NNES?
7. What strategies have you used and found successful in dealing with issues pertinent to the teaching of writing to your NES students?
8. What are the strengths and weaknesses, in your opinion, of NNES teachers teaching NES students writing?
9. In what ways do you think you have benefited from teaching composition to NES students as an L2 writer?
10. Could you share with me some anecdotes you've felt strongly about while teaching Freshman Comp to NES students as a NNES teacher?

Chapter 10

# PRAGMATIC PERSPECTIVES ON THE PREPARATION OF TEACHERS OF ENGLISH AS A SECOND LANGUAGE: PUTTING THE NS/NNS DEBATE IN CONTEXT

TRACEY M. DERWING, *University of Alberta*
MURRAY J. MUNRO, *Simon Fraser University*

## 1.    INTRODUCTION

For well over a decade considerable discussion has taken place about the construct of 'native speaker' in second language pedagogy, teacher education, and research. Some writers have argued that the terminological distinction between native and non-native is in itself problematic because it cannot be adequately defined, and a few have even gone so far as to proclaim the 'death' of the native speaker (Paikeday, 1985). Others (*e.g.*, Cook, 1999) have pointed out that these terms may be used to emphasize a distinction between two categories of people, one of which is sometimes relegated to a lower status for no reason other than the kind of linguistic exposure its members happened to receive during childhood.

Much of this discussion has centred on the attitudes of teachers and administrators who may view L2 users as somehow falling short of a required standard. Indeed Medgyes (1994) comments on the unwillingness of some administrators to hire even highly proficient L2 English speakers as EFL teachers (see also Árva & Medgyes, 2000). Cook (1999), in particular, has indicated that non-natives are sometimes inappropriately compared with natives, arguing against the unfairness of judging L2 users in terms of a

E. Llurda (Ed.), *Non-Native Language Teachers. Perceptions, Challenges and Contributions to the Profession*,
179—191.

standard that they can never achieve (*i.e.*, they can never truly become 'native', no matter how proficient in English they become.)

The writers who have commented on these matters have heightened readers' awareness of stereotyping and the belittling of non-native speakers and have made a strong case for continuing to speak out against any unfair treatment and characterization of L2 speakers. At the same time, in considering the particular matter of L2 users as teachers of English, it is important to recognize that much of the material published on this issue represents a relatively narrow range of perspectives and that some of the commentary appears to be a response to circumstances in parts of the world where native speakers may automatically be accorded high status as teachers of English, even when they lack suitable pedagogical credentials.

A more diverse range of evidence may emerge, however, when the phenomenon of non-native English teachers is considered across a wider range of contexts. For instance, when Medgyes (1994) presents his carefully researched findings about English teachers in Hungary, we see an interesting distinction between pedagogically weak NS 'backpack' TESLers and NNSs who are sometimes seen as having insufficient proficiency in English. Such a contrast undoubtedly occurs in many areas around the world. But the fact remains that what is true in one country (or even city) cannot automatically be assumed to be true in the next. In fact, when scholars seek to make general statements about what NS or NNS teachers 'are like', they themselves run the risk of overgeneralization, stereotyping, and a descent into polemics.

One matter that must be considered is the training of NNS ESL teachers in inner circle countries. To assist in the development of a wider view of the issue of NNS instructors, we present here an informal case study of ESL teacher training in Canada. As teacher educators, our view of the roles of NS and NNS English language teachers is, out of necessity, pragmatic; we see many of our concerns as transcending debate about how native speakers might be defined or about what NNS teachers 'are like'. Instead, we are regularly faced with practical questions that require us to focus on the merits of individual applicants and on the outcomes of the training process:

1. Who will be admitted to TESL training programs?
2. How will students' individual needs be met?
3. What standards will candidates have to meet for graduation?

In finding answers to these questions, the issue of NS versus NNS status is irrelevant in and of itself. Instead, a focus must be placed on ensuring that future teachers have an appropriate level of proficiency in English, that they gain the requisite linguistic knowledge and skills for classroom teaching, and that they are able to employ pedagogically sound principles in the classroom. This view is consistent with that of Milambiling (2000), who argues that 'multicompetence should ... be a goal for all language teachers' (326), whether they are NSs or NNSs. In the Canadian context, then, the answers to the three key questions above are likely to be context-specific rather than general, and to arise more often from the initiatives of teacher trainers themselves than from reflection upon categories of teachers and the hypothetical merits of each.

## 2.     CONTEXT-SPECIFIC TEACHER TRAINING

In order to assess language teachers' effectiveness, one has to consider the context in which they operate. Quite different evaluations of the standards that teachers must meet might emerge, depending on local circumstances. Here it is worthwhile to examine adult ESL teacher training in two Canadian cities, Vancouver and Edmonton, against the backdrop of the general Canadian milieu.

### 2.1     ESL students in Canada

For more than a decade, Canadian immigration rates have been relatively high, given the size of the country's population (a goal of 250,000 immigrants annually in a country of 31 million). The impact is largely felt in the major cities, where the vast majority of immigrants reside. According to government policies, immigrants fall into three categories: independents (entrepreneurs and professionals), family class (relatives of previous immigrants), and refugees. The education level of adult immigrants ranges from little or none to advanced post-secondary, but on the whole, the admission process favours the educated. The majority of newcomers do not speak English or French on arrival. For arrivals in English-speaking Canada who come with little or no knowledge of English, the federal government provides access to up to 1200 hours of ESL in the Language Instruction for Newcomers to Canada (LINC) program. Although there are some variations in delivery from one province to the next, most adult immigrants in English-speaking parts of the country can attend LINC classes. In some jurisdictions, provision for opportunities to study beyond a basic level are made available by the province (*e.g.*, immigrants in Alberta are eligible for a year of government-funded ESL and academic upgrading after they have completed LINC). Thus, in addition to many private schools and specialized programs, substantial numbers of general ESL programs are available to newcomers.

### 2.1.1    Vancouver

After Toronto and Montreal, Vancouver (population over 2 million) is the third most popular destination for immigrants to Canada. It was, for example, the favoured destination of Asian immigrants, particularly in the five years prior to the handover of Hong Kong to China. The resulting changes came very quickly. In a matter of two years, some public schools with enrollments of very few ESL students had ESL populations of 70%. Because Vancouver is on the Pacific Rim and is a well-known tourist destination, it is also home to many adult ESL schools for foreign visitors.

Vancouver has a number of TESL training programs. The program under consideration here (at Simon Fraser University) offers a Baccalaureate level certificate and is directed primarily at students who have had little or no teaching experience. The program includes courses in phonetics, general linguistics, English grammar, second language acquisition, and ESL pedagogy. The students are mainly from Vancouver, many of them from an ESL background themselves. In fact, more than half of all applicants classify themselves as NNSs. The application process entails not only a written statement of purpose, but an oral interview to assess communication skills and overall suitability for the program[1]. Because almost all applicants are local, it is feasible to conduct such interviews. Interestingly, the interview process identifies several applicants each year whose English proficiency is limited to the extent that they would be unable to function effectively as teachers of high intermediate or advanced ESL classes.

### 2.1.2    Edmonton

Edmonton, a city of almost 1 million, receives fewer immigrants in total, but a higher proportion of refugees and family class immigrants than Vancouver. The Edmonton TESL program described here offers both an after-degree diploma similar to the Baccalaureate in Vancouver as well as a Master of Education in TESL. Several linguistics and introductory TESL courses are prerequisites to the Master's program. The students study research design and methods, and a minimum of four graduate level TESL courses (ranging in topic from skills-based content such as pedagogical grammar, pronunciation, L2 reading, etc., to courses that are sociopolitical in nature). In addition, the students undertake a practicum and a research project. Many of the NS students have taught English overseas and have returned to Canada to obtain professional training, while others are novices to ESL. Still others are NNS international students who plan to return to their countries of origin once they have completed the program; a few are NNSs who have made their home in Canada. In the Edmonton program, approximately 25% of the MEd students are NNSs. Applicants to the program are admitted on the basis of grade point average, TOEFL (580/237 minimum) and TSE (50 minimum) test scores, reference letters, and a letter of intent. Currently no interview is in place because many of the applicants to this program are outside Alberta at the time of application.

### 2.1.3     Features common to both programs

Although some of the students who seek admission to TESL programs in both Vancouver and Edmonton expect to teach EFL overseas, many plan to teach ESL in Canada, and all must complete a practicum course in a Canadian ESL class of adults. The primary focus of instruction, then, is to prepare them for teaching adults in an English-speaking context. Both Edmonton and Vancouver have private language schools dependent on tuition and federal adult ESL funds, as well as institutions with blended funding from provincial governments and private sources. The settings for practicum placement are varied: in both instances the range of ESL programs available extends from beginner to very advanced ESL courses. There are also occupational English courses and academic English (EAP) programs.

Just as Astor (2000) has argued that 'Because there is no such thing as an average teacher of English or any other discipline, there can be no professional differentiation among native-speaking (NS) and NNS teachers of English. The only real difference among teachers of English or ESL lies in their qualifications, not in their nativity' (p. 19), we suggest that it is virtually impossible to make any meaningful generalizations about differences between NS and NNS applicants to these TESL programs. Certainly there are no consistent differences in pedagogical backgrounds because most are inexperienced; few have any formal training in SLA theory or pedagogical practice, though there is a significant minority of local teachers who are upgrading their skills.

One variable that does present challenges is the wide variation in English proficiency among the students. In addition to NSs, who show variability in their own skills, some students who self-identify as NNSs came to Canada in early childhood and may not even be recognized in the community as L2 users of English. In contrast, other applicants have serious difficulties with oral and written English, so much so that they are not able to function effectively as teachers of advanced, or sometimes even high intermediate-level ESL classes in Canada because their knowledge of English would actually be below that of the students in such courses. This variation in linguistic proficiency poses difficulties for placements within our practicum courses.

## 2.2      Practicum Requirements

The practicum courses in Vancouver and Edmonton are very similar. Both include an initial on-campus component intended to allay student concerns and to orient the student teachers to their placements, followed by a supervised field component. In both programs, a practicum supervisor meets with the TESL faculty to discuss possible placements and then contacts institutions and individual instructors to compile a list of potential sites.

After extensive matching criteria are applied (see below), each student is assigned to a cooperating teacher. The student observes the ESL class for a few days and then, together with the teacher, works out a practicum schedule, taking into account the requirements and timetabling of the ESL class. The student informs the university facilitator once a teaching schedule has been established. Practicum students are required to attend at least two days a week for at least two hours per session. In most cases, students spend a minimum of 25 hours in the classroom, and teach for at least 10 of those hours, though they are encouraged to spend more time in the class, if possible. The cooperating teachers monitor the practicum students and give them increasing responsibilities; at the same time they provide the students with feedback on their performance. In addition, a university facilitator visits the institution to observe the student teach and to meet with both the student and the cooperating teacher. Should a problem arise at the time of the formative evaluation, a notification of concern is issued to the practicum student, both in writing and in person, outlining the difficulties observed, along with suggestions for addressing the shortcomings. Additional observations are scheduled and the practicum period may be extended. (If the problems cannot be solved, the practicum placement is terminated). Throughout the practicum there are opportunities for the students to meet to discuss their experiences. At the end of the practicum, a final observation is conducted, and an evaluation form is completed by the cooperating teacher.

## 2.3      Community expectations

TESL graduates from our programs must have the knowledge and skills to teach in a Canadian institution. Therefore, they must have a thorough understanding of teaching practices and philosophy typical in this country. Moreover, they must have a high level of proficiency in a variety of English that is intelligible to members of the local community. This doesn't mean that they must speak 'without an accent', but it does mean, for example, they must speak a variety of English (whether native or non-native) that is readily intelligible to members of the community. The English required of the TESL graduates is dictated by the needs of their ESL students. The immigrants and international students who study ESL in Vancouver and Edmonton must live, work, and attend school in these locales and thus they quite reasonably expect to be exposed to local varieties of English in order to function successfully in the communities. We should point out that there are many NNS teachers on staff in reputable colleges in both cities: they were hired because of their superior linguistic and pedagogical skills. The criterion applies in the selection of practicum supervisors who may also be NNSs.

## 2.4     Cooperating teacher expectations

In an informal poll, cooperating teachers in a provincially funded ESL institution in Edmonton were asked to comment on the NS/NNS status of student teachers who had been placed there. The cooperating teachers indicated that they expect student teachers, regardless of their status, to be capable of designing classroom tasks, providing clear explanations, and successfully answering questions. They generally agreed that both NSs and NNSs can be able teachers, but only if they have sufficient language proficiency and metalinguistic knowledge along with strong pedagogical skills. The weakest students in their memory included both NS and NNS individuals. The complaints ranged from a lack of grammatical knowledge (NSs); an overall lack of proficiency (NNSs); and weak pedagogical skills (NSs and NNSs alike). These findings are reminiscent of the views expressed by practicum supervisors surveyed by Llurda (2003, this volume). When asked whether they thought teaching or language skills were most important to teaching success, 28% felt that language skills were paramount and another 25% indicated that teaching skills were most important, while 44% indicated that both were necessary.

## 2.5     Pragmatic considerations

Given community expectations, the needs of the ESL learners, and the nature of the ESL institutions where we place our students, we are obliged to consider the practicum experiences in a very concrete manner. We make the match between student and cooperating teacher only after considering the following criteria: level of ESL students' linguistic proficiency; personality of both the cooperating teacher and TESL student; past experiences of cooperating teacher; communication skills of the TESL students (NSs and NNSs alike); gender; whether the ESL schools are private or government-sponsored; and cultural background of the ESL students.

**2.5.1    Level of ESL students' proficiency and language knowledge of TESL students**

Generally TESL students with lesser linguistic proficiency are not placed in advanced ESL classrooms. For such teachers, the practicum experience can be intimidating; they worry that the ESL students will ask them questions they cannot answer, and in some instances, they worry that the ESL students' proficiency may outstrip their own. Indeed, they sometimes find that they lack some important aspects of tacit knowledge of English usage, although their awareness of explicit grammatical rules may exceed that of many NSs. On the other hand, other TESL students (including NSs) may have explicit knowledge gaps that would prevent them from effective performance in a TOEFL preparation course, for example. Students' performance in TESL courses with respect to metalinguistic knowledge and presentation skills, in particular, is considered when placements are made in order to facilitate as positive an experience as possible. Following observations conducted by the practicum supervisor and the cooperating teacher, linguistic gaps, whether explicit or implicit, are pointed out to the students as areas for further work.

**2.5.2    Personalities of TESL student and cooperating teacher**

Shy, somewhat apprehensive students are usually placed with nurturing cooperating teachers, while more assertive students are placed with teachers who expect a high degree of independence. Both university programs maintain a relationship with a core of cooperating teachers who volunteer to take practicum students on a regular basis. The practicum supervisors are familiar with their classrooms and their personal styles and are thus in a position to make recommendations in consultation with the instructors within the TESL programs, who have a sense of the nature of the students to be placed.

**2.5.3    Past experiences of the cooperating teacher**

Sometimes teachers are paired with TESL students whose performance is extremely weak and in fact whose practicum experience has to be curtailed. We consider it important to maintain good relationships with the cooperating programs. To ensure that teachers who have had a recent bad experience will not refuse to take a TESL student in the future, we promise that we will attempt to assign one of our more promising students to their classrooms in the following session. On occasion a cooperating teacher has not provided the level of guidance that students require; under those circumstances we endeavour to exclude that individual's classroom from future placements.

## 2.5.4    Gender

Although there is no official policy of gender matching, we must consider gender issues when placing students. Some of our international students may feel uncomfortable with a teacher of the opposite sex. To avoid any potential difficulties, we take gender into account; however, this issue certainly doesn't preclude mixed placements. Women instructors are much more heavily represented in ESL classrooms than are men; thus some of our male students have been placed with women, of practical necessity.

## 2.5.5    Cultural background of ESL students

Although we do not condone any kind of discrimination, we recognize that many newcomers to Canada bring with them values that are in conflict with official multiculturalism policy. These prejudices are sometimes expressed openly by students in ESL classes. Our primary concern is that our TESL students not be exposed to unfair treatment when they are still novices. A harmful experience with a difficult class might have long-lasting effects. Two kinds of problems involving discrimination on the basis of cultural background may arise. First, the ESL students may reject instruction from an individual whom they do not accept because of his/her ethnic background. For example, there have been instances in which tension arose because of bullying of Asian practicum students by some East European ESL students. Amin (1997) cites evidence that some ESL learners in a study she conducted in Toronto rejected teachers who belonged to a visible minority (that is, they were readily identified as being from a non-Caucasian background). Although we cannot eliminate this type of response entirely, we consult with cooperating teachers as much as possible regarding the perceived receptivity of their classes.

Second, there is the issue of disruption in the class because of ethnic or political conflicts among the ESL students. It takes an experienced ESL instructor to deal with such disagreements to ensure that they do not escalate into major incidents. Novice instructors find teaching to be enough of a challenge, without adding mediation to their responsibilities. Naturally, in time, practicum students will have to deal with such issues in their own classrooms, and we discuss at length the types of difficulties that can arise in our courses, but for the purposes of the practicum we feel it necessary to arrange as close to optimum a teaching experience as possible.

### 2.5.6    Private versus public institutions

In some ESL schools in which students pay high tuition fees, administrators may believe that their students will not stand for less than ideal teaching. This notion is independent of any evidence, but we are careful to send TESL students with some previous experience and clear evidence of strong teaching skills to those programs. Administrators in public institutions are more likely to regard acceptance of student teachers as part of their mandate because they feel they have a responsibility for professional development of the field of ESL teaching.

### 2.5.7    Pragmatic constraints

A number of mundane but important factors must also be taken into account when placing practicum students, including, but not limited to, their own course schedules, part-time employment schedules, location of residence and availability of transportation, and other personal matters.

It is important to note that all the above considerations apply to NS and NNS alike. The question of native speaker status is beside the point. The important issue is whether the student teachers can meet the requirements of the context in which we place them. If not, we would be setting them up for failure.

## 3.    CONCLUSION

A number of authors have expressed concern about negative attitudes towards NNSs that arise simply because of their non-native status. There is no question that discrimination against L2 users of English has occurred and continues to occur. In fact, there is a fairly long tradition of research in Canada that indicates that the speakers of the dominant language sometimes hold negative views of L2 users of English (Lambert, Frankel & Tucker, 1966; Kalin & Rayko, 1978; Sato, 1998). Accent discrimination has also been documented in human rights cases (*e.g.*, Munro, 2003), and discrimination on the basis of race sometimes affects students who belong to a visible minority. However, as legitimate as the concerns about these issues are, it is important to recognize that the problem of discrimination is separate from the question of whether an individual TESL student has the potential to be an effective ESL teacher. A range of knowledge and skills is required of all teachers, regardless of their L1 status. For us, and for other teacher trainers this is the most pressing concern in the recruitment and education of ESL teachers.

Medgyes (1999) appropriately raises the question of what constitutes an ideal teacher. He suggests that 'aptitude, experience, personal traits, motivation and love of students' (p. 178) are all critical to success. Beyond, that, he argues that teacher education, including English language training, is necessary to ensure competence in the English language classroom. It is clear from our experience that the latter point is most compelling. Our own students often need extra support to develop their language skills and/or awareness. This is the main source of difference across NS and NNS students. Some NNSs need vocabulary development, and are often unsure of pragmatic aspects of English language use. At the same time, they may have an excellent grasp of metalinguistic terminology and concepts. Some native speakers, on the other hand, may lack explicit knowledge of grammatical structures and may even have difficulty understanding why such knowledge is important. However, their tacit knowledge is, for the most part, satisfactory. But neither of these needs can automatically be assumed for any individual student, and, in almost all other respects, all students need similar preparation in order to teach in the Canadian context. In addition to the ubiquitous requirements of a knowledge of basic linguistics, second language acquisition, pedagogical approaches and skill-specific content, they need an understanding of how ESL is offered in Canadian adult institutions, the cultural backgrounds of ESL students, and the socio-political ramifications of ESL. These issues are complex; in order to understand their university classes, all of which are taught in English, our TESL students require a high degree of linguistic sophistication, regardless of their L1.

## 3.1    Acting versus thinking

To those faced with the kinds of practical, day-to-day problems we have described here, debate about what NSs and NNSs are 'like' or about how each group 'should' be treated can at times seem frustrating. On the one hand, it is important to recognize the need for open discussion of such issues as discrimination and bias. It is also intriguing to consider proposals such as Cook's (1999) view that notions of L2 proficiency might be defined in terms of NNS rather than NS standards. However, at present, no such standards exist. Those who engage in debate about NNS and NS teachers may see themselves as definers or prescribers of policy. However, in answering questions about who is admitted and what is to be addressed in teacher training programs, and how to establish the standards (linguistic and pedagogical) that students must meet, much of the speculative concerns about NSs versus NNSs is unhelpful. In fact, had we dwelt at length on such matters, we would never have been able to run our programs. Instead of focusing on idealistically-driven models, we believe that people concerned with NS versus NNS status should pay more attention to current teacher trainer initiatives that already seem to be addressing some of the real underlying issues. From our standpoint, the policy in Canadian teacher training programs must be driven by the needs of the ESL students, the majority of whom want to learn Canadian English as quickly as possible in order to facilitate their integration into Canadian society. Blanket statements or condemnations of either NS or NNS teachers are inappropriate. Each teaching context must be considered separately, taking into consideration the requirements of the students to be taught. Thus defining the 'best' teacher in a given setting will be determined by those needs.

## 3.2    Final consideration

As we have demonstrated here, we try to accommodate both NS and NNS student teachers within our community contexts. There is one other factor regarding the professional development of ESL/EFL teachers that may contribute to the perception in non-English speaking countries that NSs often make poor teachers. This is due to the proliferation of inferior-quality TESL/TEFL training courses that are sold via the internet or offered in intensive 'seminars' of a week or less in duration (see Watt & Taplin, 1997; Thomson, in press). Such courses are subject to very limited government regulation and are not offered through reputable institutions though in some instances they have attempted to gain the appearance of respectability by renting university facilities for their classes and by advertising that they are members of TESL Canada in their promotional material. Anyone can be a member of TESL Canada simply by paying the annual fee. Such courses usually have no admission requirements and are likely to be instructed by people with no TESL credentials whatsoever. Failure rates are zero, provided the registration fee is paid, and a 'diploma' from one of these courses is typically nothing more than a certificate of attendance. The existence of such programs has led to increased pressure on Canadian administrators to hire ESL instructors who have legitimate teaching credentials. Nevertheless, administrators in other countries may not be aware of the fraudulent nature of these certificates. Some of our own students, in fact, first took some of these programs, went overseas to teach, and then returned, only to enroll in legitimate TESL programs because they recognized the serious deficiencies in their training. The perception of native speakers as untrained and incapable of adjusting to the needs of language students may thus be fuelled in part by contact with individuals who have insufficient professional preparation and an overabundance of self-confidence.

## 4. NOTES

[1] At the time of writing, plans were underway to introduce both TOEFL and TSE requirements.

## 5. REFERENCES

Amin, N. (1997). Race and the identity of the non-native ESL teacher. *TESOL Quarterly, 31*, 580-583.

Árva, V., & Medgyes, P. (2000). Native and non-native teachers in the classroom. *System, 28*, 355-372.

Astor, A. (2000). A qualified non-native English-speaking teacher is second to none in the field. *TESOL Matters, 10* (2), 19.

Cook, V.J. (1999). Going beyond the native speaker in language teaching. *TESOL Quarterly, 33* (2), 185-209.

Kalin, R., & Rayko, D. (1978). Discrimination in evaluative judgments against foreign-accented job candidates. *Psychological Reports, 43*, 1203-1209.

Lambert, W.E., Frankel, H. & Tucker, G.R. (1966). Judging personality through speech: A French-Canadian example. *Journal of Communication, 16*, 305-321.

Llurda, E. (2003). The professional skills and beliefs of non-native speakers in English language teaching. Unpublished PhD Dissertation. Universitat de Lleida, Lleida, Catalonia.

Medgyes, P. (1994). *The non-native teacher*. London: Macmillan. (1999) 2nd edition. Ismaning: Max Hueber Verlag.

Medgyes, P. (1999). Language training: A neglected area in teacher education. In G. Braine (Ed.), *Non-native educators in English language teaching*. Mahwah, NJ: Lawrence Erlbaum Associates. 177-195.

Milambiling, J. (2000). Comments on Vivian Cook's 'Going beyond the native speaker in language teaching'. *TESOL Quarterly, 34*, 324-332.

Munro, M.J. (2003). A primer on accent discrimination in the Canadian context. *TESL Canada Journal, 20* (2), 38-51.

Paikeday, T. (1985). *The native speaker is dead!* Toronto: Paikeday Publishing Inc.

Sato, K. (1998). Evaluative reactions towards 'foreign accented' English speech: The effects of listeners' experience on their judgements. Unpublished master's thesis. University of Alberta, Edmonton, Alberta, Canada.

Watt, D. & Taplin, J. (1997). The Least a TESL program should be. *TESL Canada Journal, 14 (2)*, 72-74.

Thomson, R.I. (in press). Buyer beware: Professional preparation and TESL certificate programs in Canada. *TESL Canada Journal*.

PART IV

# STUDENTS' PERCEPTIONS OF NNS TEACHERS

# Chapter 11

# DIFFERENCES IN TEACHING BEHAVIOUR BETWEEN NATIVE AND NON-NATIVE SPEAKER TEACHERS: AS SEEN BY THE LEARNERS

ESZTER BENKE, *Budapest Business School*
PÉTER MEDGYES, *Eötvös Loránd University*

## 1.    INTRODUCTION

The NS/NNS issue has come into the focus of professional attention: various aspects thereof have been discussed in recent years. This debate has produced several taxonomies and a special NS/NNS-related vocabulary has evolved. Even the legitimacy of the key term 'native speaker' has been called into doubt (Paikeday, 1985; Medgyes, 1994; Kramsch, 1997; Braine, 1999), and the number of professionals who assert that the separation of NSs and NNSs does not bear scrutiny is on the increase. Nevertheless, the NS/NNS dichotomy is still in current use.

In his seminal book, *Linguistic imperialism*, Phillipson (1992) tries to pull down the barriers between NS and NNS teachers, yet he strengthens the distinction by establishing the demarcation line between core and periphery countries. To the core belong countries, he claims, whose first language is English, whereas the periphery includes countries in which English is spoken as a second or foreign language. Phillipson argues that linguistic imperialism holds sway by maintaining six NS fallacies, one of which is the relative ineffectiveness of NNS teachers.

A similar division is offered by Holliday's (1994) categories of BANA/TESEP. While the BANA group typically comprises private sector

E. Llurda (Ed.), *Non-Native Language Teachers. Perceptions, Challenges and Contributions to the Profession*, 195—215.

adult institutions in *B*ritain, *A*ustralasia and *N*orth *A*merica, the TESEP group includes state education at *t*ertiary, *s*econdary and *p*rimary levels in the rest of the world. By employing ethnographical research methods, Holliday asserts that an approach which works in BANA countries cannot necessarily be implemented in a culturally different environment. Although he is not directly concerned with the NS and NNS dilemma, his assumptions bear obvious relevance to the issue.

The acknowledgment of cultural differences and multiculturalism requires a critical examination of the profession's most fundamental beliefs about the role of the English language and about what constitutes native and native-like language ability. By questioning the idealized status of the NS, Kramsch highlights the benefits of being a NNS, maintaining that 'the linguistic diversity that learners bring to language learning can contribute to the multiple possibilities of self expression' (Kramsch, 1997: 386). Learning a foreign or second language, therefore, does not constrain but rather enriches the mind.

This debate carries profound implications for the work of the classroom teacher as well. Most relevant from the perspective of the present study is the first full-length book (Medgyes, 1994), which is wholly devoted to the NS/NNS dichotomy and its impact on teacher education. Investigating differences in teaching attitudes between the two groups of teachers, Medgyes relies on data obtained from comprehensive questionnaire surveys and interviews. The differences are discussed around the focal points of personal characteristics, language proficiency, attitude to teaching the language as well as attitude to teaching culture. The results strongly suggest that these differences are in large measure due to linguistic factors.

Another book primarily concerned with the NS/NNS teacher issue (Braine, 1999) expounds hitherto unknown views held by NNS educators in ELT. This unique combination of autobiographical narratives, theoretical articles and research findings raises sociopolitical and sociocultural concerns and ponders their implications for teacher education.

While the NS/NNS issue has been extensively studied from the teacher's point of view, less has been written about learners' attitudes to teachers who come from divergent language backgrounds. Based on the findings of research elaborated in Medgyes (1994), the present study attempts to examine whether the differences as viewed by NS and NNS teachers respectively are in line with the learners' perceptions. A recent study (Árva & Medgyes, 2000) suggests a possible mismatch between stated and actual behaviour, a fact which may well account for divergencies in the results. Nevertheless, differences in language proficiency, allocated roles in the language class and teaching styles between NS and NNS teachers are confirmed by the empirical data obtained from classroom observations.

Thus far, this literature review has focussed on theoretical findings concerning the NS/NNS issue on the assumption that such findings can impinge on teaching practice. However, the reverse may also be true: practical problems may well designate areas for research. An area which has sparked off heated debate in the past decade concerns the socio-political constraints related to the employment and non-employment of NNSs. In defiance of NS superiority, numerous papers and research accounts in professional journals demand equal job opportunities. Regrettably, such voices often fall on deaf ears at the decision-making levels of educational institutions the world over.

The growing interest in the question of NS and NNS teachers is also acknowledged by the inclusion of the topic in the TESOL Research Agenda (June 2000) as an item in 'Priority Research Areas and Questions'. In this TESOL document, the following NS/NNS-related questions are offered for further research:

- What challenges do NNSs face in teacher education and professional development in and outside the United States?
- To what extent, if any, are issues related to NNS professionals addressed by the TESOL teacher preparation curriculum?
- What kinds of support system are in place to assist novice teachers (NSs and NNSs alike) to successfully make the transition from preservice programs to the job situation?
- In what ways can TESOL programs capitalize on the skills and resources that NNSs bring to the TESOL classroom?
- How can collaboration between NNS and NS teachers be facilitated?

Harking back to earlier research indicated above, the present study wishes to contribute to the NS/NNS debate by seeking answers to the following questions:

- In the ESL/EFL learners judgment, which are the most characteristic features of NS and NNS teachers?
- In which aspects of teaching behaviour are the differences between the two groups the most apparent?
- To what extent do learners' perceptions correspond to those held by the teachers themselves?

## 2.    THE STUDY

### 2.1    The respondents

A total of 422 Hungarian learners of English, all NSs of Hungarian, participated in the study. The selection of respondents was determined by two factors:

- All of them had been exposed to more than a year of English language instruction offered by both NS and NNS teachers.
- They were at minimum lower intermediate level of proficiency.

The characteristics of respondents are reported in percentages in Table 1.

As shown in Table 1, the largest proportion of respondents came from ordinary or bilingual secondary schools, either grammar or vocational. Among the institutions of higher education, different kinds of colleges and universities were included. Language learners from private language schools are also represented in the study. (For a detailed list of participating schools, see Appendix A.)

To ensure easier access to data collection and a higher return rate, nearly three fourths of the respondents were recruited from Budapest and the rest from the countryside. This imbalance may also be justified by the geographical distribution of native teachers: the capital city and other large cities offer better employment possibilities and more favourable conditions as compared to rural educational institutions. Since two thirds of the respondents attended secondary school at the time of the survey, the majority of the population under study is below 20 years of age. In terms of gender, the proportion is well-balanced, with 47.9% males and 51.7% females. On average, the respondents were fairly experienced learners, and their English-language proficiency level ranged between intermediate and advanced. Considering the fact that all of them were studying English in Hungary, it is no surprise that they had been exposed to NS teacher instruction to a much lesser extent than to instruction provided by fellow Hungarians. The high percentage of the missing answers provided for 'years of NS teacher's instruction' is the result of data omission. The categorization of the apparent diversity of answers would have posed a serious threat to the reliability of the study. No subject, however, with less that a year's NS instruction was included in the sample.

*Table 1.* Participant characteristics

|  |  |  | Frequency | Percent |
|---|---|---|---|---|
| School type | Secondary school (vocational+grammar) |  | 59 | 14.0 |
|  | Bilingual secondary school (vocational+grammar) |  | 205 | 48.6 |
|  | College (teacher training, business) |  | 26 | 6.2 |
|  | University |  | 92 | 21.8 |
|  | Private language school |  | 32 | 7.6 |
|  | Missing |  | 8 | 1.9 |
|  |  | Total | 422 | 100 |
| Location of school | Budapest |  | 305 | 72.3 |
|  | Outside Budapest |  | 117 | 27.7 |
|  |  | Total | 422 | 100 |
| Age of participant | <20 |  | 276 | 65.4 |
|  | 20-30 |  | 131 | 31.0 |
|  | 30> |  | 14 | 3.3 |
|  | Missing |  | 1 | 0.3 |
|  |  | Total | 422 | 100 |
| Gender | Male |  | 202 | 47.9 |
|  | Female |  | 218 | 51.7 |
|  | Missing |  | 2 | 0.5 |
|  |  | Total | 422 | 100 |
| Years of English studies | <5 |  | 82 | 19.4 |
|  | 5-10 |  | 250 | 59.2 |
|  | 10> |  | 80 | 18.9 |
|  | Missing |  | 10 | 2.5 |
|  |  | Total | 422 | 100 |
| Years of NS teacher's instruction | <2 |  | 219 | 51.8 |
|  | 2-3 |  | 119 | 28.2 |
|  | 4-5 |  | 51 | 12.1 |
|  | 6> |  | 10 | 2.5 |
|  | Missing |  | 23 | 5.4 |
|  |  | Total | 422 | 100 |
| Level of language proficiency | Lower intermediate |  | 27 | 6.4 |
|  | Intermediate |  | 92 | 21.8 |
|  | Upper intermediate |  | 179 | 42.4 |
|  | Advanced |  | 100 | 23.7 |
|  | Missing |  | 24 | 5.7 |
|  |  | Total | 422 | 100 |

## 2.2    The instrument

The research instrument applied was a multi-item questionnaire. (For a translated version of the questionnaire, see Appendix B.) As pointed out above, the main purpose of the study was to investigate learners' perceptions of the differences between NS and NNS teachers of English, and the process of questionnaire development was facilitated by the results of two earlier studies (Medgyes, 1994; Árva & Medgyes, 2000). For fear of getting lost in details, only those aspects of teaching which had been found relevant by the studies referred to above were included in the questionnaire. (For the perceived differences in teaching behaviour between NS and NNS teachers, see Appendix C.) After the draft questionnaire was piloted on a small sample, several modifications prompted by expert validation as well as by verbal protocols were carried out.

The final instrument was a four-page questionnaire broken down into five sections. The cover letter gave a brief rationale for the survey, instructions for the completion of the questionnaire, and a request that the questionnaire be completed and returned within a week. To increase the level of reliability, the researchers' own learners were not involved in the survey and personal identification was not required.

The first section of the questionnaire contained eight questions which asked for background information (see 2.1). The second and third sections each contained a set of 23 items, one designed for NNS and an identical set for NS teachers. The respondents had to apply a five-point Likert-type scale to assess the extent to which these statements, in their view, characterized NNS and NS teachers, respectively. The statements covered classroom management issues as well as personal, albeit teaching-related, characteristics. The fourth section comprised eleven provocative statements which referred to both NS and NNS teachers within the framework of a Likert scale scoring design. The open-ended items in the last section elicited information about the potential advantages and disadvantages of NS and NNS teachers.

## 2.3    Procedures

The exceptionally high return rate (91%) of the questionnaires was possibly due to the careful selection of respondents as well as to thorough preliminary arrangements. Colleagues willing to distribute the questionnaires were asked to perform in-class administration as this allowed continuous monitoring and immediate assistance with the completion if necessary. The informal and spontaneous feedback provided by colleagues both on the questions and their learners' reactions and verbal comments also proved helpful in interpreting the results. A number of respondents expressed their wish to read the final paper—an indication that the majority took their task seriously.

For the central part of the questionnaire eliciting differences between NS and NNS teachers as well as for the concluding miscellaneous statements, means and standard deviations were calculated from students' perceptions marked on the Likert scale. To test the significance of the observed differences, a paired-sample t-test was run on the data-set.

# 3.    RESULTS AND DISCUSSION

In the sections below, the results of the data analysis of the questionnaire are presented and discussed.

## 3.1    Non-native speaker teachers

Table 2 presents learners' attitudes to and opinions about NNS teachers. The statements expressed in means and percentages are ranked according to the degree of agreement, in descending order.

*Table 2*. Responses for NNS teachers—as seen by the learners

| Statement | Likert Mean | SD | Ø answer % 0 | Strongly disagree———strongly agree % 1 | 2 | 3 | 4 | 5 |
|---|---|---|---|---|---|---|---|---|
| Assigns a lot of homework | 4.04 | 1.23 | 2.4 | 5.7 | 11.6 | 3.3 | 29.6 | 47.4 |
| Prepares conscientiously for the lessons | 3.94 | 1.12 | 2.6 | 3.8 | 10.9 | 8.8 | 37.4 | 36.5 |
| Corrects errors consistently | 3.72 | 1.22 | 2.1 | 3.3 | 20.9 | 7.8 | 33.9 | 32.0 |
| Prepares learners well for the exam | 3.51 | 1.15 | 2.9 | 3.8 | 22.5 | 9.5 | 43.1 | 18.2 |
| Assesses my language knowledge realistically | 3.50 | 1.20 | 3.1 | 5.2 | 19.9 | 15.6 | 33.9 | 22.3 |
| Relies heavily on the coursebook | 3.22 | 1.36 | 2.6 | 12.3 | 27.5 | 2.1 | 37.7 | 17.8 |
| Is interested in learners' opinion | 3.19 | 1.31 | 2.1 | 7.3 | 35.3 | 5.5 | 30.8 | 19.0 |

| | | | | | | | | |
|---|---|---|---|---|---|---|---|---|
| Puts more emphasis on grammar rules | 3.16 | 1.28 | 2.1 | 8.1 | 33.9 | 4.5 | **36.7** | 14.7 |
| Sticks more rigidly to lesson plan | 3.13 | 1.13 | 2.4 | 4.5 | 36.5 | 5.2 | **45.0** | 6.4 |
| Is too harsh in marking | 3.13 | 1.17 | 2.5 | 13.0 | **47.6** | 6.6 | 24.4 | 5.9 |
| Sets a great number of tests | 3.09 | 1.33 | 2.6 | 11.1 | 33.2 | 4.5 | **33.4** | 15.2 |
| Prefers traditional forms of teaching | 3.06 | 1.14 | 4.1 | 7.3 | 29.4 | 18.2 | **32.5** | 8.5 |
| Applies pair work regularly in class | 3.05 | 1.35 | 2 | 12.1 | **34.8** | 2.8 | 32.7 | 15.6 |
| Uses ample supplementary material | 3.03 | 1.28 | 2.6 | 9.0 | **38.6** | 3.1 | 33.9 | 12.8 |
| Applies group work regularly in class | 2.81 | 1.30 | 2.4 | 14.7 | **39.6** | 2.8 | 30.8 | 9.7 |
| Directs me towards autonomous learning | 2.73 | 1.19 | 2.3 | 14.5 | **36.5** | 13.5 | 27.5 | 5.7 |
| Runs interesting classes | 2.7 | 1.21 | 2.1 | 10.0 | **52.1** | 1.2 | 26.5 | 8.1 |
| Is happy to improvise | 2.64 | 1.22 | 2.4 | 16.8 | **38.4** | 12.6 | 22.5 | 7.3 |
| Speaks most of the time during the lesson | 2.62 | 1.2 | 2.6 | 13.5 | **49.1** | 2.1 | 26.5 | 6.2 |
| Provides extensive information about the culture | 2.6 | 1.28 | 2.1 | 16.8 | **45.5** | 6.2 | 18.5 | 10.9 |
| Focuses primarily on speaking skills | 2.54 | 1.18 | 2.5 | 15.9 | **47.2** | 5.2 | 24.2 | 5.0 |
| Prefers teaching 'differently' | 2.38 | 1.08 | 2.4 | 19.4 | **43.8** | 17.1 | 12.8 | 4.5 |
| Is impatient | 1.99 | 1.15 | 2.6 | **41.5** | 34.6 | 6.2 | 11.1 | 4.0 |

The bold type in the table indicates the view of the majority of the respondents who agreed or disagreed with the statement. Thus, the top part of the table lists the most characteristic features of the NN teacher, whereas characteristics regarded as the least typical are presented in the lower part of the table. It is interesting to note that 77%, 73.9% and 65.9% of the respondents claimed, on the one hand, that NNS teachers would always or often give a lot of homework, plan their lessons thoroughly, and consistently check for errors. On the other hand, the relatively low means for the last two items indicate that NNS teachers never or rarely lose their patience (76.1%) and tend to apply middle-of-the-road methods (63.2%).

## 3.2 Native speaker teachers

As opposed to Table 2, Table 3 shows learners' judgments about NS teachers.

*Table 3.* Responses for NS teachers—as seen by the learners

| | Likert | | Ø answer % | strongly disagree————strongly agree % | | | | |
|---|---|---|---|---|---|---|---|---|
| Statement | Mean | SD | 0 | 1 | 2 | 3 | 4 | 5 |
| Focuses primarily on speaking skills | 3.96 | 1.31 | 2.9 | 5.7 | 12.1 | 4.7 | 32.2 | 42.4 |
| Is happy to improvise | 3.68 | 1.41 | 2.1 | 6.6 | 18.0 | 8.1 | 32.5 | 32.7 |
| Provides extensive information about the culture | 3.62 | 1.38 | 2.4 | 8.1 | 22.0 | 4.0 | 28.7 | 34.8 |
| Is interested in learners' opinion | 3.53 | 1.39 | 2.5 | 11.4 | 18.2 | 4.7 | 33.6 | 29.6 |
| Applies group work regularly in class | 3.48 | 1.31 | 2.6 | 7.8 | 23.7 | 3.1 | 39.3 | 23.5 |
| Runs interesting classes | 3.42 | 1.43 | 2.4 | 12.8 | 21.8 | 2.6 | 32.9 | 27.5 |
| Prepares conscientiously for the lessons | 3.41 | 1.26 | 2.7 | 8.5 | 24.6 | 8.8 | 28.9 | 26.5 |
| Prefers teaching 'differently' | 3.38 | 1.37 | 2.2 | 8.5 | 20.1 | 14.7 | 34.8 | 19.7 |
| Assesses my language knowledge realistically | 3.36 | 1.17 | 3.3 | 5.9 | 20.9 | 19.2 | 34.1 | 16.6 |
| Applies pair work regularly in class | 3.34 | 1.41 | 2.4 | 13.5 | 22.3 | 2.6 | 36.0 | 23.2 |
| Uses ample supplementary material | 3.24 | 1.36 | 2.6 | 10.2 | 29.6 | 5.2 | 31.8 | 20.6 |
| Corrects errors consistently | 3.21 | 1.26 | 3.0 | 7.1 | 30.8 | 10.0 | 32.7 | 16.4 |
| Speaks most of the time during the lesson | 3.00 | 1.37 | 2.1 | 13.5 | 35.8 | 2.4 | 30.1 | 16.1 |
| Sticks more rigidly to lesson plan | 2.76 | 1.46 | 2.4 | 21.8 | 34.4 | 5.2 | 17.5 | 18.7 |
| Prepares learners well for the exam | 2.76 | 1.28 | 3.4 | 16.8 | 34.1 | 9.7 | 27.5 | 8.5 |
| Directs me towards autonomous learning | 2.52 | 1.18 | 2.9 | 25.6 | 29.4 | 13.0 | 23.9 | 5.2 |

| Prefers traditional forms of teaching | 2.36 | 1.19 | 2.6 | 26.5 | 32.7 | 22.5 | 8.1 | 7.6 |
|---|---|---|---|---|---|---|---|---|
| Assigns a lot of homework | 2.33 | 1.27 | 2.5 | 28.0 | 41.5 | 3.6 | 16.6 | 7.8 |
| Is too harsh in marking | 2.28 | 1.18 | 3.3 | 27.5 | 39.3 | 10.0 | 15.2 | 4.7 |
| Relies heavily on the coursebook | 2.18 | 1.15 | 2.1 | 41.9 | 29.6 | 3.6 | 12.6 | 10.2 |
| Puts more emphasis on grammar rules | 2.03 | 1.19 | 2.2 | 36.7 | 41.2 | 4.5 | 11.1 | 4.3 |
| Sets a great number of tests | 1.97 | 1.46 | 2.6 | 42.9 | 33.9 | 5.9 | 10.4 | 4.3 |
| Is impatient | 1.92 | 1.28 | 2.5 | 52.6 | 24.6 | 4.7 | 6.4 | 9.2 |

Not surprisingly, NS teachers' preoccupation with practising the speaking skills figures at the top of the list ('strongly agree' and 'agree' together amounting to 74.6%). This is followed by their preference for supplying cultural information and a flair for deviating from their lesson plan (63,5%). The results at the bottom of the scale suggest that NN teachers are very patient, just as much as their NS colleagues. In addition, it was generally agreed that the NS is a patient, permissive and experimenting type of teacher, reluctant to set tests and spend time on grammar development. Mention should also be made about the high proportion of indecisive answers that the statement 'prefers traditional forms of teaching' elicited. It seems that, in spite of the numerous modifications carried out during the validation process of the questionnaire, this statement remained a red herring for reasons unbeknown to the researchers.

## 3.3    Comparing results

Having performed the t-test, it turns out that with the exception of one item ('is impatient' $t = .809$, $p = .419$), all the rest reveal statistically significant differences ($p < .05$) in teaching behaviour between NS and NNS teachers. Thus it may be said that NNS teachers, on the whole, are more demanding, thorough and traditional in the classroom than their NS colleagues, who are more outgoing, casual and talkative. An interesting point: both groups of teachers were found to be patient—equally patient, as a matter of fact!

## 3.4    Miscellaneous statements

As indicated earlier, the fourth section of the questionnaire consisted of provocative claims about NS and NNS teachers. Table 4 shows the means and the percentages for each statement, arranged from the highest in descending order.

*Table 4.* Responses to miscellaneous statements

| Statement | Likert | | Ø answer % | Strongly disagree—strongly agree % | | | | |
|---|---|---|---|---|---|---|---|---|
| | Mean | SD | 0 | 1 | 2 | 3 | 4 | 5 |
| It is important that we should be able to translate. | 4.40 | 0.95 | 1.9 | 2.6 | 2.6 | 8.5 | 23.5 | 60.9 |
| In an ideal situation both native and non-native teacher should teach you. | 4.40 | 1.04 | 1.6 | 3.1 | 4.5 | 8.8 | 15.2 | 66.8 |
| A non-native teacher can give more help for a beginner. | 3.87 | 1.10 | 1.6 | 3.6 | 7.6 | 22.3 | 30.1 | 34.8 |
| A native speaker teaches speaking skills, conversation more effectively | 3.78 | 1.11 | 1.9 | 3.6 | 9.5 | 23.9 | 29.1 | 32.0 |
| Native speakers should teach at a more advanced level.1 | 3.65 | 1.06 | 1.7 | 4.0 | 8.1 | 30.3 | 32.0 | 23.9 |
| It does not matter what the teacher's native language is, the only thing that matters is how they teach. | 3.53 | 1.13 | 1.7 | 3.3 | 14.9 | 32.2 | 22.5 | 25.4 |
| There is no harm in the teacher using Hungarian every now and then. | 3.43 | 1.22 | 1.9 | 5.2 | 20.9 | 23.2 | 23.9 | 24.9 |
| It is essential that everything should be in English in an English lesson. | 3.42 | 1.14 | 1.4 | 7.6 | 10.9 | 30.8 | 31.3 | 18.0 |
| A non-native speaker teaches writing skills more effectively. | 3.04 | 1.19 | 2 | 12.3 | 18.0 | 32.7 | 23.2 | 11.8 |
| I would be ready to trade a non-native teacher for a native any time. | 2.48 | 1.33 | 3.8 | 30.3 | 21.3 | 22.3 | 12.3 | 10.0 |
| I wish I had only non-native teachers of English. | 1.43 | 0.93 | 1.9 | 75.6 | 11.6 | 5.0 | 3.3 | 2.6 |

As Table 4 shows, there are two statements with the same mean scores (4.40) at the top, which suggests that these items were agreed by the overwhelming majority of respondents. While the percentage of positive responses ('strongly agree' and 'agree' together) for 'It is important that we should be able to translate' was 84.4, 'In an ideal situation both native and non-native teachers should teach you' received 82%. With respect to disagreements, 'I would be ready to trade a non-native teacher for a native any time' was the second least popular statement with a mean score of 2.48 (only 22.3% of the respondents agreed or strongly agreed). The item bringing up the rear was 'I wish I had only non-native teachers of English' with a mean score of 1.43, and merely 5.9% of the respondents agreeing or strongly agreeing. Apart from the statement referring to the importance of translation skills, the other three mentioned above carry the same message: both NS and NNS teachers play an important role in the classroom and neither group should be dispensed with. In this regard, one respondent commented on 'I would be ready to trade a non-native teacher for a native any time' with the expletive 'Rubbish!' in capital letters. This seems to express the general view.

## 3.5      Advantages and disadvantages

### 3.5.1      Non-native speaker teachers

Many features brought up by the earlier parts of the questionnaire were reiterated in the answers to the open questions in the last section. The advantage most frequently ascribed to the NNS teacher is related to teaching and explaining grammar. It was repeatedly claimed that NNS teachers have a more structured approach to teaching grammar and are better able to deal with grammatical difficulties, especially with those encountered by Hungarian learners. Thanks to their intimate familiarity with the local educational environment, NNS teachers can provide more thorough exam preparation and stand a better chance of detecting cheats. Being on the same wavelength as their learners, as one respondent put it, they can promote language learning more effectively. Furthermore, they are of invaluable help in supplying the exact Hungarian equivalent of certain English words and developing translation skills. On the other hand, the shared native language poses certain threats as well. Several respondents observed that NNS teachers are prone to use too much Hungarian during the lessons and sidetrack in their mother tongue. A recurrent criticism was levelled against their bad pronunciation and outdated language use.

### 3.5.2    Native speaker teachers

With respect to NS teachers, learners spoke highly of their ability to teach conversation classes and to serve as perfect models for imitation. They were also found to be more capable of getting their learners to speak. Several respondents noted that NS teachers are more friendly, and their lessons are more lively and colourful than their NNS colleagues'. Lower level learners, however, often found NS teachers difficult to understand, nor was explaining of grammar considered to be one of their strengths. In the absence a shared native language, runs an argument, NS teachers tend to leave problems unexplained. On a more general plane, as NS teachers and their learners come from different cultural and language backgrounds, a communication gap between them is often created.

It must be admitted, though, that the picture is far more complex than described above, tainted with individual tastes and preferences. It often occurred that a feature highly appreciated by one learner was seen as a weakness by another. In addition, learners often expressed their views in crude and emotional terms, barely using modal auxiliaries as softeners. Here are a few quotations for illustration:

'I am absolutely positive that a native teacher is more confident and can teach the language much better.' (a 22 year-old female university learner)

'I have been able to understand native English speech since I was taught by a native. It is an acoustic delight to listen to them. ... Yet they are spoilt and are sometimes too casual.' (a 22 year-old male university learner)

'Pronunciation, pronunciation, pronunciation!' (a 17 year-old secondary school learner)

'A native speaker finds it more difficult to understand a sentence that was thought of in Hungarian but actually said in English.' (a 32 year-old male from a language school)

'Non-natives take the English lesson too seriously—as if it was a question of life or death. If you make a mistake, you die.' (a 28 year-old male college learner)

'They are sometimes not very accurate and they can't spell—especially Americans.' (a 16 year-old secondary school learner)

## 4.     CONCLUSION

The objective of the study was to conduct research on differences in teaching behaviour between NSs and NNSs, as perceived by their learners. Whereas earlier studies were grounded in teachers' perceptions, on the one hand, and classroom observation, on the other, this study investigated the differences from a third perspective, namely that of the learners of English.

Out of the three research questions asked in the introduction, two were answered in the preceding chapters. After the typical behavioural patterns were identified first for NNS teachers and subsequently for their NS colleagues, the results were compared against each other, with the aim of finding the distinguishing features between the two groups of teachers. In the light of these results, it may be said that NS and NNS teachers form two easily identifiable groups, who adopt distinctly different teaching attitudes and teaching methods.

There is only one question left unanswered: To what extent do learners' perceptions correspond to those held by the teachers? In order to be able to answer this question, the findings of Medgyes (1994) (cf. Appendix C) need to be contrasted with the results obtained in the present study. It has to be admitted, however, that not all the features represented in the table by Medgyes (1994) were included in this study, just as there were certain items which were specifically designed for our questionnaire. Differences in wording for corresponding items also warrant caution in assessing the results.

For all these words of caution, it is legitimate to compare the two sets of data, and indeed the results yield very close correspondences: an item-by-item analysis of the respective features reveals that there is an almost perfect match between teachers' and learners' perceptions. The responses to the miscellaneous statements (Table 4), but especially the final part of the questionnaire inquiring about the respective advantages and disadvantages provide persuasive evidence for the existence of distinctive features between the two cohorts of teachers.

Medgyes (1994) reiterated that the establishment of differences carries no value judgment: neither group is supposed to be better on account of their specific teaching styles. This assumption was confirmed by the learners' reactions to the provocative statements in the questionnaire: the results summarised in Table 4 seem to prove that learners appreciate both groups of teachers for what they can do best in the classroom. An overwhelming majority of the respondents argued that in an ideal situation both NS and NNS teachers should be available to teach them, stressing that they would be ill-prepared to dispense with the services of either group.

This study aimed to complement the findings produced by an examination of teachers' perceptions and classroom observation with that of the learners, thus adding the third leg of a tripod. At the same time, it cannot be denied that the scope of this study was obviously limited as it canvassed a limited number of respondents, who cannot be considered to be a representative sample. It was also restricted in geographical terms: only the situation in Hungary was explored. Therefore, similar triangulative research projects should be launched before conclusive evidence concerning the NS/NNS distinction can be obtained. One aim of the project outlined above was precisely this: to induce further research in the area.

## 5.     ACKNOWLEDGMENTS

The authors would like to express their gratitude to the respondents of the study and also to those colleagues who kindly contributed to the administration of the questionnaires.

## 6.     REFERENCES

Árva,V.& Medgyes, P. (2000). Native and non-native teachers in the classroom. *System, 28*, 355-372.

Braine, G. (Ed.) (1999). *Non-native educators in English language teaching*. Mahwah, NJ: Lawrence Erlbaum Associates.

Holliday, A. (1994). *Appropriate methodology and social context*. Cambridge: Cambridge University Press.

Kramsch, C. (1997). The privilege of the non-native speaker. *PMLA, 112*, 359-369.

Medgyes, P. (1994). *The non-native teacher*. London: Macmillan. (1999) 2nd edition. Ismaning: Max Hueber Verlag.

Paikeday, T.M. (1985). *The native speaker is dead!* Toronto: Paikeday Publishing Inc.

Phillipson, R. (1992). *Linguistic imperialism*. Oxford: Oxford University Press.

TESOL Research Agenda. (2000) Available: http://www.tesol.org/assoc/bd/0006research agenda03.html

## APPENDIX A

**List of schools participating in the study (in alphabetical order)**
Budapest Business School, Faculty of Commerce, Catering and Tourism
Budapest University of Technology and Economics
Calvinist Secondary Grammar School, Sárospatak
ELTE Centre for English Teacher Training, School of English and American Studies, Budapest
International House Language School, Budapest
Karinthy Frigyes Bilingual Secondary School, Budapest
Pázmány Péter Catholic University, English Department, Piliscsaba
Technical Vocational and Secondary Grammar School, Budapest
University of Veszprém, English Department, Veszprém

## APPENDIX B

Dear Participant,

With this survey we would like to obtain information on the attitudes of Hungarian learners of English to native and non-native teachers of English. We are interested to find out about the differences between native and non-native teachers as perceived by the learners. Please fill in the questionnaire by circling the appropriate answers and complete the questions in the final part. It will not take more than 20 minutes to answer the questions. The questionnaire is anonymous. All data will be handled confidentially, but we are happy to share our findings with you if you like.

Thank you for your help,

Eszter Benke and Péter Medgyes
e.benke@axelero.hu

    I.   Age of respondent: .............................

   II.  Gender:   male / female

  III.  Years of English study ..............................

  IV.  Level of language proficiency (based on course-book currently used):
      lower intermediate / intermediate / upper intermediate / advanced

   V.  How many non-native teachers of English have you had?
      .............................

  VI.  How many native teachers of English have you had?
      .............................

 VII.  How long have you been taught / were you taught by natives?
      .............................

VIII.  Institution where you are currently studying English
      secondary school / bilingual secondary school / college / university / language school

### On non-native teachers

Please decide whether the following statements are typical/true of your native teachers of English and indicate the extent to which you agree with them.

| | |
|---|---|
| Strongly disagree | - 1 |
| Disagree | - 2 |
| Neither agree, nor disagree | - 3 |
| Agree | - 4 |
| Strongly agree | - 5 |

### The non-native speaker teacher ...

| | | | | | | |
|---|---|---|---|---|---|---|
| 1. NNS | sticks more rigidly to lesson plan | 1 | 2 | 3 | 4 | 5 |
| 2. NNS | is too harsh in marking | 1 | 2 | 3 | 4 | 5 |
| 3. NNS | prepares learners well for the exam | 1 | 2 | 3 | 4 | 5 |
| 4. NNS | applies pair work regularly in class | 1 | 2 | 3 | 4 | 5 |
| 5. NNS | applies group work regularly in class | 1 | 2 | 3 | 4 | 5 |
| 6. NNS | prefers traditional forms of teaching | 1 | 2 | 3 | 4 | 5 |
| 7. NNS | speaks most of the time during the lesson | 1 | 2 | 3 | 4 | 5 |
| 8. NNS | sets a great number of tests | 1 | 2 | 3 | 4 | 5 |
| 9. NNS | directs me towards autonomous learning | 1 | 2 | 3 | 4 | 5 |
| 10. NNS | is impatient | 1 | 2 | 3 | 4 | 5 |
| 11. NNS | is happy to improvise | 1 | 2 | 3 | 4 | 5 |
| 12. NNS | focuses primarily on speaking skills | 1 | 2 | 3 | 4 | 5 |
| 13. NNS | puts more emphasis on grammar rules | 1 | 2 | 3 | 4 | 5 |
| 14. NNS | prefers teaching 'differently' | 1 | 2 | 3 | 4 | 5 |
| 15. NNS | relies heavily on the coursebook | 1 | 2 | 3 | 4 | 5 |
| 16. NNS | prepares conscientiously for the lessons | 1 | 2 | 3 | 4 | 5 |
| 17. NNS | corrects errors consistently | 1 | 2 | 3 | 4 | 5 |
| 18. NNS | runs interesting classes | 1 | 2 | 3 | 4 | 5 |
| 19. NNS | assigns a lot of homework | 1 | 2 | 3 | 4 | 5 |
| 20. NNS | uses ample supplementary material | 1 | 2 | 3 | 4 | 5 |
| 21. NNS | assesses my language knowledge realistically | 1 | 2 | 3 | 4 | 5 |
| 22. NNS | provides extensive information about the culture of English-speaking countries | 1 | 2 | 3 | 4 | 5 |
| 23. NNS | is interested in learners' opinion | 1 | 2 | 3 | 4 | 5 |

## On native teachers

Please decide whether the following statements are typical/true of your native teachers of English and indicate the extent to which you agree with them.

Strongly disagree      - 1
Disagree      - 2
Neither agree, nor disagree  - 3
Agree      - 4
Strongly agree      - 5

## The native speaker teacher ...

| | | | | | | |
|---|---|---|---|---|---|---|
| 1. NS | sticks more rigidly to lesson plan | 1 | 2 | 3 | 4 | 5 |
| 2. NS | is too harsh in marking | 1 | 2 | 3 | 4 | 5 |
| 3. NS | prepares learners well for the exam | 1 | 2 | 3 | 4 | 5 |
| 4. NS | applies pair work regularly in class | 1 | 2 | 3 | 4 | 5 |
| 5. NS | applies group work regularly in class | 1 | 2 | 3 | 4 | 5 |
| 6. NS | prefers traditional forms of teaching | 1 | 2 | 3 | 4 | 5 |
| 7. NS | speaks most of the time during the lesson | 1 | 2 | 3 | 4 | 5 |
| 8. NS | sets a great number of tests | 1 | 2 | 3 | 4 | 5 |
| 9. NS | directs me towards autonomous learning | 1 | 2 | 3 | 4 | 5 |
| 10. NS | is impatient | 1 | 2 | 3 | 4 | 5 |
| 11. NS | is happy to improvise | 1 | 2 | 3 | 4 | 5 |
| 12. NS | focuses primarily on speaking skills | 1 | 2 | 3 | 4 | 5 |
| 13. NS | puts more emphasis on grammar rules | 1 | 2 | 3 | 4 | 5 |
| 14. NS | prefers teaching 'differently' | 1 | 2 | 3 | 4 | 5 |
| 15. NS | relies heavily on the coursebook | 1 | 2 | 3 | 4 | 5 |
| 16. NS | prepares conscientiously for the lessons | 1 | 2 | 3 | 4 | 5 |
| 17. NS | corrects errors consistently | 1 | 2 | 3 | 4 | 5 |
| 18. NS | runs interesting classes | 1 | 2 | 3 | 4 | 5 |
| 19. NS | assigns a lot of homework | 1 | 2 | 3 | 4 | 5 |
| 20. NS | uses ample supplementary material | 1 | 2 | 3 | 4 | 5 |
| 21. NS | assesses my language knowledge realistically | 1 | 2 | 3 | 4 | 5 |
| 22. NS | provides extensive information about the culture of English-speaking countries | 1 | 2 | 3 | 4 | 5 |
| 23. NS | is interested in learners' opinion | 1 | 2 | 3 | 4 | 5 |

Please indicate the extent to which you agree with the following statements

| | |
|---|---|
| Strongly disagree | - 1 |
| Disagree | - 2 |
| Neither agree, nor disagree | - 3 |
| Agree | - 4 |
| Strongly agree | - 5 |

Please list some advantages and disadvantages emerging from being taught by a native and a non-native teacher.

| | | | | | | |
|---|---|---|---|---|---|---|
| 24. | A non-native teacher can give more help for a beginner. | 1 | 2 | 3 | 4 | 5 |
| 25. | A native speaker teaches speaking skills/conversation more effectively. | 1 | 2 | 3 | 4 | 5 |
| 26. | It does not matter what the teacher's native language is, the only thing that matters is how they teach. | 1 | 2 | 3 | 4 | 5 |
| 27. | In an ideal situation both native and non-native teacher teach you. | 1 | 2 | 3 | 4 | 5 |
| 28. | It is essential that everything should be in English in an English lesson, | 1 | 2 | 3 | 4 | 5 |
| 29. | A non-native speaker teaches writing skills more effectively. | 1 | 2 | 3 | 4 | 5 |
| 30. | I wish I had only non-native teachers of English. | 1 | 2 | 3 | 4 | 5 |
| 31. | There is no harm in the teacher using Hungarian every now and then. | 1 | 2 | 3 | 4 | 5 |
| 32. | It is important that we should be able to translate. | 1 | 2 | 3 | 4 | 5 |
| 33. | Native speakers should teach at a more advanced level. | 1 | 2 | 3 | 4 | 5 |
| 34. | I would be ready to trade a non-native teacher for a native any time. | 1 | 2 | 3 | 4 | 5 |

**Advantages:**
NS ...............................................................................
NNS ...............................................................................
**Disadvantages:**
NS ...............................................................................
NNS ...............................................................................

# APPENDIX C

Perceived differences in teaching behaviour between NESTs and non-NESTs (Medgyes, 1994: 58-59)

| NESTs | Non-NESTs |
|---|---|
| **Own use of English** | |
| Speak better English | Speak poorer English |
| Use real language | Use bookish language |
| Use English more confidently | Use English less confidently |
| **General attitude** | |
| Adopt a more flexible approach | Adopt a more guided approach |
| Are more innovative | Are more cautious |
| Are less empathetic | Are more empathetic |
| Attend to perceived needs | Attend to real needs |
| Have far-fetched expectations | Have realistic expectations |
| Are more casual | Are more strict |
| Are less committed | Are more committed |
| **Attitude to teaching the language** | |
| Are less insightful | Are more insightful |
| Focus on: | Focus on: |
|   fluency |   accuracy |
|   meaning |   form |
|   language in use |   grammar rules |
|   oral skills |   printed word |
|   colloquial registers |   formal registers |
| Teach items in context | Teach items in isolation |
| Prefer free activities | Prefer controlled activities |
| Favour groupwork/pairwork | Favour frontal work |
| Use a variety of materials | Use a single textbook |
| Tolerate errors | Correct/punish for errors |
| Set fewer tests | Set more tests |
| Use no/less L1 | Use more L1 |
| Resort to no/less translation | Resort to more translation |
| Assign less homework | assign more homework |
| **Attitude to teaching culture** | |
| Supply more cultural information | Supply less cultural information |

Chapter 12

# WHAT DO STUDENTS THINK ABOUT THE PROS AND CONS OF HAVING A NATIVE SPEAKER TEACHER?

DAVID LASAGABASTER & JUAN MANUEL SIERRA
*University of the Basque Country*

## 1.    INTRODUCTION

This paper is focused on the teaching of English as a foreign language in what Kachru (1985) defines as the Expanding Circle, that is to say, an example which would fit within the myriad of countries where English is learnt as a foreign language, as English in Europe is still considered to be a *foreign* rather than a *second* language by both linguists and society at large (Graddol, 2001). This Expanding Circle is put forward by Kachru in opposition to the Inner Circle (those countries in which English represents the first language of the population, such as Canada, USA, Australia, New Zealand, or Great Britain) and the Outer Circle (those wherein English is an additional language, such as Nigeria, Singapur or India). It is beyond any doubt that the increasing use of English as a lingua franca has brought about a clear decline in the proportion of the world population who speaks English as L1 (falling birth rates in English speaking countries should also be considered). According to Graddol (2001: 47), 'In the mid twentieth century, nearly 9% of the world's population grew up speaking English as their mother tongue. By 2050 that proportion wil be edging down to towards 5%'.

Graddol also states that for centuries native speakers have been in charge of establishing the standard language, but that this situation is about to change, as this percentual decline (we are far away from the time when the

E. Llurda (Ed.), *Non-Native Language Teachers. Perceptions, Challenges and Contributions to the Profession*, 217—241.

native speakers of English clearly exceeded in number those who spoke it as an L2) will have a deep impact on how English is going to be spoken, taught and learnt in the future. Graddol (1997; in Modiano, 2001) criticizes Kachru's three circles and claims that this distinction will not be useful in the twenty-first century, as it places the native speaker at the centre of global use of English and as the model of correctness. This author considers that the L2 speakers, who already clearly outnumber native speakers, will become the new ʿcentre of gravityʾ, whereas native speakers will find it very difficult to maintain their position as ʿrepresentatives of the tongueʾ.

However, and although this ever more dilated presence of English throughout the world is making the use of the term native competence increasingly irrelevant (as Rampton, 1990, highlights, this term has come in for a great deal of criticism), especially in the places where several languages are in contact (Lasagabaster, 1999), the touchy debate concerning whether the native speaker teacher (NST) or the non-native speaker teacher (NNST) is better when it comes to teaching a foreign language always remains present. And this despite the fact that multilingualism is replacing monolingualism all over the world, especially in formal settings of learning such as the school (Lasagabaster, 1998). As Seidlhofer (1999) points out, a very good case in point of this distinction can be observed in many British and North American institutions, whose diplomas for the Teaching of English as a Foreign Language (TEFL) are different depending on whether they are aimed at NSTs or NNSTs. Similarly, the volume edited by Braine (1999), although mainly focused on NNSTs working in North America, sets many examples of the discrimination faced up by NNSTs when searching for a teaching position.

Seidlhofer (1999) also highlights that language proficiency is usually associated with teaching competence, which is why native speakers are more often than not supposed to have a clear advantage over NNSTs. She blames the communicative approach for this situation, as a result of whose implementation competence in the target language has been overemphasized with respect to pedagogic competence. Nevertheless, she considers that being a native speaker, and therefore having a very high command of the target language, does not automatically imply the ability to identify which language may turn out to be more pedagogically effective. It is obvious that a NNST has gone through the same learning experience as that of their students, which should help them to pinpoint those linguistic and non-linguistic issues that can become too high a hurdle for their students to overcome and lead them to strategies aimed at facilitating the learning process. This is not the case of the NST, who having acquired the target language as an L1, has not undergone the same process. In fact, Seidlhofer (1996; in Seidlhofer, 1999), in a small-scale empirical study carried out with teachers of English in Austria, observed that the shared knowledge of the students' L1 was an important source of confidence for the NNSTs.

In the next paragraphs we will center on a handful of research studies which have examined the NST versus NNST dichotomy. To start with, Barratt & Kontra's (2000) data will be reviewed. These authors undertook three studies, two in Hungary (116 students and 58 teachers involved) and one in China (with 100 students and 54 teachers). Most of the respondents had had a NST and were asked to freewrite about their positive and negative experiences. The most valuable characteristic of NST turned out to be authenticity, and in fact the most positive comments were concerned with authentic pronunciation, wide vocabulary, and information about culture. Both the Hungarian and Chinese students also pointed out that NSTs exhibited a very relaxed attitude towards grades and error correction. However, they were seen as little fond of grammar, and due to their lack of knowledge of the students' L1 and culture, they were believed to lack the linguistic and cultural awareness that NNSTs have, which allows the latter to predict what may happen to be difficult for the students. Nevertheless, their main complaint with regards to NSTs had to do with the fact that most of them were not language teachers and lacked experience, which is why the authors of the study conclude that NSTs should not be hired by the sake of being native speakers, but rather that they should have teaching qualifications. Despite the fact that these two countries, namely Hungary and China, are (culturally and geographically) very distant, the respondents pinpointed almost identical factors in favour of and against NSTs.

In a second study, Tang (1997) asked 47 NNSTs about this matter and the respondents went for the native speaker in the areas of speaking, pronunciation, listening, vocabulary and reading, whereas the NNST was associated with accuracy rather than fluency. These results come to terms with Medgyes's (1994), as his study reflected that vocabulary, speaking and pronunciation happened to be the toughest areas for the NNSTs, whereas they were relatively at ease with grammar and reading. NSTs were thought to resort to more real language and to supply more cultural information. Samimy & Brutt-Griffler (1999) obtained the same answers, as native speakers were seen as more fluent speakers, whereas non-native speakers found their knowledge of the students' L1 to be a definitive advantage.

To finish with our brief review, we would like to mention a recent study by Árva & Medgyes (2000), in which the authors video recorded 10 teachers of English in Hungary who were later interviewed. Five of the participants were NSTs and the other half NNSTs. The former ranked grammatical knowledge as their main gap (one of them stated that 'Most native teachers I know never really came across grammar until they started teaching it'; Árva & Medgyes, 2000: 361) as well as their lack of knowledge of the students'

L1, whereas the latter admitted having problems with pronunciation, vocabulary and colloquial expressions, but felt at home when dealing with grammar. The analysis of the recorded lessons also demonstrated that NSTs were a rich source of cultural information and that they did not automatically correct every error, while their NNST counterparts resorted more often to error correction and provided less cultural content.

The picture to be drawn from these five research studies is rather evident: those involved in the teaching profession coincide in emphasizing that NSTs are more fluent and therefore better at pronunciation, vocabulary and speaking, whereas NNSTs are more at ease with accuracy (grammar) and can take advantage of sharing their students' L1. Medgyes (Bolitho & Medgyes: 2000) puts it bluntly, as native speakers speak better English, people tend to believe that they are better language teachers. Yet several studies (Barratt & Contra, 2000; Liu, 1999; Medgyes, 1994; Samimy & Brutt-Griffler, 1999) come to the conclusion that professionals strongly believe that professionalism is what really matters, irrespective of being a native speaker of the language concerned or a non-native speaker. But what do students think about this issue? This is the question on which we will try to shed some light in this article.

Although there are several research studies in which the teachers' opinions and perceptions to this debate have been analyzed, the number of studies dealing with the students' perceptions are very scant.

## 2.      METHOD

### 2.1      Subjects

The participants in this study were 76 university students in the age range of 18-36, with a mean age of 19.7. One quarter (19) were English Philology students; another quarter were Translation-Interpretation students, 30 were studying Basque Philology, 7 were in German Philology and 1 was studying Spanish Philology. They were informed that we were conducting a research study on the NST vs. NNST debate, and that we considered that their experience and opinions would surely contribute to providing much valuable information. All the participants volunteered to take part in the study.

More than half of these students (41 subjects) were enrolled in the first year, 11 in the second year, 21 in the third and only 3 in the fourth year of their specializations. The majority of them were female (60 participants; 78.9% of the sample), as is usually the norm in Humanities, whereas the percentage decreased considerably in the case of the male participants:

21.1% of the sample, that is to say, 16 students. The respondents were asked about the number of years they had spent studying English, and their answers ranged from 4 to 15 years, with an average of 9.2 years.

## 2.2 Instruments

The data were collected by means of both close (see Appendix A) and open (see Appendix B) questionnaires. We have distinguished between a close and an open questionnaire, because in the former the respondents just had to choose their degree of (dis)agreement with the proposed statement, whereas in the latter they were free to jot down their own ideas after some discussion.

In the close questionnaire the undergraduates worked on an individual basis and were asked about their opinion (whether they were more keen on a native or on a non-native teacher/lecturer) as regards the following: language skills, grammar, vocabulary, pronunciation, learning strategies, culture and civilization, attitudes and assessment, and this with respect to primary, secondary and tertiary education, as differences exist among teachers of different educational levels (Llurda & Huguet, 2003). Students were given five possibilities (a five-point Likert scale was used) with regard to each of the 42 statements included in the questionnaire so that they could show their opinion about the issue concerned: Strongly Agree (SA), Agree (A), Neither Agree Nor Disagree (NAND), Disagree (D) and Strongly Disagree (SD). However, and for the sake of clarity, these five categories will be reduced to three when analysing the results of the tables, in an attempt to make its interpretation more reader-friendly. Hence, the percentages of both the Strongly Agree (SA) and Agree (A) categories will be added to establish a unique category, those of the Strongly Disagree (SD) and Disagree (D) categories will become the second category, and the third one will correspond to the Neither Agree Nor Disagree (NAND) category.

As can be seen in the questionnaire, some items make reference to a native speaker and some others to a non-native speaker, so as to avoid mechanical answers on the part of the students. As a result of this some items were recodified (6-9, 18-21, 26-29, 34, and 37-42). In this way we facilitate the reading of the results by always referring to the category native speaker. Similarly, it has to be highlighted that, although in the questionnaire the assessment area was split up into six categories (listening, reading, speaking, writing, pronunciation and grammar), a mean was obtained for the purpose of clarity.

## 2.3 Procedure

Both questionnaires were completed in class. All the students were studying English as a subject at university, the English Philology and Translation students in one group, and the other philology students in another group. The participants firstly dealt with the close questionnaire in the belief that some of the issues put forward in it could lead them to a more rich and productive debate when it came to carrying out the open questionnaire. The students were given 15-20 minutes to cope with the close questionnaire. They were asked to avoid *politically correct* answers and try to be as honest as possible in their answers.

As for the open questionnaire, students were given 20-30 minutes for its completion. Once they had finished the close questionnaire, we briefly encouraged the students to express their opinions freely in small groups, trying to elaborate on the matters dealt with individually in the close questionnaire. They formed 17 groups of about 4 to 5 people and discussed the advantages and disadvantages of having either a NST or a NNST. After seeking for agreement within their groups, they had to summarize their opinions by writing their response in English.

A word of caution should be given when it comes to summarizing the students' opinions after the group discussion, as individual students' personal views and perceptions could be influenced and/or shaped by other students' opinions within the group. This entails a risk which has to be acknowledged; however, we do think that the richness of the debate and the wider range of issues dealt with is worth taking this risk. Moreover, if one or more students were in disagreement with the group, they could also express their opinion in a few words.

## 3. HYPOTHESES

Bearing in mind the aforementioned research studies, in this study the following three hypotheses are put forward:

HP1. In general students will not show a clear preference for either NSTs or NNSTs.

HP2. The respondents will prefer a NST in the specific areas of vocabulary, pronunciation, speaking, culture and civilization, attitudes and assessment, and a NNST in the areas of grammar, listening, reading and learning strategies.

HP3. There will be no differences in the students' preference when primary education (PE), secondary education (SE) and tertiary education (University) are compared.

HP4. With regard to the open questionnaire, we expect them to be consistent with the results apportioned in the close questionnaire. Thus the participants will acknowledge the advantages of NSTs in areas such as pronunciation, language authenticity and knowlege of English speaking countries' culture, whereas they will consider the the NNSTs' strengths inherent to the sharing of the students' L1 and as a facilitator on the foreign language learning process.

## 4. RESULTS

### 4.1 Results concerning the close questionnaire

In order to test our first three hypotheses, the percentage of answers given by the students in each of the aforementioned five categories will be considered in this section. However, and for the sake of clarity, these five categories will be reduced to three (as previously explained in section 2.2.) when analysing the results of the tables, in order to help the reader with the interpretation.

Concerning our first hypothesis, *HP1: In general students will not show a clear preference for either NSTs or NNSTs*, the results are exhibited in table 1:

*Table 1.* In general I would prefer a native speaker as a teacher

|                             | Percentage |
|-----------------------------|------------|
| Strongly Disagree           | 1.3%       |
| Disagree                    | 2.6%       |
| Neither Agree Nor Disagree  | 35.5%      |
| Agree                       | 47.4%      |
| Strongly Agree              | 13.2%      |

Half of the sample (50.6%) prefer a NST, 35.5% have no clear preference, and only 3.9% would choose a NNST. Therefore the general trend seems to indicate a preference for native teachers, although the percentage of those who have no clear-cut preference is rather high too. The next table refers to the same statement but considering different educational levels:

*Table 2.* I prefer a NST in PE, SE and at university. In general I prefer both

|                     | SD    | D     | NAND  | A     | SA    |
|---------------------|-------|-------|-------|-------|-------|
| Native in PE        | 4.1%  | 28.4% | 23%   | 33.8% | 10.8% |
| Native in SE        | 1.3%  | 10.5% | 27.6% | 47.4% | 13.2% |
| Native at University| 0%    | 2.7%  | 29.3% | 42.7% | 25.3% |
| In general, both    | 1.4%  | 5.4%  | 21.6% | 35.1% | 36.5% |

A clear trend can be observed in these results, as the higher the educational level, the greater the preference towards a NST. Thus, although in PE there is a slight imbalance in the results (32.5% of the students would rather have a NNST, 23% have no definitive answer, and 44.6% would prefer a NST), this tendency sharpens in SE (60.6% in favour of a NST) and is even more definitive at university level (68% would prefer a native lecturer). However, it is worth mentioning that almost 30% of the students chose the NAND option with respect to SE (27.6%) and university (29.3%). When students were offered the possibility of having both a NST and a NNST, those who agreed with this proposal represented 71.6% of the sample, this one being therefore the most widely supported possibility.

As for our second hypothesis, *HP2: The respondents will prefer a NST in the specific areas of vocabulary, pronunciation, speaking, culture and civilization, attitudes and assessment, and a NNST in the areas of grammar, listening, reading and learning strategies,* the students perceptions were as follows:

*Table 3.* A NST is better for some specific areas in general

|                          | SD    | D     | NAND  | A     | SA    |
|--------------------------|-------|-------|-------|-------|-------|
| Vocabulary general       | 1.3%  | 18.4% | 34.2% | 26.3% | 19.7% |
| Pronunciation general    | 0%    | 2.6%  | 15.8% | 44.7% | 36.8% |
| Speaking general         | 1.3%  | 7.9%  | 26.3% | 47.4% | 17.1% |
| Culture and Civilization | 3.9%  | 6.6%  | 18.4% | 56.6% | 14.5% |
| Attitudes to countries   | 1.3%  | 14.5% | 47.4% | 31.6% | 5.3%  |
| Attitudes to learning    | 1.3%  | 17.1% | 56.6% | 22.4% | 2.6%  |
| Assessment general       | 3.9%  | 19.5% | 39.6% | 27.8% | 9%    |

An analysis of the results shown in Table 3 seems not to fully validate our second hypothesis. Although there is a clear preference for a NST in the areas of pronunciation (81.5%), culture and civilization (71.1%) and speaking (64.5%), the percentage in favour of a NST in the area of vocabulary (46%) clearly diminishes. And if we consider the areas of positive attitudes towards English speaking countries (36.9%), the domain of assessment (36.8%), and finally, the development of more positive attitudes towards the learning of English (25%) this tendency is not so clear, being the NAND option (47.4%, 39.6%, 56.6% respectively) the one most respondents chose. With regard to the preference for a NNST, the respondents' viewpoints are apportioned in table 4:

*Table 4.* A NNST is better for some specific areas

|  | SD | D | NAND | A | SA |
|---|---|---|---|---|---|
| Grammar general | 14.5% | 25% | 43.4% | 13.2% | 3.9% |
| Listening general | 7.9% | 18.4% | 28.9% | 34.2% | 10.5% |
| Reading general | 2.6% | 10.5% | 61.8% | 19.7% | 5.3% |
| Strategies general | 9.2% | 36.8% | 32.9% | 18.4% | 2.6% |

The figures in this table indicate that only in the area of listening the students expressed their preference for a NST (44.7%); the NAND option was second (28.9%) and the preference for a NNST was the least voted with a 26.3%. On the contrary, the highest percentage (46%) showing preference for a NNST was in response to item 30 (*In general a native speaker would give me more strategies / ideas to learn better),* being NAND the second option (32.9%) and the NST choice last (21%). As for reading and grammar, respondents did not take sides in the dispute: in both cases the NAND option captured most of the students' responses, 61.8% and 43.4% respectively. In the area of grammar, however, the second highest percentage is in favour of the NNST (39.5%) whereas, when deciding on reading, the second position is taken by these in favour of a NST (25%), and the NNST option only reaches a 13.1%.

In the case of our third hypothesis, *HP3: There will be no differences in the students' preference when primary education (PE), secondary education (SE) and tertiary education (University) are compared,* the students' responses are exhibited in tables 5 and 6. The former encompasses the items in which the NST was supposed to be preferred by the students, and the latter, those in which the NNST was hypothesized to be the best option.

*Table 5.* Differences in the educational levels (PE, SE and university)

|  | SD | D | NAND | A | SA |
|---|---|---|---|---|---|
| Vocabulary PE | 1.3% | 18.4% | 50% | 22.4% | 7.9% |
| Vocabulary SE | 1.3% | 14.7% | 34.7% | 38.7% | 10.7% |
| Vocabulary university | 1.3% | 10.7% | 37.3% | 29.3% | 21.3% |
| Pronunciation PE | 0% | 5.3% | 31.6% | 39.5% | 23.7% |
| Pronunciation SE | 0% | 2.6% | 26.3% | 47.4% | 23.7% |
| Pronunciation university | 0% | 3.9% | 15.8% | 51.3% | 28.9% |
| Speaking PE | 1.3% | 5.3% | 40.8% | 42.1% | 10.5% |
| Speaking SE | 1.3% | 5.3% | 38.2% | 43.4% | 11.8% |
| Speaking university | 2.6% | 7.9% | 32.9% | 40.8% | 15.8% |

The data exhibited in table 5 above do not fully confirm our third hypothesis. There is an increasing tendency in favour of the NST as the educational level is higher. Thus, in the area of vocabulary the percentages range from 30.3% in PE or 49.4% in SE to 50.6% at university. As regards pronunciation, the differences cover from 63.2% in PE to 71.1% in SE and 80.2% at university. Finally, as for speaking, the differentiating percentages are 52.6%, 55.2% and 56.6% respectively.

However, there are differences in this increase of the respondents' preferences regarding vocabulary, pronunciation and speaking. The highest variation corresponds to the area of vocabulary, where between PE and university the difference is 20.3%. This variation is slightly lower when it comes to pronunciation: PE and university differ in 17%. Speaking is the area where the increase on the preference is the lowest: 4% between PE and university. Finally, it is worth mentioning that in the three areas it is always the level of PE where the option NAND gets a higher percentage if compared with SE and TE.

*Table 6.* Differences in the educational levels (PE, SE and university)

|                      | SD    | D     | NAND  | A     | SA    |
|----------------------|-------|-------|-------|-------|-------|
| Grammar PE           | 11.8% | 31.6% | 43.4% | 11.8% | 1.3%  |
| Grammar SE           | 6.7%  | 26.7% | 53.3% | 12%   | 1.3%  |
| Grammar university   | 9.2%  | 18.4% | 47.4% | 22.4% | 2.6%  |
| Listening PE         | 6.6%  | 19.7% | 34.2% | 32.9% | 6.6%  |
| Listening SE         | 7.9%  | 13.2% | 38.2% | 32.9% | 7.9%  |
| Listening university | 10.5% | 10.5% | 34.2% | 30.3% | 14.5% |
| Reading PE           | 3.9%  | 17.1% | 59.2% | 11.8% | 7.9%  |
| Reading SE           | 3.9%  | 13.2% | 61.8% | 15.8% | 5.3%  |
| Reading university   | 3.9%  | 9.2%  | 57.9% | 22.4% | 6.6%  |
| Strategies PE        | 10.5% | 40.8% | 36.8% | 10.5% | 1.3%  |
| Strategies SE        | 7.9%  | 39.5% | 35.5% | 15.8% | 1.3%  |
| Strategies university| 9.2%  | 31.6% | 32.9% | 23.7% | 2.6%  |

The results exhibited in table 6 maintain the trend observed in table 5, as there are differences in the students' preferences when the three educational levels are compared. The increasing tendency in favour of the NST as we ascend the educational level, which was shown by the data in table 5, is maintained when the areas of grammar, listening, reading and strategies are considered. The most striking results are those in the area of grammar, where the preference for a NNST in PE is 43.4% (whilst the NST obtains only 13.1%). On the contrary, when we look at the university level this tendency is not maintained, as can be seen in the percentages: 27.6% of the sample prefers a NNST, and a very similar percentage, 25%, supports the NST option. Therefore, the effect of the educational level is very outstanding: the higher the linguistic proficiency required, the more voted the NST option is.

## 4.2 Results concerning the open questionnaire

The total number of sentences produced by the students in the seventeen groups was 119, distributed as follows: 70 statements described the students' favourable judgements while 49 accounted for the disadvantages, and this with respect to both NSTs and NNSTs. If we take into account these two categories, the number of positive comments on NSTs amounts to 46, whereas NNSTs obtained 29. With regard to the cons of having a NST, participants generated 25 statements while the disadvantages of having a NNST were synthesized into 20. Students produced more responses to talk in favour of NSTs (46 vs. 28), negative statements being very balanced (25 for NSTs vs. 20 for NNSTs).

*Table 7.* Groups' statements

| No. of groups | Total no. of statements | No. of favourable statements | No. of unfavourable statements | NST Pros | NST Cons | NNST Pros | NNST Cons |
|---|---|---|---|---|---|---|---|
| 17 | 119 | 70 | 49 | 46 | 25 | 28 | 20 |

As far as the students' positive perceptions of NSTs are concerned, table 8 presents a rankordered summary of the participants' positive categories of responses. Two of them, pronunciation and cultural knowledge of English speaking countries clearly stand out representing 76% (13 groups) and 53% (9 groups) respectively:

*Table 8.* Students' positive comments about NSTs

| Categories | No. of groups |
|---|---|
| Pronunciation | 13 |
| More cultural knowledge of English speaking countries | 9 |
| Teaching certain areas | 7 |
| Listening | 6 |
| More knowledge of vocabulary | 5 |
| Speaking | 5 |
| Bilingualism | 2 |
| Writing | 1 |
| Reading | 1 |
| Educational levels | 1 |

In line with the studies by Barrat & Kontra (2000) our students valued the authenticity of NSTs with regard to pronunciation, vocabulary (including slang and idioms) and usage as we can see in the following responses:

- A native teacher has better pronunciation. (G3)
- More knowledge of idioms and vocabulary. (G6)
- Good knowledge of the language. (G9)

As far as the four skills are concerned participants expressed the following opinions:

- You get used to understanding natives. (G1)
- Listening to a native teacher is better to improve our listening. (G8)
- They have more experience in writing and reading. (G2)
- They speak better English than the non-native teacher. (G1)

Another advantage reported by the students was that having a NST would make them use more English:

- It's almost compulsory to speak in English (it's good to improve). (G7)
- You must ask him/her in English. (G9)
- You must speak in English all the time. (G13)

Our respondents also viewed NSTs as a resource they could refer to in order to augment their knowledge of other cultures:

- You can learn more about English speaking countries' culture. (G1).
- You can ask him/her about their country; it's more enjoyable. (G2)
- You get closer to their culture. (G7)

Some groups highlighted the NST's specific abilities *to teach* and *assess* certain areas:

- They can teach you strategies to learn the language. (G2)
- They teach you slang, idioms, etc. (new expressions). (G7)
- There could be more accuracy when testing pronunciation. (G3)
- They correct your grammar or pronunciation mistakes. (G7)

Other groups elaborated on the benefits of knowing the students' mother tongue, the effects of the L2 on the L1 or the suitability of NSTs for certain educational levels:

- If the native teacher knows our mother tongue he is better to explain the grammar and the doubts you have. (G8)
- Better fluency when he can't speak Spanish. (G10)
- It's better a native teacher when you are 5 or 6. (G11)

Table 9 exhibits the rank ordering of the negative categories of responses with regard to NSTs. Two themes—intelligibility and monolingualism—lead the ranking with the hot issue of NSTs' qualifications and teaching skills as a close runner-up.

*Table 9.* Students' negative comments about NSTs

| Categories | No. of Groups |
| --- | --- |
| Intelligibility | 8 |
| Monolingualism | 8 |
| Qualifications/teaching ability | 7 |
| Teaching style | 3 |
| Learning process | 1 |

As for intelligibility, although the participants attached great importance to the authenticity of NSTs' pronunciation, they also saw clear disadvantages in native articulation:

- If they have a non-standard English, it's really difficult to understand them. (G2)
- We think that they don't speak standard English. (G4)
- The pronunciation is more difficult to understand. (G13)

The participants had different degrees of bilingualism (Basque-Spanish) and most of them had some knowledge of other foreign languages besides English. With this linguistic background in mind, it is hardly surprising that the respondents critically acknowledged the disadvantages of monolingual NSTs. Especially relevant is the high percentage of sentences showing awareness of the importance of translation:

- When you have a low level maybe you can't understand him/her, if he/she doesn't know another language you know. (G1)
- They can't translate some words or idioms. (G4)
- In case the teacher doesn't know our language, you have problems to solve doubts. (G8)

Seven groups showed their concern over the capacity of NSTs to teach effectively:

- Normally, they don't have a degree in English. (G3)
- Their English can be very good but sometimes they haven't got the knowledge to explain it. (G12)
- They aren't aware of the difficulties of grammar. (G3)
- Sometimes they explain the grammar worse. (G1)

This students' distress has been dealt with by several authors, Thus, our students' comments come to terms with Astor's (2000: 18), who postulates professionalism as the only possible answer:

For a teacher to be competent only in one aspect—command of English—is not sufficient because the teaching of English requires more than intuitive knowledge of English grammar and syntax. A good teacher of English—or any other language, for that matter—should have a cognitive knowledge of the grammar and syntax of the target language; in other words, the teacher should be a linguist, or be linguistically educated. However, a teacher of English should be a specialist in pedagogy, psychology, and methodology as well.

Three groups touched upon NSTs' teaching styles or some of their psychological characteristics:

- A native teacher doesn't correct your pronunciation as much as a non-native teacher. (G3)
- A native teacher is more demanding when correcting mistakes in an examination. (G5)
- They demand more knowledge. (G9)

Finally, one group neatly summarized the difficulties of learning a foreign language:
- They never have studied English and they don't know the difficulties to learn it. (G4)

Our students thus seem to echo Widdowson's words, when he states the following:

For although native speakers obviously have the more extensive experience as English language users, the non-native speakers have had experience as English language learners. They have been through the process of coming to terms with English as another language. (Widdowson, 1992: 338)

The following table depicts the rank-ordered summary of the participants' positive categories of responses with respect to the NNST. We would like to point out that the areas of strategies/process of learning (12 groups) and bilingualism (7 groups) are the most often cited ones:

*Table 10.* Students' positive comments about NNSTs

| Categories | No. of Groups |
|---|---|
| Strategies/Learning process | 12 |
| Bilingualism | 7 |
| Grammar | 3 |
| Intelligibility | 2 |
| Achievable model | 1 |

Concerning the process of learning, a summary of the most conspicuous comments follows:

- They can understand better the mistakes we make, and why we make them. (G2)
- They have learnt before, so they have more experience to teach. (G3)
- A non-native teacher can compare the way of explaining the language
- with our mother tongue. (G5)
- They can teach us more strategies to learn. (G4)

When the participants reflected on the role played by the teacher's knowledge of their L1, that is to say, the benefits of having a bilingual teacher, they made abundant comments such as:

- If you have a problem with the meaning of a word, for example, she/he can translate into a language you know. (G1)
- They can explain to you in your own language. (G8)
- A non-native teacher from your own country can help you better understand English by comparing it to your language. (G11)

The domains of grammar and intelligibility were also mentioned.

- They provide better explanations for grammatical items. (G3)
- Listening is easier. (G13)
- If you speak quite badly, your teacher can understand you. (G13)

The students also made reference to the NNST as an achievable model (Cook, 1999):

- They make you realise you can get a good level with a language which is not your mother tongue. (G6)

In table 11 the respondents' negative viewpoints about the NNST are hierarchically ordered. As expected, the results show the other side of the coin if we compare this table with their preferences in table 5, which is why pronunciation arises as the main stumbling block for NNSTs:

*Table 11.* Students' negative comments about NNSTs

| Categories | No. of Groups |
|---|---|
| Pronunciation | 11 |
| Assessment/Teaching style | 3 |
| Vocabulary | 2 |
| Speaking | 1 |
| Language proficiency | 1 |
| Cultural knowledge | 1 |

Undoubtedly pronunciation is an area which really worries them:

- They can have very good pronunciation, but they won't have the original English accent. (G2)
- Sometimes pronunciation and their sentences sound artificial. (G7)
- If the teacher have pronunciation mistakes, the students may learn them. (G5)

Some groups expressed their concern for assessment and the NNST's teaching style, some of their comments putting it bluntly:

- You need more effort to pass the subject. (G1)
- You learn less. (G10)
- You don't practice much English. (G13)

Finally, they elaborate on areas such as vocabulary, culture and language proficiency. To set a few examples:

- They don't use colloquial expressions in their classes. (G3)
- They can't provide as much cultural knowledge as a native teacher. (G6)
- They don't have the same knowledge as the native speaker. (G9)

## 5.     CONCLUSIONS

Although the debate about the question of whether native or non-native speakers are better language teachers may appear as irrelevant and even counterproductive, as the studies by Medgyes (1994), Samimy and Brutt-Griffler (1999) and Liu (1999) conclude, it seemed to us that our students' perceptions about this matter should in any case be taken into account. Whereas the previously quoted three studies examined professionals' opinions (all of them with teaching experience), we were of the opinion that our students' perceptions should also be considered, as they could be different from that of those involved in the teaching world.

When students were asked if in general they would prefer a NST[1], 60.6% of them chose this alternative. However, when they were given the possibility of having both a NST and a NNST, the percentages were even higher 71.6%. These results coincide with Medgyes's (1994) conclusion, when he stated that had his students been given the latter option in his questionnaire, it would have been the most popular choice. In Llurda and Huguet (2003), Catalan non-native teachers also preferred this option when they were asked how many NNSTs and NSTs they would hire if they owned their own language school, with the particularity that primary teachers were much more favourable of NSTs than secondary teachers. Similarly, and speaking in general terms, our respondents went for the NST in the areas of pronunciation, culture and civilization, listening, vocabulary and speaking, whereas they preferred the NNST in the areas of grammar and strategies. In the rest of the areas, namely attitudes towards English speaking countries, attitudes towards the learning of English, assessment and reading the students did not take sides.

Our third hypothesis was not confirmed, as the students did show differences when the different educational levels were compared. In fact, respondents preferred a NST at university level in most areas, whereas this was not the case in PE. For example, common sense led us to hypothesize that in the domain of pronunciation their preferences would favour the NST from PE onwards, because it is widely believed that pronunciation is more easily acquired at an early age. Curiously enough, their choice was higher at university (80.2%) than in primary education (63.2%). These results seem to validate the design of the questionnaire, as the differentiation between educational levels turns out to be significant.

The conclusions to be drawn from the open questionnaire underline some important aspects and fully confirm our fourth hypothesis, as the results coincide with those obtained in the close questionnaire. Firstly, our students were clearly concerned about the benefits of a NST in pronunciation and culture. Our students' concern about pronunciation might be tempered by Mattix's (2000) proposal, who remarks that the usual anxiety showed by students in this area should be alleviated and on no account should it stigmatize L2 speakers by making them believe that language is identity. It is a fact that the immense majority of our students are aware of the impossibility of achieving a native accent in a formal context such as ours. Furthermore, Cook (1999) underlines the difficulties attached to the definition of a native accent (that of a Geordie, a Cockney, a Texan, a Nigerian, a New Zealander, ...?): a utopian endeavour indeed. Paradoxically enough, when students commented on the negative aspects of a NST, 8 groups out of 17 admitted that a native accent brought about intelligibility problems, in fact the top negative aspect in the open questionnaire.

Secondly, when the participants took their time to reflect and debate on the advantages of having a NNST, the results (70% of the groups) clearly showed that students highly valued the NNSTs as a resource of learning strategies throughout the process of learning English, and McNeill (this volume) further confirms this point. On the other hand, only one group commented on the benefits of the NST as language strategies provider.

Thirdly, the importance attached to the NNST being (at least) bilingual was neatly stated. These results come to terms with Seidlhofer (1999: 235), when she states that 'This makes non-native teachers uniquely suited to be agents facilitating learning by mediating between the different languages and cultures through appropriate pedagogy'. As a matter of fact, the importance of fostering cross-language comparisons and more discussion in class about the different languages of the students is once again underlined (Lasagabaster & Sierra, 2001), and in this respect the NNST has a clear advantage over the NST when the latter does not speak the students' L1. Tang (1997: 579) concludes that NNSTs 'not only play a pedagogical role in their classrooms, but they also serve as empathetic listeners for beginning and weak students, needs analysts, agents of change, (...)'. Most of the students' perceptions coincide with the advantages attributed to the NNST by Megdyes (1992): imitable models, more effective teaching of learning strategies, providers of more information about the language, anticipation of language difficulties, more empathy to the needs and problems of learners and benefits from sharing the learner's mother tongue.

Cook (1999) proposes the use of teaching methods that acknowledge the students' L1 and cites task-based learning as especially appropriate when dealing with what he calls *emphasis on the classroom internal goals*, so that students may develop their own goals rather than L2 user goals, that is to say, 'abilities that students acquire through L2 learning that can be defined independently of native speaker models' (Cook 1999: 198). In this way, proposals intended to make students benefit from the interface between mother tongue and foreign language learning should be encouraged. The implementation in the classroom of instruments such as students' diaries—which facilitate the difficult process of making explicit the students' procedures of reflection and help to construct the syllabus cooperatively (Sierra, 2001)—can contribute to change students' perceptions and assist them to find their own voice.

Fourthly, 7 groups expressed their preoccupation about the lack of professional qualifications and ability to deal with the teaching of grammar on the part of NSTs. In this sense Astor (2000) claims that professional judgement should be the only parameter under consideration when judging both the NST and the NNST's performance, as is the norm in any other discipline. The inclusion of consciousness raising activities in the L2 classroom (*e.g.*, debates or any other pedagogical intervention aimed at making explicit students' own learning experiences with NSTs and/or NNSTs) could be a possible solution to make students—and perhaps employers who hire people without pedagocial training—aware of the importance of the *ability to teach* rather than *only native(-like) proficiency* in the target language.

Last but not least, we would like to underline that we believe that this field of research is relevant for all those involved in the teaching of a foreign language, as these results should help us to reflect on our everyday work and help both NSTs and NNSTs to become aware of their weaknesses and strengths, which is a first step to endeavour to overcome the hurdles we may come across in our classes. And above all, they clearly show us what students believe, a very important question that has often been set aside and which should turn out helpful to beef up our teaching. For example, it is a fact that many NSTs do not learn the local language or become familiar with the local culture (Bolitho & Medgyes, 2000), a question widely mentioned as a handicap for the NST by students and which should make NSTs change their attitudes in this respect. As Barrat & Kontra (2000: 22) put it, 'The more the NS teachers learn about the host language, the better they will be able to teach (*i.e.*, to predict students' difficulties)'.

# 6. NOTES

[1] For further analysis of the effect of specialism (students who could become teachers of English in the short run versus students with other future perspectives) and previous learning experience (experience or not of a NST), see Lasagabaster & Sierra (2002).

# 7. REFERENCES

Árva, V. & Medgyes, P. (2000). Native and non-native teachers in the classroom. *System, 28*, 355-372.

Astor, A. (2000). A qualified non-native English-speaking teacher is second to none in the field. *TESOL Matters, 10*, 18-19.

Barratt, L. & Kontra, E.H. (2000). Native-English-speaking teachers in cultures other than their own. *TESOL Journal, 9* (3), 19-23.

Bolitho, R. & Medgyes, P. (2000). Talking shop: from aid to partnership. *ELT Journal, 54*, 379-386.

Braine, G. (1999). *Non-native educators in English language teaching.* Mahwah, NJ: Lawrence Erlbaum Associates.

Cook, V.J. (1999). Going beyong the native speaker in language teaching. *TESOL Quarterly, 33,* 185-209.

Graddol, D. (1997). *The future of English?* London: British Council.

Graddol, D. (2001). The future of English as a European language. *The European English Messenger, X* (2), 47-55.

Kachru, B.B. (1985). Standards, codification, and sociolinguistic realism: the English language in the outer circle. In R. Quirk & H.G. Widdowson (Eds), *English in the world: Teaching and learning the language and literatures.* Cambridge: Cambridge University Press. 11-30.

Lasagabaster, D. (1998). *Creatividad y conciencia metalingüística: Incidencia en el aprendizaje del inglés como L3.* Leioa: Universidad del País Vasco - Euskal Herriko Unibertsitatea.

Lasagabaster, D. (1999). El aprendizaje del inglés como L2, L3 o Lx: ¿En busca del hablante nativo? *Revista de Psicodidáctica, 8,* 73-88.

Lasagabaster, D. & Sierra, J.M. (Eds.) (2001). *Language awareness in the foreign language classroom.* Zarautz: Universidad del País Vasco - Euskal Herriko Unibertsitatea.

Lasagabaster, D. & Sierra, J.M. (2002). University students' perceptions of native versus non-native speaker teachers. *Language Awareness, 11,* 132-142.

Liu, J. (1999). Non-native-English-speaking professionals in TESOL. *TESOL Quarterly, 33,* 85-102.

Llurda, E. & Huguet, A. (2003). Self-awareness in NNS EFL primary and secondary school teachers. *Language Awareness, 12* (3&4), 220-233.

Mattix, M. (2000). Going further beyond the native speaker model: a remark concerning language models. *TESOL Quarterly, 34,* 328-329.

Medgyes, P. (1992). Native or non-native: who's worth more? *ELT Journal, 46,* 341-349.

Medgyes, P. (1994). *The non-native teacher.* London: Macmillan. (1999) 2nd edition. Ismaning: Max Hueber Verlag.

Modiano, M. (2001). Linguistic imperialism, cultural integrity, and EIL. *ELT Journal, 55,* 335-346.

Rampton, M.B.H. (1990). Displacing the 'native speaker': expertise, affiliation, and inheritance. *ELT Journal, 44* (2), 97-101.

Samimy, K.K. & Brutt-Griffler, J. (1999). To be a native or non-native speaker: Perceptions of 'non-native' students in a graduate TESOL program. In G. Braine (Ed.), *Non-native educators in English language teaching.* Mahwah, NJ: Lawrence Erlbaum Associates. 127-144.

Seidlhofer, B. (1996). 'It is an undulating feeling . . .' The importance of being a non-native teacher of English. *Vienna English Working Papers, 5* (1&2), 74-91.

Seidlhofer, B. (1999). Double standards: Teacher education in the expanding circle. *World Englishes, 18* (2), 233-245.

Sierra, J. M. (2001). Project work and language awareness: insights from the classroom. In D. Lasagabaster & J. M. Sierra (Eds.), *Language awareness in the foreign language classroom.* Zarautz: Universidad del País Vasco - Euskal Herriko Unibertsitatea. 177-198.

Tang, C. (1997). The identity of the non-native ESL teacher. On the power and status of non-native ESL teachers. *TESOL Quarterly, 31* (3), 577-579.

Widdowson, H.G. (1992). ELT and EL teachers: matters arising. *ELT Journal, 46* (4), 333-339.

# APPENDIX A. (CLOSE QUESTIONNAIRE)

## Native versus Non-native Teachers
- Age:
- Specialization:
- Academic year:
- Gender: ___ Male ___ Female
- Mother tongue (L1): ___ Basque ___ Spanish
  ___ Basque & Spanish
- How good is your knowledge of the following languages?:
  Basque: ___ Little ___ Good ___ Very good
  Spanish: ___ Little ___ Good ___ Very good
  English: ___ Little ___ Good ___ Very good
  Others: ___ Little ___ Good ___ Very good
- Have you ever been to an English speaking country? ___ Yes ___ No
- Have you ever had a native speaker of English as a teacher?
  ___ Yes ___ No
- How long have you been studying English? ___ years

Here are some statements about the Native versus non-native teachers issue. Please say whether you agree or disagree with these statements. There are no right or wrong answers. Please be as honest as possible. Answer with ONE of the following:

SA = Strongly Agree (Circle SA)
A = Agree (Circle A)
NAND = Neither Agree Nor Disagree (Circle NAND)
D = Disagree (Circle D)
SD = Strongly Disagree (Circle SD)

|  | (5) | (4) | (3) | (2) | (1) |
|---|---|---|---|---|---|
| **General** | | | | | |
| 1. In general I would prefer a native Speaker as a teacher | SA | A | NAND | D | SD |
| 2. In primary education I would prefer a native Speaker as a teacher | SA | A | NAND | D | SD |
| 3. In secondary education I would prefer a Native speaker as a teacher | SA | A | NAND | D | SD |
| 4. At university I would prefer a native Speaker as a teacher | SA | A | NAND | D | SD |
| 5. If I could choose, I would prefer to have both a native and a non-native teacher | SA | A | NAND | D | SD |

**Grammar**

6. In general a non-native teacher
is better at Explaining grammar. . . . . . . . . . . . SA    A    NAND  D    SD
7. In primary education a non-native
teacher is Better at explaining grammar. . . . . . SA    A    NAND  D    SD
8. In secondary education a non-native
teacher is Better at explaining grammar. . . . . . SA    A    NAND  D    SD
9. At university a non-native teacher
is better at explaining grammar. . . . . . . . . . . . SA    A    NAND  D    SD

**Vocabulary**

10. In general I would learn more
vocabulary with a native teacher . . . . . . . . . . SA    A    NAND  D    SD
11. In primary education I would learn
more vocabulary with a native teacher. . . . . . . SA    A    NAND  D    SD
12. In secondary education I would learn
more vocabulary with a native teacher. . . . . . . SA    A    NAND  D    SD
13. At university I would learn more
vocabulary with a native teacher. . . . . . . . . . . SA    A    NAND  D    SD

**Pronunciation**

14. In general my pronunciation would be
better with a native teacher . . . . . . . . . . . . . . SA    A    NAND  D    SD
15. In primary education my pronunciation
would be better with a native teacher. . . . . . . SA    A    NAND  D    SD
16. In secondary education my pronunciation
would be better with a native teacher. . . . . . . SA    A    NAND  D    SD
17. At university my pronunciation would
be better with a native teacher. . . . . . . . . . . . SA    A    NAND  D    SD

**Listening**

18. In general my listening would be
better with a non-native teacher . . . . . . . . . . . SA    A    NAND  D    SD
19. In primary education my listening
would be better with a non-native teacher. . . . . SA    A    NAND  D    SD
20. In secondary education my listening would
be better with a non-native teacher. . . . . . . . . . SA    A    NAND  D    SD
21. At university my listening would be
better with a non-native teacher. . . . . . . . . . . . SA    A    NAND  D    SD

**Reading**
22. In general my reading skills would
    be better with a native teacher . . . . . . . . . . . .   SA   A   NAND   D   SD
23. In primary education my reading skills
    would be better with a native teacher. . . . . . . .   SA   A   NAND   D   SD
24. In secondary education my reading skills
    would be better with a native teacher. . . . . . . .   SA   A   NAND   D   SD
25. At university my reading skills would
    be better with a native teacher. . . . . . . . . . . . .   SA   A   NAND   D   SD

**Speaking**
26. In general I would speak more fluently
    if i had a non-native teacher . . . . . . . . . . . . . .   SA   A   NAND   D   SD
27. In primary education I would speak more
    fluently if i had a non-native teacher. . . . . . . . .   SA   A   NAND   D   SD
28. In secondary education I would speak more
    fluently if i had a non-native teacher. . . . . . . . .   SA   A   NAND   D   SD
29. At university Ii would speak more fluently
    if i had a non-native teacher. . . . . . . . . . . . . . .   SA   A   NAND   D   SD

**Learning strategies**
30. In general a native speaker would give
    me more strategies/ideas to learn better . . . . . .   SA   A   NAND   D   SD
31. In primary education a native speaker would
    give me more strategies/ideas to learn better. . .   SA   A   NAND   D   SD
32. In secondary education a native speaker would
    give me more strategies/ideas to learn better. . .   SA   A   NAND   D   SD
33. At university a native speaker would
    give me more strategies/ideas to learn better. . .   SA   A   NAND   D   SD

**Culture and civilization**
34. I would learn more about english speaking
    countries with a non-native speaker . . . . . . . . .   SA   A   NAND   D   SD

**Attitudes**
35. I would have more positive attitudes towards
    english speaking countries and their speakers
    if i had a native teacher . . . . . . . . . . . . . . . . . .   SA   A   NAND   D   SD
36. I would have more positive attitudes towards
    the learning of English if i had a native teacher . .   SA   A   NAND   D   SD

**Assessment**

37. A non-native teacher would assess my listening
    comprehension better than a native speaker . . .  SA     A     NAND  D       SD
38. A non-native teacher would assess my reading
    comprehension better than a native speaker . . .  SA     A     NAND  D       SD
39. A non-native teacher would assess my speaking
    better than a native speaker . . . . . . . . . . . . . . .  SA     A     NAND  D       SD
40. A non-native teacher would assess my writing
    better than a native speaker . . . . . . . . . . . . . . .  SA     A     NAND  D       SD
41. A non-native teacher would assess my
    pronunciation Better than a native speaker . . . .  SA     A     NAND  D       SD
42. A non-native teacher would assess my knowledge
    of grammar better than a native speaker . . . . . .  SA     A     NAND  D       SD

## APPENDIX B. (OPEN QUESTIONNAIRE)

Experience with a native teacher:    \_\_\_\_ yes \_\_\_\_ no
*Would you prefer a native or a non-native teacher?*

NATIVE TEACHER

Pros                                   Cons

NON-NATIVE TEACHER

Pros                                   Cons

Chapter 13

# 'PERSONALITY NOT NATIONALITY': FOREIGN STUDENTS' PERCEPTIONS OF A NON-NATIVE SPEAKER LECTURER OF ENGLISH AT A BRITISH UNIVERSITY

DOROTA PACEK
*The University of Birmingham*

## 1.     INTRODUCTION

There are a number of controversies surrounding the issue of native speaker teachers (NST) and non-native speaker teachers (NNST). Firstly, although the terms NST and NNST have been extensively used, they remain rather contentious. The literature on the subject points to the difficulties of distinguishing between NSs and NNSs, and the vagueness of the definitions (see, for example, Edge, 1988; Phillipson, 1992a, 1992b; Medgyes, 1994). Moreover, the terms NS and NNS have been criticized for being evaluative and judgemental, ascribing power to NSTs, while presenting the NNSTs as 'lacking' something, thus being 'worth' less than NSTs. However, it seems that the terms NS/NNS, despite all their drawbacks, are the reality which cannot be simply 'magicked-away'; such a distinction certainly does exist in the minds of general public not directly engaged in the NS/NNS debate.

Secondly, in the last decade there has been an on-going discussion among scholars involved in TESOL discourse regarding the relative advantages and disadvantages of NSTs and NNSTs of English (Phillipson, 1992a, 1992b; McKay, 1992; Rampton, 1990; Prodromou, 1992; Widdowson, 1992, 1994; Medgyes 1994). The belief in the superiority of a NST has been called into question on several grounds. First, there is a

E. Llurda (Ed.), *Non-Native Language Teachers. Perceptions, Challenges and Contributions to the Profession*, 243—262.

changing view of the role of English in the world; it is no longer regarded as the property of NSs only. Moreover, intuition-based approaches to linguistics fostered by the Chomskyan school have been strongly criticized. There has been a growing realization that NSs do not always have accurate insights into all aspects of English: they need access to English-English dictionaries, thesauri, encyclopedias of English and computer corpora in order to make reasonable generalizations about how English is used. Secondly, there is the view that NSs imported into an educational system to teach English often do not adapt sufficiently well to the host educational environment for pedagogic reasons, including teaching methods and materials. Thirdly, NSs often do not fit into the host country educational system for cultural reasons, such as differences in 'classroom culture', attitudes and beliefs concerning teacher/student roles, or criteria for a 'good' teacher.

By contrast, it has been pointed out in the literature that despite relative deficiency in foreign language competence, NNSTs have certain advantages over NSTs. They share their students' first language, and therefore can use it to their advantage when necessary, they can often anticipate their students' language problems and empathize with their difficulties, since they went through the process of acquiring the foreign language themselves. Moreover, as they come from the same cultural and educational background, they have similar attitudes to student/teacher roles in the classroom. All the above arguments assume situations where NSTs teach abroad, and NNSTs teach in their home country; the relative merits of a NNST teaching English in an English-speaking country, however, would be less obvious. The advantages of a NNST teaching at home do not hold in the particular situation of students surveyed for the purpose of this paper; their teacher does not share the $L_1$, cultural or educational background with her students, as they come from many different countries from the Far East, Europe and Latin America.

Despite academic doubts about the assumption that NSs are best teachers of their mother tongue, anecdotal evidence, and some research, show that the prevailing conviction among language learners, their parents, or even people directly involved in language education, is that the best teacher of a language is a NS. Medgyes (1994), for example, has shown through a series of interviews and surveys, that the NST is still the preferred choice in English-speaking countries. When learners go abroad, their expectation is that they will be taught the language by native English speakers. Although Medgyes' research refers primarily to commercial language schools, his conclusions also ring true in the case of an academic environment.

Informal chats with international students at the University of Birmingham, clearly indicate that students embarking on their chosen university course in Britain often do so for two main reasons. Firstly, they believe that British university education might give them better prospects in their future careers, and secondly, they also hope to dramatically improve their English language ability by studying through the medium of English. It is clear from students' comments that while a NNST is often the norm in their countries (particularly in the Far East), they assume that when studying in an English-speaking country they will be taught English language by NSTs. Therefore, a NNS lecturer in English language and linguistics at a British university certainly goes against students' expectations. Moreover, the advantages ascribed to NNSTs teaching at home do not fully apply here, so students might have even more reason for dissatisfaction and disappointment. It seemed worthwhile to explore the issues which had emerged in informal chats with students, so a small-scale survey among Birmingham University international students was undertaken in order to find out what exactly two different groups of learners expected from an English language teacher (ELT), and to establish what students' reactions to the fact of being taught by a NNS were. In particular, the aim was to investigate (1) whether students' attitudes to a NNST would be as negative as could be expected under the circumstances, and (2) to find out if such factors as students' age, gender, nationality and, by extension, their educational background, had any bearing on their views.

## 2.     BACKGROUND INFORMATION

Before describing the survey itself and discussing its outcomes, it is perhaps worth saying a few words about the teacher concerned, and the character of the Unit where the study was conducted. Students who participated in the survey will be described in some detail in section 3.1.

The teacher comes from an East European country, and has been teaching English language, linguistics and ELT methodology for 20 years; first in her home country, and subsequently at Birmingham University. She has some limited knowledge of several European languages, and has been involved in teaching/running a teacher-training programme for Japanese secondary school teachers of English (JST), and other courses for Japanese students for 11 years. She has visited Japan on several occasions, meeting Ministry of Education officials, school teachers, and visiting schools. Thus, she has a sound knowledge of the Japanese educational system and tradition, and is conversant with all aspects of ELT curriculum in Japanese schools, teaching conditions and requirements that teachers have to meet there. Moreover, since she has been involved in teaching English to Japanese for many years, she is familiar with typical language difficulties that Japanese students encounter.

The English for International Students Unit (EISU) is a part of the Department of English at the University of Birmingham and it provides in-sessional English language and study skills courses for international students and members of staff at the University of Birmingham, as well as pre-sessional academic English courses for foreign students who need to improve their knowledge of the language before joining university courses of their choice. Moreover, the Unit runs several tailor-made courses for specific groups of learners (Business English Course, Study Abroad Programme for Japanese undergraduates, In-service Teacher Training Course for Japanese Teachers of English, and others).

## 3.      METHOD

### 3.1     Student sample

Two groups of students were surveyed for the purpose of this study: vocabulary class students and the JST programme participants. This was done for two main reasons. Firstly, they are quite different in many respects, as will be outlined below. It was therefore interesting to see if their views would differ in any way, and if so, how. Secondly, it was felt that the survey would be more balanced and less biased towards any specific type of learner, if reactions of two types of student were compared.

The vocabulary class, like all other in-sessional classes, is free and open to all, and therefore it tends to be quite large; between 50-200 students typically attend. It takes place once a week over a period of 20 weeks (2 terms x 10 sessions), and each session lasts for an hour. The student population is very diverse: they come from a wide range of disciplines, a variety of cultural and educational backgrounds, they have different levels of language proficiency, and there is a mixture of undergraduates, postgraduates, and members of staff. They come from many different countries representing three main geographical areas of the Far East, Europe, and Latin America.

The JST course is a tailor made, in-service teacher-training programme for Japanese secondary school teachers of English, sponsored by the Japanese Ministry of Education. Groups are small (5-12), the course lasts 11 months, and there are several classes/lectures each day. The main aims of the course are:

a) to improve the participants' language skills;
b) to introduce them to those areas of linguistics directly relevant to ELT;

c) to introduce them to a range of methods for developing CLT in Japan;
d) to give them an understanding of traditional and contemporary British culture.

Students of both groups can be characterized as follows:

*Table 1.* A comparison of vocabulary class and JST students

| Vocabulary class | JST course |
|---|---|
| Studying/researching various subject areas | All secondary school teachers of English |
| Highly motivated, as classes are not compulsory | Highly motivated |
| From all over the world, thus having different educational backgrounds and expectations | All from one country with a specific educational background |
| Language proficiency from intermediate to advanced | Language proficiency from intermediate to advanced |
| Age groups from 18-19 year old undergraduates to mature students and staff members | Age group 35-45 year olds on average |

As can be seen, there are quite a few differences between the two groups that can be broadly put into two categories. Firstly, courses as such differ in their duration, intensity, and type, and in whether they are compulsory (JST) or optional (vocabulary class). Moreover, in terms of contact hours, the vocabulary class students meet their teacher once a week for an hour only, while the JTS group attend a variety of classes with the lecturer, meeting her several times per week for 2-6 hours per day. Secondly, the two groups differ in terms of the type of students attending (age, country of origin, educational background, students/researchers in a variety of subject areas versus teachers of English). As will be shown below, the character of the courses, and students' nationality in particular, had a substantial bearing on the way they perceive NNSTs.

## 3.2     Instrument

The survey consisted of two independent parts (for questionnaires, see Appendix A). In both cases the purpose of the survey was clearly explained in covering letters, questionnaires were anonymous, and students were asked to be as honest and objective in their answers as possible. Although questionnaires were anonymous, students were invited to give their age, gender, and nationality, since the intention was to explore not only the prevailing feelings, but also to discover whether there would be any differences in responses according to these three categories.

The aim was to compare students' initial comments on the most/least important characteristics of a foreign language teacher (FLT) with their later views on relative merits/demerits of a NNST in a concrete situation. Thus, the first questionnaire was aimed at finding what, in students' views, were the most and the least important characteristics of an FLT in general. The second questionnaire was designed to elicit answers in three particular areas: a) what students' initial reactions were to the fact that their teacher was a NNS of English, b) if their attitude had changed after the courses had finished, and c) what, according to students, were the most important advantages/disadvantages of having a NNS lecturer. Interesting differences in responses were noted, depending mainly on the students' countries of origin, and on whether they were vocabulary class students, or Japanese teachers of English. After presenting results, an attempt will be made to identify reasons for differences in both groups' reactions, as well as differences in answers to the first and second questionnaires.

## 3.3    Procedure

During each vocabulary class students are asked to sign a register. On the basis of ten week register (one term's teaching), two separate questionnaires were sent a week apart via internal post to 57 students who had been identified as regular attenders (a week and two weeks after the course had finished). In the case of the first questionnaire 43 responses were obtained (75.4% return rate), and in the case of the second one, 38 answers were received (66.7% return rate).

As far as the JST programme is concerned, the questionnaires were given to the five participants present in Birmingham during the penultimate and last weeks of the programme, and, at the same time, 68 questionnaires were sent via e-mail to ex-participants of the JST programme (*i.e.* 73 in total). 39 responses were received to the first questionnaire (57.5% return rate), and 46 responses to the second one (63% return rate).

Both questionnaires were sent to all the students one week apart, so that respondents would not be unduly influenced by the answers they had given to the first one. The aim was to make both questionnaires seem unconnected. It was hoped that by conducting the survey in two parts, it would be possible to trace any (in)consistencies in students' responses and to establish how students' general feelings, divorced from any specific situation, translated into their reactions when they were faced with the actual situation of being taught a foreign language by a NNS.

## 4.    RESULTS

As indicated earlier, the first questionnaire was meant to be a 'setting the scene' exercise, with the aim of identifying what students typically considered to be the most/least important characteristics of an FLT in general, abstract terms, while the second one was aimed at eliciting students' reaction to a NNST in a concrete situation. The results obtained for both questionnaires are presented below.

### 4.1    Results concerning questionnaire 1

As far as the *most* important characteristics of an FLT are concerned, the most common answers can be subsumed under the following headings, in descending order:

*Table 2.* Most important features of an FLT according to Far East and European/Latin American students

| Categories | Total | Far East | Europe/ Lat. Am. |
|---|---|---|---|
| Sensitivity to students' needs and problems | 33 | 18 | 15 |
| Patience/kindness/helpfulness | 20 | 18 | 2 |
| Sense of humour | 16 | 16 | 0 |
| Sound knowledge of language system | 23 | 16 | 7 |
| Clear explanations | 31 | 15 | 16 |
| Clear pronunciation | 24 | 15 | 9 |
| Well prepared | 23 | 12 | 11 |
| Imaginative, enthusiastic and motivating | 15 | 11 | 4 |
| Good communicator | 21 | 6 | 15 |
| Variety of teaching methods and materials | 20 | 4 | 16 |
| Knowledge of everyday/idiomatic language | 14 | 3 | 11 |

As already mentioned, the students came from three areas: the Far East (22 students), Europe (14) and Latin America (7). Quite unexpectedly, the views of students from Europe and Latin America, despite substantial differences in their respective cultural and educational traditions, seemed to be very much alike, at the same time being quite different to those represented by students from the Far East. It was rather surprising that no substantial divergence of opinions between European and Latin American students was identified, but, in a sense, quite fortunate. Since there were 22 Far East students, and 21 European/Latin American ones, their views could be grouped together, providing a well-balanced ground for comparison.

It is interesting to note quite significant differences in responses given by Far East and European/Latin American students. There seem to be only three categories where there is a (relatively) close correspondence between reactions given by both groups of students: 'sensitivity to students' needs and problems', 'clear explanations' and 'well prepared'. Other than that, Far East students seem to value personal features of character most (sensitivity, kindness, patience, sense of humour, enthusiasm), rather than the knowledge of the language or a variety of teaching methods. As far as European/Latin American students are concerned, the importance of most features is almost completely reversed. While 'personality' categories are almost insignificant, the knowledge of the language and pedagogic skills, as well as good communication skills, feature quite prominently in the second group's responses.

The *least* important characteristics were listed as follows:

*Table 3.* Least important features of an FLT according to Far East and European/ Latin American students

| Categories | Total | Far East | Europe/ Lat. Am. |
|---|---|---|---|
| Gender | 12 | 4 | 8 |
| Age | 10 | 4 | 6 |
| Looks/appearance | 9 | 3 | 6 |
| Native pronunciation | 7 | 5 | 2 |
| Variety of teaching methods and materials | 6 | 4 | 2 |
| Patience and kindness | 6 | 1 | 5 |
| Detailed grammatical knowledge | 5 | 1 | 4 |

As can be seen by comparing the results in Tables 2 and 3, some categories (variety of teaching methods/materials, patience/kindness, and grammatical knowledge) are mentioned as both most and least important. This is due to the fact that different 'geographical' groups consider different characteristics as less or more important.

Although the list of most important features is quite straightforward, the second one is less easy to interpret. It is not clear if the features at the bottom of the list, or some other possible features not mentioned at all, can be interpreted as those considered relatively unimportant (as only few students, or none at all, mentioned them as *least* important), or, in fact they are so unimportant that few/no students even thought of mentioning them. In retrospect, the questionnaire would have perhaps given a more comprehensive answer if, on top of open-ended questions, students had also been given a list of different characteristics, and asked to tick the most/least important ones. The results would have been easier to interpret and compare. Perhaps, though, the fact that certain characteristics appear at all is worth noting.

Due to the difficulties in interpreting the data regarding the least important features of an FLT, only the most important characteristics have been focussed on here. One interesting outcome of this questionnaire is that there seems to be a great divergence of opinions; although age and gender did not seem to have much impact on students' attitudes, nationality and, by extension, students' educational background, seem to play an important role in how they perceive an FLT.

JST responses differed in some respects from those given by vocabulary class students in general, and also to some extent from those given by the Far East students, of whom 9 were Japanese.

*Table 4.* Japanese teachers' responses

| Categories | Number of responses |
|---|---|
| Sound knowledge of language system | 39 |
| Effective teaching methods | 39 |
| Supportive and kind | 37 |
| Sensitive to students' needs and problems | 31 |
| Well prepared | 28 |
| Imaginative and motivating | 27 |
| Knowledge of students $L_1$ and culture | 27 |
| Familiarity with and teaching about target culture | 19 |
| Tolerance for language mistakes and ambiguity | 12 |
| Ability to produce own teaching materials | 9 |
| Use of authentic materials | 5 |

First of all, JSTs gave more reflective answers, rather than limiting themselves to listing most/least important characteristics. Secondly, their responses clearly show a teacher's point of view, rather than a learner's, as was the case with vocabulary students. Despite these differences, a proportion of the answers seems to be quite similar to those given by vocabulary Far East students. For example, a large number of JSTs mentioned the fact that teachers should be supportive and kind (37), sensitive to students' needs and problems (31), or imaginative and motivating (27). Also, sound knowledge of the language system was rated high by Far East students, and came top in JST responses (39), and good lesson preparation was rated relatively high by Far East (12) and JST respondents (28). However, effective teaching methods featured low in Far East students' responses (4), but came top in the other group of vocabulary students (16), and was cited by all 39 teachers. Some categories mentioned by vocabulary group, such as 'clear pronunciation', 'sense of humour', 'good communicator' or 'knowledge of idiomatic language' were not mentioned at all by JSTs, while some others, not listed by students were brought up. Quite a few teachers, for example, felt that the knowledge of their students' first language and culture was important (27). Many said that foreign language teachers should be familiar with, and introduce to students, the target language culture (19), and that teachers should display tolerance for language mistakes and ambiguity (12).

## 4.2    Results concerning questionnaire 2

The results of the second questionnaire will now be described, firstly to compare answers given by the two groups of respondents, and secondly, to look at how answers to the two questionnaires relate to each other. As a reminder, the objectives of the second questionnaire were to identify students' initial reaction to a NNST, to find out if their attitudes have changed by the end of the course, and to identify typical views on advantages/disadvantages of a NNST.

Of the total number of vocabulary class students, 18 had not realized the lecturer was a NNS until they were asked to fill in the questionnaire. Of the remaining 20 initial reactions, seven responses indicated that students had not been concerned about the prospect of being taught by a NNS, while 13 had been worried/negative about it.

**Initial reactions: (numbers in brackets indicate the number of similar answers).**

*Unconcerned:*

'Other lecturers were British, so it did not matter that one wasn't'. (4)

'I don't care if she was not English. My teacher [back home] is also not English and she is very good'. (2)

'I thought if she teaches here, she must be good'. (1)

*Negative:*

'I came to England to be taught by English'. (6)

'I was very surprised and disappointed'. (4)

'Non-native can never be as good teacher as native'. (3)

After one term of teaching, of 13 students with initial negative reactions, four changed their mind and became positive, while the other nine responses became mixed, rather than outright negative. Of the 18 who did not initially realise that the lecturer was a NNS, 10 were positive and 8 were mixed/negative at the end of the course.

**Reactions after the end of the course:**

Typical comments were as follows:

*Positive:*

'She was better than English lecturers because she had more patience and explained more clearly. Other teachers speak very fast and don't care about students'.

'She knows other languages, so she understands our problems better. Also, she is a good teacher'.

'I liked the way she taught better than other lecturers'.

'She speaks and explains more clearly'.

*Mixed/negative:*

'Her English is less idiomatic and her accent is not native, but she has good methods of explaining and teaching'.

'Her pronunciation is not native, but easier to understand'.

'She doesn't speak like native speaker, so she cannot be a good model for us'.

'English people should teach in England'.

'They probably not have enough English teachers, so they have to use non-native'.

It is clear that the positive remarks above, and the positive parts of the mixed comments, refer mostly to the way/methods of teaching and explaining new concepts, while the negative remarks relate mainly to various aspects of language proficiency, or point to a conflict between students' expectations that while in England, they would be taught English by NSs, and the situation where they are faced with a NNST.

The most interesting part of the questionnaire is the one which reveals students' beliefs concerning advantages and disadvantages of NNSTs. When asked what they expected initially to be the advantages/disadvantages of a NNST, the vast majority gave rather vague answers like 'I didn't know', 'will not be as good as native', 'I didn't think about it', or no answer at all. Of those few (7) who did give more concrete answers, most (5) seemed to regard lack of fluency and non-native pronunciation as the main drawbacks, while on the positive side they mentioned better understanding of foreign students' language problems (4). After the course had finished they had a much clearer idea of what they considered to be advantages/disadvantages of the NNS lecturer. As far as *advantages* are concerned they mentioned sensitivity to students' problems, variety of teaching methods, patience, tolerance, clearer explanations and pronunciation, detailed knowledge of grammar, and several others, while main *disadvantages* mentioned were non-native pronunciation, less idiomatic/ colloquial language, and lower awareness of the origin of some idioms/expressions. A more detailed analysis of students responses will be presented in section 4.3.

I would now like to turn to the JST responses. As far as their initial reactions are concerned, only 3 participants were slightly worried that their main lecturer was a NNS, while the remaining 43 were not concerned about it at all; they were more worried about various aspects of the academic side of the course, and whether they would be able to communicate in English, and cope with living in a different culture.

**Reactions after the end of the course:**

All were positive/very positive. Typical comments:

'We had an **advantage** of having non-native teacher, as she knows very well about frequent and typical mistakes we make. She also has more sympathy for foreign students living and studying in Britain' (my emphasis).

'I feel very relaxed with her because she understands us better than anybody else'.

'I felt very relieved when I learned that my course teacher was non-native, because I felt kinship with her'.

'I feel that a non-native speaker can be a better teacher than a native speaker. I believe the most important thing is the teacher's personality, not nationality'.

**Advantages and disadvantages:**

Anticipated advantages and disadvantages mentioned by JST course participants were broadly similar to those listed by vocabulary class students, although there were some differences. JSTs, for example, put on top of their list of advantages such features as empathy with, and better understanding of Japanese students' cultural background, or a variety of teaching methods, while disadvantages were hardly mentioned at all: two participants listed poorer familiarity with the British culture, and two non-native pronunciation. Actual advantages/disadvantages as perceived by JSTs after the end of the course correspond to a large extent with those outlined by vocabulary students. However, on the very top of almost all JSTs' lists some other advantages, not featured in the vocabulary students' responses, were mentioned:

'A good model for us, an actual example of non-native teacher teaching English in England. This encourages me that I can also be a good teacher of English'.

'Positive approach to students from Asian culture, because she knows different cultures and no culture is superior to others'.

'Speaks clearer than native, so is easier to understand, and shows more understanding for non-native teachers, and knows better our expectations'.

'Non-native speaker can teach NNS teachers more effectively, because we have had similar/same worries, effort, difficulties which NSTs cannot experience'.

'She understands our background better, so can give us more good ideas about ELT methodology than native speakers'.

'She gave me many good ideas for working with ALTs (Assistant Language Teachers) effectively, and gave me a lot of confidence as a non-native teacher in Japan'.

'She was a very successful model for us, non-native speakers, not only for methodology but also for confidence'.

## 4.3     Discussion of results

As mentioned earlier, the JST programme participants were positive from the start, becoming even more so after the course had ended. By contrast, of the 31 vocabulary students who initially were either unaware of the fact that the lecturer was a NNS, or had a negative attitude, 14 become positive, and 17 remained sceptical, but not as negative as they had been initially (Figure 1).

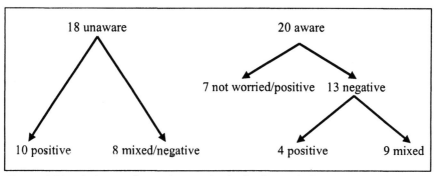

*Figure 1.* Vocabulary students' change of attitude after end of course

Both initial and final differences between the two groups could be explained by factors such as:

- group size and length/intensity of teaching;
- type of student;
- differences in cultural/educational backgrounds.

## 4.3.1     Group size and length/intensity of teaching

As the vocabulary class is very large, and students only have one contact hour with the lecturer per week for the duration of one term (10 weeks), they have a relatively limited opportunity for frequent interaction with her. Because the sessions are, by necessity, less interactive than in the case of small group teaching, there is little time for the lecturer to get to know her students well, and vice versa. Thus, it is possible that the main impression students get, is that the lecturer has a 'strange accent' in comparison with other lecturers, and their NS friends. It is interesting to note, however, that many of the students had not realised that the lecturer was not a NS until they were asked to fill in the questionnaire. There might be two reasons for this: either some students have a better 'ear' for accents than others, and they picked up the difference, or some of them might have made comments about foreign accent only with the hindsight—after they had realised that the lecturer was a NNS. The same might be true for their comments about less idiomatic or colloquial language. Another point worth noting, however, is that comments about accent/pronunciation can be found in both positive and negative categories. In other words, non-native accent is seen as an advantage by some students, as they find it easier to understand (and perhaps imitate), while some others see it as a disadvantage, as it is not 'authentic' (and not worth imitating).

The JST programme participants, unlike the vocabulary students, are taught in small groups, and the course lasts for eleven months. Therefore, they are much more familiar with the lecturer, have many more opportunities to interact with her individually, the sessions are very interactive, and there is ample opportunity for both sides to get to know each other well. This might result in a situation where the Japanese teachers are less concerned about pronunciation, for example, as they realize that there are more important things they can learn from the lecturer. Also, as practicing teachers of English, they might be more aware of the fact that native-like pronunciation is almost impossible to attain, and that other models are also acceptable. They seem to subscribe to the view that a non-native pronunciation, as long as it is comprehensible to others (both native and non-native speakers), could in fact be a better model for learners of a language, as it is more achievable.

### 4.3.2    Type of student

Another possible reason for different views between the two groups might be that the JSTs have a variety of academic subjects with the lecturer, including language improvement classes, areas of linguistics relevant to their teaching training, as well as ELT methodology, and various aspects of Britain, including media, education, social structure, multiculturalism, and many others. Therefore, they do not see the lecturer just as a language teacher, but as somebody who can offer them new perspectives in many other areas relevant to them as teachers of English.

Vocabulary students on the other hand, meet the lecturer just for the language classes. This might be the reason why more of them consider having a NST important, although the nationality factor also plays a part, an issue which will be considered later. They are either undergraduate or postgraduate students, or visiting academics, and none of them is a language teacher. Since they have no experience of teaching a foreign language, the views expressed by them in the questionnaires represent the point of view of language learners only, which, of course, is as valid as that of Japanese teachers.

What also seems to be important is the fact that JSTs can be said to have 'dual personalities'; they are students for the duration of the JST programme, but back in Japan they are teachers of English with several years' practice. Therefore, their attitude to the NNS lecturer is different to that of the vocabulary students, in that they view the issue from both angles, although the 'teacher' perspective seems to be more prevalent than the 'student' one.

From the JST comments, it is clear that they predominantly want assurance that they will be able to cope as NNS teachers; they need more confidence and effective solutions to their teaching problems. Their mostly positive remarks about the NNS lecturer point to the fact that they see her as an effective role-model and a 'confidence booster'; if she can do it in England, we can do it in Japan. The fact that the number of negative comments regarding the lecturer's language proficiency is minimal, despite the fact that all JSTs rated 'sound knowledge of language system' very high, might indicate that either they consider the lecturer to be very proficient in English, or that they recognise the fact that it is not necessary to be a NS, or NS-like to be able to teach a language, and do it successfully.

One issue is perhaps interesting to note here. It seems that respondents from the Far East, whether vocabulary students or language teachers, need more reassurance that they will be able to cope as (language) learners than their European/Latin American counterparts. JSTs' responses cited above clearly show this, as well as the fact that 'personality' features (sensitivity, kindness, patience, sense of humour) rated high in all Far East students responses, and relatively low in answers by other geographical groups.

### 4.3.3     Differences in cultural/educational backgrounds

As vocabulary class students represent many nationalities, from the Far East, Europe and Latin America, their attitudes towards NNSTs have been influenced by, and formed in, different cultural and educational settings. As indicated in Table 2, students' responses differed greatly depending on the area/country they came from. One of the differences that has not been mentioned earlier is that of students' beliefs concerning the view that a language teacher should be a NS. While many European/Latin American students expressed such a preference, only a few of the Far East, and none of the nine Japanese vocabulary students, considered it important. It is clear from conversations with European students that they are used to relatively frequent contacts with NSs and NSTs, both in their native countries, and through travelling abroad. Therefore, they have expectations that, especially while in Britain, they should be taught the language by a NS. The Far East students, on the other hand, are accustomed to the fact that the standard FLT in their schools is a NNS. Even if they do have contacts with NSs at schools, those usually play a role of language assistants, rather than classroom teachers. They are expected to act as informants on such aspects of the language as naturalness or appropriacy, or as a motivation and justification for students to use English in the classroom, rather than being involved in regular teaching following local syllabuses and textbooks. In Far East educational systems it is also more common to teach through more traditional methods, where NS-like fluency, communication skills, and teaching the language are less valued than pedagogic skills and the ability to teach *about* the language. In effect,

Far East students might realise that those aspects of the language can be successfully taught by NNSTs, and therefore do not necessarily consider NSs as better teachers, or a requirement.

## 4.4     Comparison of questionnaire 1 and 2

Let us now return to Questionnaires 1 and 2. Some inconsistencies in students' responses can be identified, depending on whether they were asked to consider an abstract concept of an FLT in general (Questionnaire 1), or whether they were faced with the actual situation of being taught English by a NNS (Questionnaire 2). Students' responses presented in Table 1 will be examined and compared with those given to the second questionnaire, to identify differences. Only the vocabulary class reactions will be analysed here, as there were no significant changes of attitude in the first and second questionnaires in the case of JST course participants. Also, it will be assumed that what students identified in Questionnaire 1 as the 'most important features' of an FLT are to them the most desirable/advantageous ones, and therefore can be translated into their views, after the end of the course, on the main advantages of NNST in Questionnaire 2. Such an assumption cannot be made in the case of 'least important features', as compared to disadvantages. Firstly, 'least important' cannot be interpreted as most disadvantageous, and secondly, as mentioned earlier, the responses regarding 'least important' features of an FLT were difficult to interpret even in their own right.

As a reminder, 43 students replied to Questionnaire 1, 22 of which were from the Far East, and 21 from Europe/Latin America; 38 responses were received to Questionnaire 2, with 20 Far East, and 18 European/Latin American students.

Generally speaking, it can be said that students' expectations regarding desirable features of a language teacher have been met by the NNST. Some categories, such as 'clear pronunciation', 'sound knowledge of language system', and 'well prepared' match almost exactly. In several other cases, some of the features students mentioned in Questionnaire 1 as desirable became even more prominent. Categories relating to teaching methods, and the teacher's attitude seem to have increased in importance in Questionnaire 2: 'variety of teaching methods and materials' increased by 10 points, and 'patience/kindness/ helpfulness', and 'imagination/enthusiasm/motivation' were also considered as more important than in Questionnaire 1. Perhaps students realised that those characteristics of the lecturer helped them to become better, higher motivated and more secure learners. In other cases, the relation between answers to Questionnaires 1 and 2 seems to indicate that either students' expectations were not fully met, or that they simply did not consider some of the categories as important as they had initially, and thus fewer students mentioned them at all. Table 4 indicates that there were some differences between students' initial views on an FLT, and their reflections on advantages of a NNST.

*Table 5.* Comparison of Questionnaire 1 & 2 results

|  | Quest. 1 (most important features) | Quest. 2 (advantages) |
|---|---|---|
| Sensitive to students' needs and problems | 33 | 27 |
| Clear explanations | 31 | 24 |
| Clear pronunciation | 24 | 25 |
| Sound knowledge of language system | 23 | 24 |
| Well prepared | 23 | 24 |
| Good communicator | 21 | 15 |
| Patience/kindness/helpfulness | 20 | 26 |
| Variety of teaching methods and materials | 20 | 30 |
| Sense of humour | 16 | 3 |
| Imaginative, enthusiastic and motivating | 15 | 24 |
| Knowledge of everyday/idiomatic language | 14 | 6 |

## 5. CONCLUSION

The survey has shown that students' approach to the issue of NNST differed to some degree, depending on whether they were considering it in more abstract terms (Questionnaire 1), or whether they were faced with an actual case of being taught by a NNS (Questionnaire 2). What, in many cases, was low priority in the first survey, became high priority in the second one, and vice versa.

As far as differences in both groups' reactions are concerned, it is perhaps not surprising that teachers' responses differed quite markedly from those given by vocabulary class students. By virtue of their profession, they have a better insight into, and different perspective on all aspects of language teaching and learning, and their views on relative merits/demerits of NNSTs are a reflection of their own position as NNSTs.

Returning to the two research questions posed in the introduction, perhaps the most uplifting finding of the survey is, that by and large, both groups have been less negative/critical of a NNST than had been expected. Generally speaking, while it seems more acceptable for students to have a NNST in their home country, when they go abroad they expect to be taught by NSs. Despite this, quite a proportion of students had an either positive or mixed reaction to a NNST, with few entirely negative ones. Moreover, many vocabulary students' initial negative attitude to a NNST changed into mixed/positive by the end of the course.

Students' age, gender and nationality/educational background were also expected to influence to a large degree the way they view a NNST. The survey has confirmed that students' cultural and educational backgrounds play an important role in what characteristics of a NNS they perceive to be more or less important, and whether they consider having a NS as a teacher essential or not. By contrast, age and gender did not seem to have any bearing on students' views. While it is not surprising that gender was not a factor here, it was assumed that age would actually influence respondents' views. The expectation was that older respondents would be less keen on interactive, and eclectic teaching methods, and that they would feel more strongly that the 'best' language teacher is a NS, than the younger generation. However, the results obtained did not bear it out.

Both the unexpectedly favourable views regarding a NNST, and the lack of strong feelings against NNSTs among older respondents indicate that if a NNST can meet students' expectations by introducing appropriate teaching methods and by displaying personality features favoured by the learners, most of them can actually be persuaded that being taught by a NNST can be a rewarding and positive experience.

The replies to the survey, although intriguing, left some questions unanswered, particularly as to *why* students had given particular responses, such as 'I liked the way she taught better than other lecturers', 'Non-native can never be as good teacher as native', or 'I was very surprised and disappointed (with the NNST)'. There is much scope for further research here.

## 6.    REFERENCES

Edge, J. (1988). Natives, speakers and models. *JALT Journal, 9* (2), 153-157.
McKay, S. (1992). *Teaching English overseas.* Oxford: Oxford University Press.
Medgyes, P. (1994). *The non-native teacher.* London: Macmillan. (1999) 2nd edition. Ismaning: Max Hueber Verlag.
Phillipson, R. (1992a). *Linguistic imperialism.* Oxford: Oxford University Press.
Phillipson, R. (1992b). ELT: The native speaker's burden? *ELT Journal, 46* (1), 12-17.

Prodromou, L. (1992). What culture? Which culture? Cross-cultural factors in language learning. *ELT Journal, 46* (1), 39-50.

Rampton, M.B.H. (1990). Displacing the 'native speaker': expertise, affiliation, and inheritance. *ELT Journal, 44* (2), 97-101.

Widdowson, H.G. (1992). ELT and ELT teachers: matters arising. *ELT Journal, 46* (4), 333-339.

Widdowson, H.G. (1994). The ownership of English. *TESOL Quarterly, 28* (2), 377-88.

# APPENDIX A

## Questionnaire 1
Age          ....................
Sex          .................... (M/F)
Country of origin  ......................
1. According to you, what are the most important characteristics of a foreign language teacher?
2. What are the least important ones?

## Questionnaire 2
1. What was your **initial** reaction after arriving in Britain, when you learned that the main lecturer on your course was a non-native speaker (NNS) of English?
2. What did you think **then** the advantages of having a NNS lecturer **would** be?
3. What did you think the disadvantages **would** be?
4. Has your attitude changed by the end of the course?
5. Looking back, what were the advantages of a NNS lecturer?
6. What were the disadvantages?

PART V

# NNS TEACHERS' SELF-PERCEPTIONS

Chapter 14

# MIND THE GAP: SELF AND PERCEIVED NATIVE SPEAKER IDENTITIES OF EFL TEACHERS

OFRA INBAR-LOURIE
*Beit Berl College*

## 1.     BACKGROUND

Language is seen as a marker of group identity. Social identity and ethnicity are deemed to be largely maintained by language, group membership and group identity creating a 'we' and 'they' differentiation (Gumperz, 1982). Individuals who are dissatisfied with the real or assumed attributes of the power or resources of the language community to which they belong may try to assimilate into another language group, often chosen since it appears to offer a more positive group identity for the individual (Giles & Johnson, 1987).

There may be instances where a gap is created between the group an individual identifies with and the status attributed to the individual by others, *i.e.*, between one's self identity as compared with one's perceived identity (Louw-Potgieter & Giles, 1987). This phenomenon is noticeable in the case of native and non-native language speakers who ascribe themselves as belonging to either the native or non-native group of a certain speech community whilst being perceived differently by members of that community (Davies, 2003). The reasons for this gap vary: some may be pertinent to all language speakers, whereas others may be particular to speakers affiliated with distinct social or professional groups. Since native/non-native labeling is of paramount relevance to language teachers,

E. Llurda (Ed.), *Non-Native Language Teachers. Perceptions, Challenges and Contributions to the Profession*, 265—281.

this paper will report on research on self versus perceived native and non-native identities of teachers of English as a Foreign Language and the scope and nature of the identity gap.

## 1.1     Language identity—self and perceived

Identity is generally defined as referring to 'who or what someone is, the various meanings someone can attach to oneself or the meanings attributed to oneself by others' (Beijaard, 1995: 282). Group or collective identity is seen as 'the culture-embedded self-definitions of individuals related to others—both in terms of inclusion and exclusion—through which they interpret their condition' (Ben-Rafael, 1996: 188).

Language and identity are intertwined, for language choice signals membership in an ethnic, political, social, religious, professional or national speech community and allows the individual to share the cultures, values and social prestige represented by the language (Kramsch, 1998). Since many of the world's societies are multilingual, the concept of individual, collective and multilingual identity is currently deemed fundamental to making sense of individual social phenomena. Identity construction is perceived as a dynamic intricate process, closely related to and affected by social, cultural and economic processes (Leung, Harris & Rampton, 1997; Ogulnick, 2000; Uchida & Duff, 1997). Norton (2000) defines identity as 'how a person understands his or her relationship to the world, how that relationship is constructed across time and space, and how the person understands possibilities for the future' (5). An example of the above can be found in Lvovich (1997) who provides a biographical account of the emergence of her multilingual identities and its effect on her personal existence.

Language identity research draws from social psychological identity theories and processes of group membership, particularly from Tajfel (1978) who sees identity as evolving from group membership. In cases where membership in a certain group does not satisfy the social identity individuals uphold, an attempt to change group identity may occur. This change may or may not materialize, thereby affecting the reinterpretation of the group's social identity by the individual. Giles & Coupland (1991) provide an extensive analysis of the role language plays in forming ethnic and cultural identity. Basing their views on Tajfel's social identity theories, they emphasize the proximity between language and ethnicity and the potential instability of ethnic linguistic identity.

Individuals who are dissatisfied with the real or assumed attributes of the power or resources of the language community to which they belong may try to assimilate into another language group, the group likely to be chosen being the one which appears to offer a more positive group identity (Giles &

Johnson, 1987; Clement & Noels, 1992). There may be instances where a noticeable gap is created between the group an individual identifies with and the status attributed to the individual by others, implying power relations among the judges and those being judged. In such cases the 'self', *i.e.*, the individual, and the 'dominant', *i.e.*, the community, may have contradictory views as to the ethnic identity of the defined, causing a 'defined in' or 'defined out' dilemma. McNamara's (1987) study of Israeli immigrants to Australia who identified themselves as Israelis but were perceived by others as having a Jewish rather than an Israeli affiliation, provides an example of such a situation.

The 'Dominated as Defined by Self and the Dominant' model by Louw-Potgieter & Giles (1987) depicts this predicament (Table 1 below). In case of native/non-native recognition, the underlying assumption is that the individual may gain, or risk to losing, resources of some kind as a result of being granted native or non-native identity.

*Table 1.* The dominated as defined by self and the dominant

| Self definition (provided by the dominated) | Other definition (provided by the dominant) | |
|---|---|---|
| | Defined in | Defined out |
| Defined in | A | B |
| Defined out | C | D |

Source: Louw-Potgieter & Giles, 1987: 263.

Yet, acceptance or rejection of claims to native speaker status by members of the speech community may be impeded by failure to recognize native or non-native speakers as such. This is due to the speaker exhibiting 'near native' qualities (Coppieters, 1987) or 'pseudo native speaker' features (Medgyes, 1994), which include elements such as native-like pronunciation, high-level language abilities (particularly regarding idiomatic language) and confident language use. Conversely, mistaken identities may also occur among self-ascribed native speakers as a result of social conventions as to who qualifies for native speaker status. Other reasons that may account for this confusion are the interlocutors' low level of language knowledge and subsequent expectations in terms of the speaker's ability, gaps in conceptual knowledge between the interacting parties, their relationship and reciprocal status, such as in the case of language teachers and learners (Medgyes, 1994).

In recent years there has been much discussion of the pertinence of power issues to identity formation in language learning. Norton (1997) states that 'power relations play a crucial role in social interactions between language learners and target language speakers' (3), since through languages learners gain access to social networks thereby negotiating their identity. Drawing on theory by Bourdieu (1977) Norton (1997; 2000) thus sees identity in terms of the learners' investment, which changes overtime depending on the social context and the power relations that shape it. Power is linked to resources. According to Bourdieu (1991) resources are the 'capital' people have access to. This capital may be economic, cultural, social or symbolic, and has context-dependent value. Access to such resources provides opportunities for future development, hence affecting the individual's desire to affiliate and identify with one language rather than another (Heller, 1988; Goldstein 1995). Since the notion of acquiring native speaker status later in life has recently been argued for (Davies, 2003; Skutnabb-Kangas, 2000), the choice to become a native speaker and affiliate with a speech community is regarded as a viable option

## 1.2      Language identity among language teachers

Application of the power issues discussed above to language teachers is particularly relevant and intriguing, for being part of the target language community may provide teachers with access to resources in the sense implied by Bourdieu (1991). These include first and foremost acknowledged language competence that entails better hiring opportunities, increased pay and improved social status. A possible conflict, however, may arise between the language teachers' chosen identity versus their perceived identity by other speakers of the language—both native and non-native—as well as by their students. Hence language teachers may identify themselves as either native or non-native speakers of the language they teach while the public deems otherwise. Perceived identity was found to play an important role in constructing teachers' self identity, for EFL teachers' assumptions as to how others perceive their English native speaking identity was one of the reasons underlying the teachers' native or non-native self-ascriptions. (Inbar-Lourie, 1999).

Since English is a world lingua franca it allows native English teachers access to material incentives and prestige (Pennycook, 1998). Consequently, teachers are more likely to strive for native speaking affiliation, as is evident for example in the struggle of World Englishes speakers for native speaker recognition (Nayar, 1994). Furthermore, in the case of high status languages, judgments by native speaker teachers as to the qualifications of their non-native colleagues are more rigid due to their reluctance to share their wealthy resources with outsiders (Inbar-Lourie, 1999).

Conversely, focus on the positive attributes of teachers who are non-native English speakers in terms of familiarity with the local language and culture and the language acquisition process have also been noted (*e.g.* Seidlhofer and Widdowson, 1998).

## 1.3     The identity gap among language teachers

Language teachers are clearly aware of the crucial significance of native non-native labeling to their professional status as well as the possible gap between self and perceived identities. Seven TESOL professionals of varied L1 backgrounds teaching in a university ESL program in the US, were asked to compare how they perceived themselves versus how they thought their students perceived them (Liu, 1999). Findings show that in three cases of self-ascribed non-native speakers no gaps were detected, but in other cases, the teachers thought their students perceived them differently because of external features (a teacher of Asian origin was perceived by his students as a non-native speaker contrary to his own ascription), or because of bilingual background. Results are interpreted in terms of power relations projecting themselves into the native/non-native dichotomy.

Other variables noted to affect language teachers' perceived native or non-native identities by others are pronunciation, familiarity with the target language and its culture, self-efficacy in teaching the various subject matter components and perceptions as to who qualifies as a native speaker of the language (Amin, 1997; Braine, 1999; Greis, 1985; Medgyes, 1999). In addition, the identity gap may emanate from factors which evolve from the particular learning-teaching context as well as from variables related to the teachers and learners and the interaction between them: the learners' language knowledge, their age and socioeconomic background, their exposure to and encounters with native speakers; the teachers' status in the social strata of the learning context, teachers as role models and as experts in the subject area.

Pronunciation is reported to play a crucial role in determining native identity: 'Pronunciation may most obviously provide clues for non-native status since it is formed in early age and may be the least conscious element is speech' (Gimson, in Paikeday, 1985: 23). It is also the most evident indicator of group membership both within and outside of the speech community (Paikeday, 1985), and has been referred to as 'the accent bar' (Kachru, 1982). Non-English accent is reported by foreign-trained teachers enrolled in a recredentialing program in Ontario to be one of the most difficult barriers they encounter. The teachers, who are required to adopt Canadian sounding pronunciations, voice discontent, arguing that shedding their accents denies them of their identities (Mawhinney & Xu, 1997).

Criteria for determining norms used to judge 'native-like' speech or norms of intelligibility, however, whether British, American, New Zealand or Indian, are unresolved (Eayrs, 1994; Taylor, 1991). In addition, in foreign language contexts where the target language is not spoken, ignorance on the part of the learners as to what constitutes 'proper' native-like pronunciation may diminish its relevance for determining the teacher's perceived native or non-native identity.

Differences as to the teacher's perceived native speaker identity were also seen to depend on the learners' age. In a research on EFL teachers in Israel (Inbar-Lourie, 1999), E., a non-native speaker teacher born in Russia says: 'The younger kids can't tell the difference between my accent and that of the native speaker teachers. The older pupils ask me where I learned to speak English so well' (147). The mere teaching position may, however, establish the language teacher's perceived status of the all-knowing expert, whose linguistic ability (including 'proper' pronunciation) cannot be questioned (Medgyes, 1994).

Familiarity with the target language culture can also affect the language teacher's perceived identity. Greis (1985) notes, however, that the non-native students and their parents may reject non-native language teachers as authentic representatives of the target culture and its people despite their efforts. Surprisingly, this also applies to native speaking English teachers whose country of birth is not considered 'native' in certain foreign language contexts. When asked to identify their EFL teachers as native/non-native speakers of English, 99% of students participating in a survey in Slovakia stated that only teachers born in the US or the UK can always be classified as native speakers. Only 10% added Indian teachers to the exclusive native-speaking group (Thomas, 1995).

The racial issue was also observed to influence the manner in which students' perceive their teachers' identities. Amin (1997) presents research findings showing that Canadian ESL teachers assume that their adult students believe that 'only white people can be native speakers of English' (580). The researcher thus concludes: 'the students' construction of their minority teachers as non-native speakers and therefore less able teachers than white teachers, has an impact on their identity formation' (581).

Since language proficiency is a major component in the subject matter knowledge of language teaching (Medgyes, 1999), the teachers' estimation of the knowledge they possess in the language and their ability to use that knowledge for different purposes is of primary importance. Greis (1985) relates to the heightened anxiety level that non-native speaking teachers may experience due to their perceived insufficient language proficiency. It has been shown that language teachers will vary in their feelings of confidence regarding their language proficiency in the target language depending, among other things, on their native or non-native background (Reves &

Medgyes, 1994). Hence non-native teachers who demonstrate self-efficacy in the subject matter may be mistaken for native speakers and vice versa.

Perceived native speaker identity among language teachers may thus be formed by factors unique to this particular group. Since the teachers' self-ascribed and native/non-native identities have meaningful consequences to their personal as well as classroom behavior (Norton, 2000), and teachers' assumptions as to their perceived identities bear significance on identity formation, it is important to further investigate the relationship between their self and perceived identities. This study thus set out to examine the possible gap between EFL teachers' self-ascribed native non-native English speaker identity and the identity they believe others ascribe to them.

## 2.     METHOD

### 2.1     Research sample and procedure

EFL teachers were asked to ascribe themselves as native or non-native speakers of English and state whether they thought others perceive them as native or non-native speakers of English. Specific mention was made of three perceiving groups: native speakers of English, non-native speakers of English, and the subjects' students. In case of incongruence between the identities respondents were asked to provide reasons for this difference in perceptions.

The research sample consisted of 102 mostly female[1] EFL teachers in the Israeli school system, with an average teaching experience of 12 years. The teachers taught EFL in primary, junior high and high school (all State schools) in a large heterogeneous city in the central part of the country. Respondents were born in 17 different countries: 39% in English speaking countries, 39% in Israel, 9% in the former Soviet Union and 13% in other countries. Fifty-four of the respondents (53%) ascribed themselves as non-native speakers of English, and 48 (47%) as native speakers of English.

The research was conducted as part of a larger study on native non-native EFL teachers' ascription. Data was collected using a self-report questionnaire with open-ended questions relating to the respondents' linguistic history and their self-ascribed and perceived English native speaker identity. In terms of perceived identity, the teachers were asked to state whether they believe others, *i.e.*, native speakers of English, non-native speakers of English and their students, perceive them as native or non-native speakers of English. In cases where a gap was evident between the self and perceived identities participants were asked to try and account for this gap.

## 3.      RESULTS

Chi-Square analysis was conducted between native/non-native self and perceived identities for each of the perceiving groups (native English speakers, non-native speakers and the teachers' students). In all cases native/non-native self-ascription was found to differ significantly from the perceived identities ($p<.001$).Yet, while hardly any difference was found between respondents who ascribed themselves as native speakers and their perceived ascription, considerable gaps emerged between non-native self and perceived identities particularly when the assumed perceivers were the respondents' students. Findings for each of the perceiving groups are reported below.

### 3.1      Perceived native/non-native identity by *native speakers*

Findings showed that in 46 cases (95.85%), self-ascribed native speakers thought other native speakers perceive them in the same way, *i.e.*, as native speakers, and in two cases, differently, as non-native speakers. Self-ascribed non-native speakers felt that in 43 (82.7%) of the cases native speakers perceive them in the same way, *i.e.*, as non-native speakers, and in 9 cases differently as native speakers, $\chi^2$ (1, N=100) = 62.19 ($p < .0001$) (Table 2).

*Table 2.* Native/non-native self and perceived-ascriptions *by native speakers of English*[1]

| Perceived Identity | Self-ascribed NS identity | Self-ascribed NNS identity | Row Total | P |
|---|---|---|---|---|
| Perceived identity | 46 | 9 | 55 | 62.19**** |
| as NS | 95.8% | 17.3% | 55% | |
| Perceived identity | 2 | 43 | 45 | |
| as NNS | 4.2% | 82.7% | 45% | |
| Column | 48 | 52 | 100 | |
| Total | 48% | 52% | 100% | |

**** $p < .001$      [1]missing cases = 2

### 3.2      Perceived native/non-native identity by *non-native speakers*

Results presented in Table 3 indicated that in all of the cases (48) self-ascribed native speakers thought that non-native speakers in general perceive them in the same way, *i.e.*, as native speakers, $\chi^2(1,N=100)=32.43$ ($p<.001$). Self-ascribed non-native speakers felt that in only 26 (50%) of the cases non-native speakers perceive them in the same way, *i.e.*, as non-native speakers, while in the same number of cases (26, 50%) their perceived identity by non-native speakers is that of native speakers, contrary to their own self-ascription.

*Table 3.* Native/non-native self and perceived ascriptions *by non-native speakers of English*[1]

| Perceived Identity | Self-ascribed NS identity | Self-ascribed NNS identity | Row Total | P |
|---|---|---|---|---|
| Perceived identity as NSs | 48 | 26 | 74 | 32.43*** |
| | 100% | 50% | 74% | |
| perceived identity as | 0 | 26 | 26 | |
| NNSs | 0% | 50% | 26% | |
| Column | 48 | 52 | 100 | |
| Total | 48% | 52% | 100% | |

\*\*\*\* *p* < .001        [1]missing cases = 2

## 3.3    Perceived native/non-native identity by *my students*

Respondents related to how the students each of them teaches (from beginners in primary school to advanced in high school) perceive their teacher's identity. Results showed that in all cases except one (47 cases, 97.9%), self-ascribed native speakers thought their students' perception and their own are identical. On the other hand, self-ascribed non-native speakers felt that in 18 cases (34.6%) their students perceive them in the same way they do, while in the majority of the cases (34, 65.4%) their students perceive them as native speakers, contrary to their own self-ascription, $\chi^2$ (1, N = 100) = 17.2 ( $p$ < .0001). Results are presented in Table 4.

Table 4. Native/non-native self and perceived ascriptions by the *respondents' students*[1]

| Perceived Identity | Self-ascribed NS identity | Self-ascribed NNS identity | Row Total | P |
|---|---|---|---|---|
| Perceived identity as NSs | 47 | 34 | 81 | 17.164**** |
| | 97.9% | 65.4% | 81% | |
| Perceived identity as NNSs | 1 | 18 | 19 | |
| | 2.1% | 36.4% | 19% | |
| Column | 48 | 52 | 100 | |
| Total | 48% | 52% | 100% | |

\*\*\*\* *p* < .001        [1]missing cases = 2

When comparing the perceived ascriptions (Table 5) it is evident that with regard to non-native speakers, the participants' responses indicate a hierarchy in the gap between self- and perceived ascriptions: more students than non-native speaking teachers, and more non-native than native speaking teachers, perceive English teachers who ascribe themselves as non-native speakers of English differently. In other words, students are the most likely to perceive their teachers as native speakers, even if the teachers do not perceive themselves as such, followed by non-native speakers. As to native speaker identity, findings show consensus in almost all cases between the self- and perceived identities of native speaking teachers. Thus, all the observers involved tend to agree with the teachers' own identities as long as they claim to be native speakers of English.

*Table 5.* A comparison of the results for native/ron-native self-ascription with perceived ascriptions by *native and non-native English speakers and students.* (N=100)

| Perceived identity by: | NS self-ascription | | | | NNS self-ascription | | | |
|---|---|---|---|---|---|---|---|---|
| | Same | | Different | | Same | | Different | |
| | N | % | N | % | N | % | N | % |
| NS | 46 | 95.8 | 2 | 4.2 | 43 | 82.7 | 9 | 17.3 |
| NNS | 48 | 100 | 0 | 0 | 26 | 50 | 26 | 50 |
| My students | 47 | 97.9 | 1 | 2.1 | 18 | 34.6 | 34 | 65.4 |

## 3.4    Gap between self- and perceived ascriptions

Respondents were asked to account for the gap between self-ascribed and perceived native/non-native identities wherever such a gap exists. Seven reasons were provided, four of which were found to account for 90.3% of the cases. The reason most frequently stated was lack of knowledge on the part of the observers (34.3% of the cases). Statements related to the respondents' students were 'The students don't really understand the difference between a native and non-native speaker', and 'Though I was born in the Ukraine the students in my school think I come from England'. Such statements were provided more often by primary school teachers who teach beginners than by teachers of older more advanced students and by teachers teaching in low socioeconomic neighborhoods, where exposure to English speakers is limited. With regard to the non-native public in general, a typical comment by non-native speakers (perceived as native speakers) was 'People perceive me according to their own knowledge'.

The second most salient explanation mentioned in 24.5% of the cases was the speakers' accent, either native or non-native. The statements provided were 'People are fooled by my accent' accounting for non-native self-ascription and perceived native identity, versus 'my accent sounds strange because I am originally from Pakistan', when accounting for the gap between native speaker self-ascription and non-native perceived identity.

Language fluency was considered another major reason for possible gaps in identity in which non-native speakers were presumed to be native speakers (23.5% of the reasons). The fourth reason mentioned by 8% of the participants emanates from the participants' professional status: 'Because I am an English teacher!' was the simple explanatory declaration provided by one of the respondents.

Other reasons mentioned were: studies in an English medium school and confidence in language use—both accounting for mistaken native speaker identity; personality traits—outgoing personality on one hand seen as accounting for the gap between non-native self ascription versus perceived native speaker identity, and introverted shy characteristics ('I'm too humble') seen to account for the opposite situation.

Thus the reasons for a discrepancy between self and perceived native speaker identity can stem from the speaker's language knowledge and professional status, as well as from the perceiver's lack of awareness as to native speaker competencies.

## 4.     A VALIDATION STUDY: PERCEIVED NATIVE SPEAKER IDENTITIES

Since the findings reported above regarding the nature of a gap between self and perceived identity were based solely on the teachers' assumptions as to how others perceive them, a validation study was conducted in order to examine how EFL teachers are in point of fact perceived.

### 4.1     Method

Data was collected from members of a large English teaching staff in an urban junior high and high school (N=16), as well as from a number of the teachers' students aged 12-17 studying in grades seven to eleven in the same school (N=31). The data collection instrument for the teachers was a self-report questionnaire in English requiring the English teachers to first ascribe themselves as native or non-native speakers of English, and then ascribe each of their colleagues in the same way. Randomly chosen students (1-3 per teacher) replied to another questionnaire (in Hebrew), in which they were asked whether they think their English teacher is a native or non-native speakers (the term provided in both languages).

Results were analyzed per teacher, comparing self-ascribed native/non-native identity with the teacher's identity as perceived by (a) EFL colleagues on the English teaching staff who consider themselves either native or non-native speakers of English, and (b) the teachers' students.

## 4.2    Results

Findings (displayed in Table 6) showed that agreement between self-ascription and colleagues' ascription was evident in 87% of the cases, while self-ascription and students' ascriptions were identical in 75% of the cases. Total agreement was apparent in the case of native speaker self-ascription and perceived identity. The hierarchical continuum reported in the previous study regarding the descending order of judgments by the three groups is observable in this set of data as well: native speaker teachers tend to label non-native speaker colleagues as native speakers less often than do non-native speaker teachers, who in turn are less apt to do so than students.

*Table 6.* Self-Ascription, Colleagues' Ascription and Students' Ascription colleagues: N=16; students: N=31)

| Teacher | Self | Perceived by NS | Perceived by NNS | Perceived by students |
|---------|------|-----------------|------------------|------------------------|
| H1 | N | N(n=3) | N (n=12) | 2 Grade 9 - N |
| V | NN | NN (n=4) | NN (n=11) | 1 Grade 7 - N |
|  |  |  |  | 1 Grade 8 - NN |
| D1 | N | N (n=1)NN (n=2) | N (n=11) | 2 Grade 11 N |
| H2 | N | N (n=3) | N (n=12) | 2 Grade 8 - N |
| S | NN | NN(n=4) | NN (n=11) | 1 Grade 11 - NN |
|  |  |  |  | 1 Grade 10 - NN |
| L | NN | NN(n=4) | NN (n=11) | 1 Grade 7 -not sure |
|  |  |  |  | 1 Grade 8 - NN |
| D2 | NN | NN (n=4) | NN (n=11) | 2 Grade 7 - NN |
| I | NN | NN(n=4) | NN(n=11) | 1 Grade 9- NN |
| N1 | NN | NN(n=4) | NN(n=11) | 1 Grade 7 - NN |
|  |  |  |  | 1 Grade 8 - NN |
| N2 | NN | NN(n=4) | NN (n=9) | 2 Grade 8 - N |
|  |  |  | Not sure (n=2) | 1Grade 8 - NN |
| H3 | NN | NN (n=4) | NN (n=11) | 2 Grade 9 - NN |
| O | NN | NN (n=4) | NN (n=11) | 1 Grade 8-NN |
|  |  |  |  | 1 Grade 7 N |
| N4 | nearl | NN (n=2) | NN (n=2) | 1Grade 7 N |
|  | y N | N (n=1) | N (n=9) | 1Grade 8 N |
| M | N | N (n=3) | N(n=12) | 2 Grade 10- N |
| B | NN | NN(n=4) | NN(n=11) | 1Grade 10- NN |
|  |  |  |  | 1Grade12 NN |
| T | NN | NN(n=4) | NN(n=11) | 1 Grade 11 - NN |

This phenomenon is illustrated in the case of N2, who ascribes herself as a non-native speaker of English and is so labeled by 100% of the native speaking colleagues. Two of the 11 non-native speaker colleagues, however, are unsure of this teacher's native identity, while two of the three students labeled their teacher a native speaker. Borderline cases present difficulty for all parties involved: N4 ascribes her identity as being nearly native. Both native and non-native colleagues are likewise undecided in the way they perceive her identity. The two students, however, agree as to their teacher's native speaking ascription.

These findings are congruent with the teachers' assumptions as to how they are perceived in terms of native non-native identity by the three groups, and validate the assumed behavior pattern among the observers. The somewhat reduced scope of the gap found in this study between self-ascribed and perceived identities among the teachers can probably be attributed to both the familiarity among the participants and to their sensitivity as language professionals to language speakers and language varieties. In terms of the students the characterizing tendencies noted in the previous report are clearly apparent in this study as well.

## 4.3    Discussion

The findings confirm the existence of an assumed gap between self and perceived identities among EFL teachers. This gap is most apparent in the case of non-native English speakers, often perceived as native speakers by other non-native speakers and by their students. The reasons brought forth by the teachers to account for the gap and the systematic patterns amongst the perceivers provide insight as to native non-native identity formation among language teachers. Findings of the validation study confirm the teachers' speculations regarding their perceived identity and its inherent features, thus rendering credibility to these assumptions.

The most prominent observable phenomenon emerging from the study is the multi-identity reality teachers function in and accept as a natural part of their professional existence. It is likewise interesting to note the teachers' awareness of and sensitivity to the power granted to them as part of their professional status, manifested in what they assume to be their students' perceptions. At the same time, teachers are also conscious of the limitations of this context-dependent authority, and of the fact that the native speaker status bestowed upon them is more salient among less informed individuals.

Needless to say native/non-native English speaking identity is just one of the identity constructs these individuals hold and have to grapple with: examination of merely the language domain will most probably reveal that both native and non-native speakers of English are also labeled as native or non-native speakers of other languages, either of the dominant language (Hebrew) or of an array of other tongues. This phenomenon is more prevalent in immigrant multilingual societies such as in the case of the research site, and obviously has meaningful ramifications for each and every individual.

Since the focus of this study is self and perceived native/non-native identities results need to be considered within the wider spectrum of the native speaker concept. Given the inconsistent and often conflicting views as to what constitutes native speaker identity (see for example Davies, 2000; Elder, 1997), the lack of consensus observed in this study as to native or non-native classification is hardly surprising. Native/non-native labeling, specifically among self-ascribed non-native speakers, was seen to fluctuate according to the perceiver, the context and the speakers' attributes.

In addition, analysis of the reasons provided for the gap shows that though the most frequent ones (accent and language knowledge) may be pertinent to mistaken identities in general, some of the explanations provided are nonetheless unique to the research sample of EFL teachers. This aspect corroborates previous findings as to the need to consider specific populations and their inherent characteristics when examining native speaker phenomena.

Hardly any disparity was observed among self-ascribed native speakers regarding their own identities and those of self-proclaimed non-native speakers. Thus adherence to a dichotomous native/non-native English speakers' division is clearly evident among native speakers, who do not accept into their midst individuals lacking native speaker characteristic as they perceive them. Since being a native English speaker entails access to valuable assets, the warding off of *pseudo* native speakers by proclaimed native speakers can be interpreted as the guarding of potentially valuable resources by privileged native speakers. One may assume, however, that with the massive spread of English currently accepted norms of native speaker status will be revisited and perhaps revised to include populations presently excluded from the native speaker speech community. Such a process will relocate the locus of power and control among English speakers, transforming and reshuffling notions of hitherto perceived native and non-native identities.

In terms of the 'The Dominated as Defined by Self and the Dominant' model (Louw-Potgieter & Giles, 1987: 263), these results show that when the teachers define themselves as part of the group, *i.e.*, self-ascribed native speakers, they are generally also 'defined in' by others. On the other hand, while 'defined out' EFL teachers (*i.e.*, self-ascribed non-native speakers) are perceived in the same manner by legitimate members of the speech community (the 'dominant'), they are often viewed differently and 'defined in' by non-members (non-native speakers and students). These latter populations of judges are excluded, however, from the model since it is confined to perceivers belonging to either the dominated or dominant speech communities, not recognizing the function of a third party (or parties) in formulating linguistic identities. Thus a more comprehensive model needs to take into consideration other individuals who function as relevant observers and judges in the contextual framework under examination.

Hence, perceived native speaker identity is not a generalizable phenomenon but rather the product of the interaction between the judge and the person being judged and the relevant knowledge both parties bring to the joint encounter.

## 5.    NOTES

[1] About 80% of the teachers in Israeli Jewish State schools are females (Ministry of Education, 2003).

## 6.    REFERENCES

Amin, N. (1997). Race and the identity of the non-native ESL teacher. *TESOL Quarterly, 31,* 580-583.

Beijaard, D. (1995). Teachers' prior experiences and actual perceptions of professional identity. *Teachers and Teaching: Theory and Practice, 1* (2), 281-294.

Ben-Rafael, E. (1996). The paradigm of Jewish identities. In Y. Kashti, F. Eros, D. Sekers & D. Zisenwine (Eds.), *A quest for identity - Post-war Jewish biographies.* Tel Aviv University. 187-203.

Bourdieu, P. (1977). The economics of linguistic exchanges. *Social Science Information, 16,* 645-668.

Bourdieu, P. (1991). *Language and symbolic power.* Oxford: Polity Press.

Braine, G. (Ed.) (1999). *Non-native educators in English language teaching.* Mahwah, NJ: Lawrence Erlbaum Associates.

Clement, R. & Noels, K.A. (1992). Towards a situated approach to ethnolinguistic identity: The effects of status on individuals and groups. *Journal of Language and Social Psychology, 11,* 203-232.

Coppieters, R. (1987). Competence differences between native and non-native speakers. *Language, 63* (3), 544-573.

Davies, A. (2000). What second language learners can tell us about the native speaker: identifying and describing exceptions. In R.L. Cooper, E. Shohamy & J. Walters (Eds.), *New perspectives and issues in educational language policy: A festschrift for Bernard Spolsky.* Amsterdam: John Benjamins. 91-112.

Davies, A. (2003). *The native speaker: Myth and reality.* Clevedon: Multilingual Matters.

Eayrs, M. (1994). Teaching correct pronunciation. *IATEFL Newsletter, 125,* 15-17.

Elder, C. (1997). The background speaker as learner of Italian, modern Greek and Chinese: Implications for foreign language assessment. Unpublished doctoral dissertation. Department of Linguistics and Applied Linguistics, University of Melbourne.

Giles, H. & Coupland, N. (1991). *Language: Contexts and consequences*. Milton Keynes: Open University Press.

Giles, H. & Johnson, P. (1987). Ethnolinguistic identity theory: A social psychological approach to language maintenance. *International Journal of the Sociology of Language, 68*, 66-99.

Goldstein, T. (1995). Nobody is talking bad. In K. Hall & M. Bucholtz (Eds.), *Gender articulated: Language and the socially constructed self.* New York: Routledge. 375-400.

Greis, N. (1985). Towards a better preparation of the non-native ESOL teacher. In *On TESOL '84: Selected papers from the 18th convention of teachers of English to speakers of other languages*. Washington DC: TESOL. 317-324.

Gumperz, J.J. (1982). *Discourse strategies*. Cambridge: Cambridge University Press.

Heller, M. (1988). *Codeswitching: Anthropological and sociolinguistic perspectives*. New York: Mouton de Gruyter.

Inbar-Lourie, O. (1999). The native speaker construct: Investigation by perceptions. Unpublished doctoral dissertation. Tel-Aviv University, Tel-Aviv, Israel.

Kachru, B.B. (1982). *The other tongue: English across cultures*. Oxford: Pergamon.

Kramsch, C. (1998). *Language and culture*. Oxford: Oxford University Press.

Leung, C. Harris, R. & Rampton, B. (1997). The idealized native speaker, reified ethnicities, and classroom realities. *TESOL Quarterly*, 31 (3), 543-560.

Liu, J. (1999). From their own perspectives: The impact of non-native ESL professionals on their students. In G. Braine (Ed.), *Non-native educators in English language teaching*. Mahwah, NJ: Lawrence Erlbaum Associates. 159-176.

Louw-Potgieter, J. & Giles, H. (1987). Imposed identity and linguistic strategies. *Journal of Language and Social Psychology, 6*, 261-286.

Lvovich, N. (1997). *The multilingual self: An inquiry into language learning*. Mahwah, NJ: Lawrence Erlbaum Associates.

Mawhinney, H. & Xu, F. (1997). Reconstructing the professional identity of foreign-trained teachers in Ontario schools. *TESOL Quarterly, 31* (3), 632-639.

McNamara, T.F. (1987). Language and social identity: Israelis abroad. *Journal of Language and Social Psychology, 6* (3&4), 215-228.

Medgyes, P. (1994). *The non-native teacher*. London: Macmillan. (1999) 2nd edition. Ismaning: Max Hueber Verlag.

Medgyes, P. (1999). Language training: A neglected area in teacher education. In G. Braine (Ed.), *Non-native educators in English language teaching*. Mahwah, NJ: Lawrence Erlbaum Associates. 177-196.

Ministry of Education, Culture and Sports. (2003). The Economics and Budgeting Division. http://207.232.9.131/minhal_calcala/misparim2003.htm#4

Nayar, P.B. (1994). Whose English is it? *TESL-EJ, 1* (1), 1-5.

Norton, B. (1997). Language, identity, and the ownership of English. *TESOL Quarterly, 31* (3), 409-429.

Norton, B. (2000). *Identity and language learning: Gender, ethnicity and educational change*. London: Longman/Pearson Education.

Ogulnick, K. (2000). *Language crossings: Negotiating the self in a multicultural world*. New York: Teachers' College Press.

Paikeday, T.M. (1985). *The native speaker is dead!* Toronto: Paikeday Publishing Inc.

Pennycook, A. (1998). *English and the discourses of colonialism*. London: Routledge.

Reves, T. & Medgyes, P. (1994). The non-native English speaking ESL/EFL teacher's self-image: An international survey. *System, 22* (3), 353-367.

Seidlhofer, B. & Widdowson, H.G. (1998). Applied linguistics, pragmatics, and language pedagogy. In R. Beaugrande, M. Grosman & B. Seidlhofer (Eds.), *Language policy and language education in emerging nations*. Stamford, CN: Ablex. 3-13.

Skutnabb-Kangas, T. (2000). Linguistic genocide in education or worldwide diversity and human rights? Mahwah, NJ: Lawrence Erlbaum Associates.

Tajfel, H. (1978). *The social psychology of minorities* (Minority Rights Group Report No. 38). London: Minority Rights Group.

Taylor, D.S. (1991). Who speaks English to whom? The question of teaching English pronunciation for global communication. *System, 19* (4), 425-435.

Thomas, D. (1995). *A survey of learner attitudes towards native speaker teachers and non-native speaker teachers of English in Slovakia* (part 2) http://cksr.ac.bialystok.pl/flattic/ptt/apr95/thomas.html.

Uchida, Y. & Duff, P.A. (1997). The Negotiation of teachers' sociocultural identities and practices in postsecondary EFL classrooms. *TESOL Quarterly, 31* (3), 451-486.

Chapter 15

# NON-NATIVE SPEAKER TEACHERS OF ENGLISH AND THEIR ANXIETIES: INGREDIENTS FOR AN EXPERIMENT IN ACTION RESEARCH

KANAVILLIL RAJAGOPALAN
*State University at Campinas*

> hi, there, i'm a taiwanese who live in hualien, i love sea, speeding motorcycle, music (tarvis, uzjsme doma, tom waits, julie dolphin, yo la tengo, rufus.....), and i love sculpture. i want to make friends with anyone who is a native speaker of english, if you're interested, please write email to me.

>> —Message retrieved from the Internet (http://fl.hfu.edu.tw/ss/_disc1/0000008c.htm)

## 1. INTRODUCTION: THE TRAUMA OF BEING A NNST

Non-native speaker teachers (NNSTs) are typically treated as second class citizens in the world of language teaching. The problem is especially acute in the realm of teaching English as a *foreign* language (EFL)[1]. A possible explanation for this unfortunate state of affairs is not all that far to seek: in today's world, English is not just another language; it is the hottest selling commodity on the foreign language teaching market. A close look at the history and expansion of the EFL industry since the end of World War II and the emergence of the new world order shows how the multi-billion dollar language market, with its tentacles reaching out far and wide—indeed

E. Llurda (Ed.), *Non-Native Language Teachers. Perceptions, Challenges and Contributions to the Profession*, 283—303.

to practically every nook and corner of this terrestrial globe, has been meticulously monitored and zealously manipulated by the powers that be to favor certain vested interests (Phillipson, 1992; Pennycook, 1994, 1998)[2].

One of the main reasons why NNSTs came to be marginalized and often discriminated against is that, from the very beginning, there has been a systematic campaign—often camouflaged as serious academic research—to ensure special 'trading privileges' for native speakers in the ever-expanding and increasingly competitive language market. The native speakers were said to be the true custodians of the language, the only ones authorized to serve as reliable models for all those wishing to acquire it as a second or a foreign language. And so effective has that campaign been that, until recently, NNSTs were themselves, by and large, resigned to their pariah status in spite of the fact that they constitute today no fewer than 80 per cent of the total ELT workforce worldwide (Canagarajah, 1999a). Many found no alternative but to get used to living with low self-esteem and the resultant job-related stress.

This paper explores the need to help NNSTs overcome their (often unconfessed) complex of inferiority. It presents data from quantitative as well as qualitative research undertaken with a view to assessing the exact extent of the problem(s) faced by NNSTs and, based on the preliminary feedback from a project currently under way, suggests ways of helping NNSTs better cope with their lack of self-confidence and self esteem.

Section 1 is devoted to a quick look at the genealogy of the discrimination faced by NNSTs as well as the intellectual climate that made it possible for such callous and wide-spread discrimination to take place practically unopposed. Section 2 presents partial results from a survey conducted in Brazil, a country that belongs to so-called 'expanding circle' in terms of Kachru's well-known division of countries according to the status accorded to English (Kachru, 1985). Section 3 discusses the outline of and preliminary results from an experiment in action research (still in its embryonic stage) geared towards empowering NNSTs and enabling them to overcome their anxieties. Finally, in Section 4, I shall present arguments as to why I think there is an urgent need to make a concerted effort to dispel the myth of the native speaker by, among other things, denouncing it as ideological through and through (Rajagopalan, 1997) and look for alternative conceptual tools for the teaching of EFL as well as the assessment of learner proficiency in it.

## 2.     HOW THE NNSTS CAME TO BE MARGINALIZED

The native speaker has for long reigned supreme in the world of EFL, safely ensconced in a lofty position of unassailable authority and absolute infallibility from where, until very recently, s/he could contemplate the kingdom below and proclaim confidently: 'I am Monarch of all I survey and my right there is none to dispute'. As Mey (1981: 70) noted with some concern: 'Native speaker is the final criterion of matters linguistic: his verdict settles all disputes, be they about sentences, linguistic postulates, innate ideas, or what have you. Like the kings of old, Native speaker can do no wrong. He is above all laws: he is the Law himself, the Rule of the Realm [...]'.

From the 1960s through 1980s, language teaching in general, and EFL teaching in particular, came heavily under the influence of theoretical linguistics where the dominant paradigm happened to be Generative Grammar. Chomsky and his followers had elevated the figure of the native speaker to the status of literally the be-all and end-all of all theorizing about language. From suppliers of raw data for the field linguists to work on, they became the very object of linguistic theory. To theorize about language was to delve into the mind of the native speaker, period. For the natives know their language. And, as far as the linguist interested in understanding the workings of grammar was concerned, the simple message was: 'That is all ye know on earth and all ye need to know'. Thus idolized, the native speaker became the potent and awe-inspiring trademark of the billion-dollar EFL industry world wide, whose soft imperialist underbelly remained largely unnoticed until, in the early 1990s, scholars like Phillipson (1992) and Pennycook (1994, 1998) took the bold initiative of blowing the whistle. English itself had by then become a commodity and the idea of native-speakerhood had been transformed, as it were, into a certificate of quality, of authenticity, of hundred percent genuineness, of the coveted product on sale (Prospective buyers were routinely warned not to be beguiled by cheap counterfeits and asked to double check the factory seal for any possible violation).

Not that Chomsky himself is to be held directly responsible for what language teachers and teacher educators did with one of his prized concepts. But the fact remains that, in the world of language teaching in general and EFL teaching in particular, the one most lasting (and unfortunately, in many quarters, still enduring) spin-off from the great revolution in linguistics was what I have elsewhere referred to as the 'apotheosis of the native speaker' (Rajagopalan, 1997). For the native, by definition, never errs (which in itself is, come to think of it, a truly divine attribute), given the axiomatic claim that s/he is to be regarded as the only reliable source for 'all and only the grammatical sentences' of the language in question.

Like Marlowe's Mephistopheles who said to Faustus '[...]where we are is hell, And where hell is, there must we ever be', the all-powerful native speaker might have said: 'What I speak is the language [that you are after] and the language is *whatever* I speak'. So to learn English as a foreign language was to ape the native speaker as best as one could, knowing full well that all one could hope for was to be caught out later rather than sooner. In the heyday of generative grammar and teaching methodologies directly inspired by it (and, in a more concerted fashion, with advent of so-called communicative teaching methodologies that followed in their wake), it was not uncommon to find teachers overly anxious to teach their students strategies of hesitation and rephrasing sentences half-way through the utterance, notably techniques of humming and hawing the way the natives do—'uhm', 'oops', 'sort of', 'kind-a-like', 'I mean', and so on—encouraging the unsuspecting learners to pick up in the process some very nasty and most irritating verbal tics (Rajagopalan, 2001a: 82). The underlying principle was: if you can't be a native, at least try to *pass for* one. The fact that Chomsky himself was, most of the time at least, speaking of an idealized native speaker—not to be confused with the ones in flesh and blood that normally walk the face of the earth—did little to discourage or deter these doting worshippers of the nativity scene, who preferred to overlook the inconvenient detail.

For most NNSTs of English though, the whole idea of native-speakerhood has over the years only served as a dreadful nightmare, a veritable incubus. After all, all through their professional training, most of them were taught to regard the native speaker 'as the ultimate state at which first and second language learners may arrive and as the ultimate goal in language pedagogy'. (Van der Geest, 1981:317) In fact, it is not difficult to come across NNSTs who have been literally brainwashed into believing that their highest goal should be to be so proficient in the language as to be welcomed into the community of native speakers as 'regular' members. Unlike the native, the non-native was *human*—in fact, all too human, if only for the reason that s/he was prone to err and who therefore was eternally at the mercy of the native who alone had the power to pardon. It was in this sense that the EFL enterprise became an extension of 19<sup>th</sup> century European colonialism and its flipside called imperialism (which, incidentally, in their crude form at least, had by now fallen into disrepute). As Phillipson (1992: 1) warned: '[...] whereas once Britannia ruled the waves, now it is English which rules them. The British empire has given way to the empire of English'.

This covertly imperialist dimension of the world-wide EFL enterprise had the immediate consequence of relegating the non-native to a condition of 'second class citizenship' in the EFL profession from which there was no hope of any redemption or emancipation[3]. The closest the NNSTs could ever hope to get to being a native was to be graced with the honourable title of a 'near native', the linguistic equivalent of a knighthood, condescendingly distributed amongst the doting admirers of the royalty. Yet, a near native was by definition someone who lacked the hundred per cent authenticity of a full-blooded native and was, for this reason, branded a 'pseudo-native' by Medgyes (1994), that is to say, a rather clever impostor who is nonetheless bound to be caught in due course—although Medgyes (1994: 17) himself underscored the fact that occasionally the pseudo natives' proficiency 'may even surpass the native's in one or several aspects'. Indeed the fact of not being a native speaker and, worse still, of never being able to become one no matter how hard they tried, often became a source of anxiety and job frustration, tormenting their lives around the clock and making them constantly feel the tantalizing sensation of hankering after an unattainable ideal[4].

Luckily, things are beginning to change. Linguistics is no longer regarded as the privileged site for language teachers to turn to for fresh ideas on going about their business (Rajagopalan, 2003a). Nor is generative grammar the dominant paradigm in contemporary linguistics any longer. Moreover, thanks to the important work of scholars such as Phillipson, Pennycook and several others, there has been a growing awareness among EFL professionals all over the world of the ideological implications of the very enterprise they have been engaged in. Far from being an innocent theoretical reference point in language teaching, the figure of the native speaker is increasingly being seen today as a concept shot through with ideological, indeed often *racist*, connotations. And, with more and more people becoming aware of the ideological use of the concept, the native speaker is no longer the cynosure of all eyes but is on the road to steady decline (Rampton, 1990; Canagarajah, 1999a; Graddol, 1999). And, as far as English as an *international* language is concerned, the very concept of native speaker is becoming of doubtful utility even as a reference point (McKay, 2002) (more on this below).

While these developments are indeed most welcome and long overdue, there is still a lot of work to be done by way of empowering the NNSTs and encouraging them to rethink their own roles in EFL. There is an urgent need to help them overcome the profoundly pernicious deficit model of their own professional competence which was thrust upon them as part of an insidious agenda and which, over the years, many came to accept and silently learned to live with. The gravity of the situation may be gauged from the fact clearly brought to light by the survey reported in the section below—that many NNSTs try to cover up their nagging inferiority complex by pretending (and deluding themselves in the process) that they are perfectly at ease with their subaltern condition.

## 3.    A PEEK INTO THE MINDSET OF NNSTS AND THEIR PROFESSIONAL FEARS

With a view to assessing the exact extent of the damage done to the EFL teaching enterprise as a result of the unconditional adulation of the native and the consequent relegation of NNSTs into second class citizenship, the present writer undertook a survey in Brazil, the largest country in South America and one of the major players in the geo-politics of the region. As already noted, English is very much a foreign language in this country, although thanks to the extremely complex north-south relations that have evolved over the years in the Americas, the precise role of English is anything but easy to define (Rajagopalan, 2003b; Rajagopalan, forthcoming-2; Rajagopalan & Rajagopalan, forthcoming). The survey consisted of both quantitative and qualitative means of data collection. The quantitative side of the survey was based on a questionnaire consisting of 8 questions, posed in Portuguese, the country's national language and the first language of the vast majority of the respondents. Around 500 copies of the questionnaire were sent out, of which some 90% were returned in time for the processing and tabulation of result. The decision to use the vernacular was prompted by the one major concern throughout the data collection stage: to let the respondents feel maximally at ease with themselves, given the special status of English in their professional lives and the likelihood that a questionnaire in English may subconsciously make them less forthcoming in their responses (see Appendix A for a translation of the original questionnaire into English).

It was clearly understood right from the very outset that the primary objective of the early quantitative phase of the survey was confirmatory rather than exploratory. In other words, there already was an educated guess as to the kind of results to be obtained. The use of the questionnaire was motivated by a desire to make sure that the intuitive expectations of the researcher, based on experience in ELT in a wide range of teaching contexts, did correspond to the views of the particular cross-section of NNSTs that was targeted for the study. And a quick look at the results shows that, by and large, they indeed did.

A preliminary analysis of the results did, however, spring some surprises as well. Questions 6 and 7 overwhelmingly elicited what appeared to be inconsistent answers. While a surprisingly large percentage of the respondents (88%) categorically denied ever having been made to feel sidelined for not being native speakers of the language they were required to teach (question 6)[5], the responses several of the very same group gave to question 7 revealed that they did think they were under-prepared (answer (a)-42%), under constant psychological pressure (answer (b)-35%), undervalued as professionals (answer (c) 64%), handicapped when it came to career advancement (answer (d)52%), doomed to be chasing an impossible ideal (answer (e)-40%), or even being treated as 'second class citizens' in their workplace (answer (f)- 66%). Possible explanations of the discrepancy include—with respect to question 6—fear of being 'caught' admitting professional incompetence, the rather blunt nature of the question itself, and unsavoury associations of the Portuguese word *menosprezado(a)* in the questionnaire, used to convey the idea of *sidelined* in the English version.

Except for the surprise finding mentioned in the foregoing paragraph, the survey results practically confirmed this researcher's 'gut feelings' concerning NNSTs and their anxieties. The majority of the respondents also confirmed the hypothesis that underpinned question 5. Experience of having lived in a native speaking environment is often touted by the NNSTs as a valuable feather in the cap and an amulet against possible charges of inadequate command of the language (a fact duly reflected in hiring practices). An affirmative answer to Part (C) of question 5 (almost 100%) must therefore be seen, not necessarily as a true confirmation of the respondents' greater ease with the language but as a psychological refuge from nagging suspicions concerning their own professional preparedness.

A number of these results were either confirmed *in toto* or, more often, were replaced by more nuanced or fine-tuned versions thereof as the experiment shifted to its qualitative mode. Indeed, one thing that the experiment did prove beyond the shadow of a doubt was the superiority of the qualitative over quantitative approach to data gathering in a research context such as the one reported in this paper. With its focus on personal, less formal and open-ended interviews, where interactive dialogic exchange takes over from the arid unidirectional question-answer sequence, the qualitative approach succeeds in eliciting more spontaneous responses from the interviewees for the simple reason that they are made to feel partners in the whole endeavour rather than mere 'subjects'.

Thus, it soon became evident during the follow-up one-to-one interviews conducted during the qualitative stage of the survey, there was no verifiable correlation between the time spent in a native speaking environment and the teacher's own command of the language[6]. Some of the most fluent teachers, as it turned out, had ventured out of their country, while some others who claimed having lived in English speaking environments often showed a certain amount of difficulty in expressing themselves fluently in the foreign language. Here we have a clear indication that what really counts when it comes to assessing a teacher's self-confidence is not necessarily their actual, publicly attestable knowledge of the language, but rather the way they perceive themselves and rate their own fluency.

Finally, an interesting finding (in a way, again somewhat anticipated—whence the very presence of the point in the questionnaire) of the survey was with regard to a certain correlation between the degree of self-esteem as NNSTs with, on the one hand, the length of teaching experience of the respondents and, on the other, their teaching environments. It turned out that those with less teaching experience (and presumably from a younger generation) were less worried about their being non-natives than those who have been in the profession for upwards of 10 years. This seems to indicate that, with the recent emphasis on teacher education and cutting edge trends such as reflective teaching, action research and the like with which new entrants to the profession presumably have some nodding acquaintance, respondents belonging to younger age brackets were less encumbered by the native-speaker myth than their older colleagues. As for the pertinence of teaching environment to teacher self-evaluation, teachers from private language schools tended to underrate their own professional preparedness vis-à-vis that of NSTs (95%), whereas results from a copy cat survey (using the same questionnaire) carried out amongst professionals at work in some universities (one private and two state-run) showed that respondents in this latter category had no such qualms (80%), since they viewed teacher education in much broader terms, where linguistic competence was just one—and by no means the overriding concern—among the basic requirements.

## 4.        TOWARDS A PEDAGOGY OF EMPOWERMENT

The experiment in action research, which I shall report on in this section, is still in its very early stage and is being conducted as part of an ongoing project. In early 2001, the present researcher was asked to counsel a large, privately run English language institute on matters relating to NNSTs, especially in regard to their job-related anxieties. The institute, called the *Sociedade Brasileira de Cultura Inglesa* (henceforward *Cultura Inglesa*), one of the largest of its kind in São Paulo, Brazil, had for some time been looking for ways to get its 400 or so teachers, on full or part time contracts, to 'brush up' their own English in ways that would not make them feel threatened. The present writer was consulted on the possibility of working on a project, directed at those teachers at the uppermost echelons of the institute's internal hierarchy (referred to as the 'academic department'), most of whom dedicate themselves to ensuring quality of teaching and uniform standards across the 16 branches of the institute by providing regular in-service training and preparing teachers for examinations such as Certificate for Overseas Teachers of English (COTE), Diploma in English Language Teaching to Adults (DELTA)—conducted worldwide by the University of Cambridge Local Examinations Syndicate (UCLES). In other words, the persons amongst whom the project was to be tried out on an experimental basis themselves constituted some sort of a 'think tank' within the institute.

Perhaps a word or two concerning EFL practices in Brazil would be in order at this juncture and help put in perspective the *Cultura Inglesa* (which is present in practically every major city in Brazil, although the different regional units are autonomous with respect to one another). Alongside a handful of similar language institutes, the *Cultura Inglesas* constitute an exception to the rule as far as standards of English language teaching in Brazil go (Rajagopalan & Rajagopalan, forthcoming). As noted by Falk (1991: 8, cited in Consolo, 1996: 8), teaching standards at the *Cultura Inglesas* 'are considerably higher than those required of secondary school teachers'. Candidates to a teaching position at the *Cultura Inglesa* are expected to hold at least the Certificate of Proficiency in English (Cambridge University). Many also have Diplomas or Master's Degrees in ELT or Applied Linguistics, often from British or American universities. Naturally, they are also among the best paid in the field and make up a select minority in a profession which has precious little to celebrate in a country like Brazil, where successive governments—both military and civilian— have at best paid lip service to improving overall educational standards. Across the country, the standards of EFL teaching are nowhere near what could be considered minimally satisfactory. Kol and Stoynoff (1995: 5) observe that 'students receive only the most basic introduction to English'. Teachers are generally inadequately prepared and mostly underpaid, and consequently have little interest in investing in their own professional improvement (Gimenez, 1994; Almeida Filho, 1998; Rajagopalan & Rajagopalan, forthcoming).

As already pointed out, the initial concern of the *Cultura Inglesa-São Paulo* was to do something about a frequent complaint from members of its teaching staff concerning their lack of self-confidence when it came to expressing themselves freely in English, especially to an audience other than their regular students. An early fact-finding interview on an informal basis with some of those interested revealed their unease in the presence of 'native speakers'. Fear of making mistakes—it soon became evident that their fears in this respect were largely exaggerated, for most of them were actually quite fluent in English—often inhibited them, they said, especially on occasions when they were required to speak in public or present papers at academic conferences in the country or overseas, which they were encouraged to do every now and then by the institute (all expenses paid). In short, what they wanted was a project designed to help them out of their lack of self-confidence.

Why did they decide to ask the writer of this paper to help them out? For several reasons. To begin with, as an outsider to the institute, the present writer would not be a threatening presence in their midst. Also, as someone born and brought up in a country belonging to Kachru's 'outer circle', the present writer (whose own linguistic characterization is anything but easy, defying as it does cut-and-dried conceptual categories such as native/non-native) was viewed as an ideal interlocutor. Besides, many of the would-be participants in the project had already some idea of the author's views in relation to the concept of native speaker and its role in EFL, disseminated through published work and conference lectures.

The project, still in progress as this moment, is being carried out through periodic encounters with the target group mentioned above. To kick start discussion, texts problematizing EFL practices worldwide were recommended as prior reading. The primary objective was to, as was put to them bluntly, deliberately 'muddy the placid waters' of inherited wisdom in matters relating to a host of issues in language and language teaching, as well as some of the wider questions raised by the spread of English worldwide and their implications for fashioning language policies in host countries.

As was only to be expected, an initial reaction from EFL teachers as they are asked to look at the ideological dimension of the global enterprise in which willy-nilly they do participate is to point to their own limited sphere of action. As classroom teachers, so the typical reaction runs, there is a limit to what they can do. The implication is that they have no say in decision making, which is made at the top and passed on downwards in a one-way chain of command. The biggest challenge therefore was to convince them that, while it is indeed true that one swallow does not make a summer, it is equally the case that, unless some one swallow or another takes the first step, the rest of the swallows may prefer to sit back as well, following their natural instinct to flock together, with the rather sombre prospect that the eagerly awaited summer may, for all you know, never get started. In other words, language planning is just one end of a continuum whose other end is actual classroom practice—so that a teacher whose sphere of influence is confined to the four walls of the classroom can nonetheless play an important part in initiating a process ultimately resulting in major policy changes at the top of the hierarchy (Canagarajah, 1999b).

Although the study itself is as yet at an incipient stage, it is possible to detect some noticeable forms of engagement emerging as a working rapport is established with the group of selected teachers. An early highly encouraging result was the perception that these teachers did know at the bottom of their hearts that there was a genuine problem that needed to be addressed. The complex of inferiority experienced by NNSTs is much more widespread than might seem at first glimpse. No matter how hard individual teachers might convince themselves of their positive qualities as EFL professionals—including, as they themselves will often tell you, their clear superiority vis-à-vis many NSTs when it comes to pinpointing the inter-lingual sources of errors arising from negative transfer from L1 (as in *'Thanks God!' instead of 'Thank God'), offering didactically adequate grammatical explanations for specific usages (as in *'No sooner I had ...' instead of 'No sooner had I...' etc.)—the very idea that they can never be equal to their NS colleagues often makes them enter into a spirit of conformity or even defeatism, paving the way for frustration and lack of enthusiasm to go on investing in themselves.

It is clear that these negative consequences can only be averted if steps are taken in time to ensure that the morale of NNSTs does not tailspin beyond control, making them incapable of realizing their full professional potential. This in turn calls for carefully planned strategies of empowerment aimed at convincing NNSTs of the important contribution they can make to the teaching enterprise based on the often vastly superior linguistic experiences they have been through and what Cook (1999, this volume) calls multi-competence that they have painstakingly acquired over the years. Forced into a resignedly defensive, or even at times pitiably submissive position, many NNSTs need to be re-educated so as to recognize that many of their job-related woes are actually the result of a well-orchestrated program designed to guarantee privileged status for certain groups of people to the detriment of others.

Clearly any effort to bring about significant changes in the mindset of NNSTs (or *anyone*, for that matter) is by no means going to be an easy task or one that will yield positive results overnight. After all, what one is asking them to do is to learn to swim against the tide. The market values the native speaker; students, parents, almost everybody wants to learn the language straight from the horse's mouth—in fact, the common sense on this is quite literally also the *horse* sense. And, in our post-industrial, neo-liberal world who will dare challenge what the market dictates? The answer to this is: Just because the market is behaving in a certain way and demanding certain things it does not mean that the market itself cannot be made to perceive things differently. In other words, even the much-talked-about distinction between learners' 'wants' and 'needs' is never static or given once and for all, but subject to the winds of change from the outside. As we have already seen, some of the 'wants' of today actually had their origin on the drawing board of those who have high stakes in the EFL market. Many of the 'wants' relating to the widely attested demand for NSTs, authentic materials and a lot of other pedagogical accessories marketed as conducive to the teaching of 'communicative competence' actually began their lives as 'needs' (not of the prospective buyers but of the interested sellers), zealously kept from public notice by a truly global industry whose market monopoly crucially depended on keeping it a closely guarded secret. As Consolo (1996: 7) points out, the EFL industry is caught up in a vicious circle where the presence of NSTs—zealously disputed on the market—on the teaching staff is used as a key selling point by language institutes as they struggle to hike up their student enrolment figures. Now, the higher costs of hiring NSTs (soaring in conformity with the growing demand) make these language institutes invest in the very image of NSTs and induce learners to 'want' to be taught by NSTs rather than NNSTs. This 'spontaneous' demand from the market is then used as a justification for discriminatory hiring practices. Notice that, by now, the wheel has already gathered a momentum of its own, sufficient to keep it going as long as the supply of NSTs does not dry up. Perhaps the only thing Consolo failed to notice in his otherwise brilliant discussion of the vicious circle at work is that the wheel cannot keep turning for ever but is bound to grind to a halt sooner or later, if only for the reason that the supply is limited and cannot indefinitely meet the ever-growing demand.

In the next section, we will look at some of the arguments that can come in handy as we confront the NNSTs with the proposal that the road to salvation is right ahead of them and that they have nobody but themselves to blame if they don't take it.

## 5. SOME KEY QUESTIONS OF THEORETICAL IMPORT THAT NEED TO BE BROUGHT UP IN TRYING TO HELP NNSTS OVERCOME THEIR LACK OF SELF-CONFIDENCE

What many in the language teaching world seldom if ever pause to think is that the native speaker—with all the attributes that are characteristically credited to this extremely powerful pedagogic totem—is simply non-existent in the world of lived reality. A native meeting all the requirements of one hundred per cent authenticity and so on is a chimera that can only exist in the fertile imagination of an ivory tower theoretical linguist. And, even if one did succeed in calling forth the native from the other-world of imagination, and investing it 'with a local habitation and a name', one would still need to come to terms with the embarrassing consequence that, from the very moment of venturing out into the wild from its idyllic 'natural environment', the native is condemned to lose its precious nativity progressively. For the native retains the amulet against 'contamination' from alien tongues only so long as it sticks to the confines of its hermit-like isolation and distance from members of other speech communities. The native is, in other words, the true incarnation of the Noble Savage whose nobility is, ironically enough, predicated upon its very native savagery, that is to say, on his/her (its?) being kept insulated against any outside, civilizing contact.

As the supreme irony of it all would have it, the authenticity of the native speaker teacher (NST) can only be guaranteed to the extent to which s/he remains immune to contact with the alien tongue and also proof against being influenced by it as a result. Or, to stretch the implications of this to their utmost in an EFL context, a NST can only continue to remain a true NST by constantly resisting the tendency to 'go native' (to recall a shibboleth of colonial parlance) by excessively friendly contact with the alien subjects—which, in concrete terms must mean: a NST's authenticity is conditional upon his/her not establishing anything remotely like a working rapport with their foreign language speaking learners, lest prolonged contact with the alien tongue should deprive them of their native purity or innocence. To put matters at their simplest: a NST can only remain a NST by, paradoxically enough, not teaching (at least in any pedagogically interesting sense of the term), let alone engaging in any meaningful contact with people from other speech communities.

In other words, it is important to 're-program' generations of EFL teachers who have been brought up believing that the native is whosoever was born into a native environment or, alternatively, that native speakerhood is a matter of birthright. As we have just seen, a native claiming hundred per cent authenticity can only do so at the peril of relinquishing his/her special credentials to teach their language to speakers of other languages. This is so because the linguistic environment s/he is going to find within the four walls of the EFL classroom is one of interlanguage (Selinker, 1972, 1992). Interlingual situations are situations where the language being used is, so to speak, 'still in the making'. A teacher under such circumstances is professionally ill-equipped and pedagogically incompetent to the precise extent to which s/he fails to perceive the challenges posed by the specific interlingual context. In other words, a rigorously monolingual native (if at all such a mythical creature does exist in the real world of EFL) is precisely the opposite of what s/he is standardly claimed to be. If anything, it is the

NNSTs who have a head start here, if only for the reason that it is they who have actually been through anything like the interlingual experience that the L2 learner is being asked to go through.

Once the privileged role of NSTs in EFL has been successfully debunked or at least shown to be conditional upon a series of other factors of an ideological nature, the stage may be seen to be ready for further considerations aimed at convincing the NNSTs that it is not necessarily the case that their NST colleagues have a head start in relation to them and retain that advantage for the rest of their career. The argument here is fairly simple and straightforward. Granted that, no matter what approach to EFL you happened to have adopted in a given context (along with the methods and techniques that characteristically come with them), we all agree that the aim of any language teaching program is to help the learners develop all four of the skills, we have a right to wonder if the much bandied-about native is equally 'perfect' in all four merely in virtue of a birth-right widely credited to them. Anyone who is inclined to hasten to answer the question in the affirmative must pause to give due consideration to the crucial fact that the so-called native is native only in speaking, that too at a none-too-exciting level of practical utility (by any standard, far from the kind of competence an L2 learner is typically looking for). If part of learning to speak an L2 is to be able to do things with words, and amongst the various things we would like to do with words are such things as persuading others, or convincing, threatening, praising them and so forth, it is also important not to miss the crucial fact that such skills are not acquired in the cradle, but picked up along the way as the toddler ventures out into the real world. Or to rephrase the same argument in the more technical vocabulary of the theory of speech acts that underwrites our discussion at this point, many of the real-life activities we engage in while speaking are perlocutionary rather than illocutionary, and the former, in opposition to the latter, sit at the crossroads between the strictly linguistic and partially discursive or rhetorical (call it what you will). If this were not the case people like Dale Carnegie and Paulo Coelho would not have made the millions they did telling others—including their fellow 'natives'—how to make their lives more liveable, by just *speaking*.

With the remaining three skills, the argument is even more striking and, indeed it is surprising how many an otherwise intelligent person has glossed over it in the past. First, listening. Chomsky's idealized prototype, after which has been constructed the myth about its homelier versions in flesh and blood, was a 'speaker-*hearer*', not a 'speaker-*listener*'. Chomsky must have known only too well that it is only an 'ideal speaker-*hearer*' who could be credited with 'infinite riches in a little room', the room being the space enclosed by the native's skull and the riches being his/her competence, whose defining trait is to generate sentences endlessly, or *ad nauseam*. One does not have to be an expert on Nietzsche to see that listening is a far cry from hearing.

As for reading and writing, even professional linguists will not be caught dead considering the possibility that these skills come as part of one's native, biological endowment. Besides, there is a growing body of research evidence that shows that quite a lot of the kind of expertise we actually bring to bear on specific tasks of reading and writing are not tied to this or that language, but an expertise that cuts across language boundaries. As a matter of fact, they are better classified as *discursive* or *rhetorical* rather than *linguistic* skills, properly speaking—they are linguistic only to the extent that they are carried out in and through language; but they are rhetorical for the reason we can ill afford to ignore, viz., that they are acquired by means of years and years of practice. As Davies (2001: 277) put it, '[w]hat many [natives] lack is fluency in the written elaborate code', which, as the very Bernsteinian vocabulary he adopts suggests, has to be acquired the hard way, thus leaving the native on practically the same footing as a non-native, except perhaps for a head start with respect to the code in the narrower, Chomskyan sense of the term. Indeed, EFL teachers used to teaching advanced levels have long known how these skills draw on competencies other than the purely linguistic—notably cognitive, rhetorical, logical etc. (which are nobody's monopoly, howsoever well endowed by birth).

To sum up the argument thus far: With regard to any one of the four skills in the sense in which the L2 learner is interested in acquiring them, it is practice that, as the good old adage says, makes perfect—not genetics or birth-right. From the immediacy of face-to-face communication in the case of speech to the anonymity and psychological distance in the case of writing, one may indeed argue that what we in fact have is a cline, progressing moving away from the linguistic and toward the rhetorical. But the fact remains that, as far as the vast majority of L2 learners are concerned, what they really need is something that the native, solely in virtue of being a native, is in no way better qualified to deliver.

This brings us to the very important question of what it is our typical L2 learner *needs* (as opposed to what he *wants*, or may *say* s/he needs). It was already pointed out above, that in our world to all intents and purposes run by marketing gurus, the very distinction between *needs* and *wants* may turn out to be not all that helpful. Needs can be easily converted into wants (and vice versa), provided we use the right strategy to sell them. And one way to sell a new product is to convince your customer that it is in his/her best interests to buy it.

It is here that an awareness of the changing status of English in contemporary world becomes important as part of a strategy aimed at empowering NNSTs (Rajagopalan, forthcoming-1). The idea of a World English is still resisted by many (Phillipson, 1992) who insist that English is still monopolized by the nations of 'inner circle' and that their monopoly over world-wide networks of mass media and publishing—and translation (cf. Venuti, 1996)—industries is guaranteed by media giants such as the CNN and the BBC. While such arguments do make sense as far as they go, it is also equally necessary to convince ourselves that it is by no means a *necessarily* win-win game for those who have so far run the show. With proper shuffling and dealing, the trump cards can be distributed if not evenly (probably a utopian dream), at least making sure that they do not always end up in certain hands and not others. Also, for every dominant discursive practice, it is always possible to come up with appropriate counter-discourses, provided there is the will (Canagarajah, 1999b).

It is also open to question how far an international language can simultaneously be claimed to be the property of any one people or nation. As Widdowson put it 'It is a matter of considerable pride and satisfaction for native speakers of English that their language is an international means of communication. But the point is that *it is only international to the extent that it is not their language'*. (italics mine) (Widdowson, 1994: 385). And, statistics confirm the trend is already underway and, as it seems, irreversibly so. With non-native users of English already outnumbering so-called natives, one should not be surprised to find the language being used more and more for communication between non-native speakers world-wide in their effort to communicate to one another rather than the prototypical situation envisaged by most theories of EFL to date, which focuses on a foreign learner trying to survive in a native environment and desperately trying to make him/herself understood by the native. Curiously enough, the day may not be all that far off when those 'natives' who have not bothered to learn the new language of international communication called 'World English' will find themselves left out.

Finally, with mass migration of populations (rural exodus in many countries, movement of masses of people worldwide, in directions East-West and South-North, the very idea of monolithic languages (based on such outdated 19th century slogans as 'One Nation, One People, One Language'), is becoming a museum piece. Whether we like it not, the linguistic reality of the future is sure to be dominated by the growing presence of 'mixed languages' like 'Spanglish', 'Franglais', and the South-American 'Portuñol'. Attempts to brush them aside or characterize them as passing phenomena are underwritten by the very same ideological agenda that, in times past, justified European imperialism, whether geo-political or linguistic, its latter-day reenactment (Rajagopalan, 1999).

This last question also underscores the need to help EFL professionals all over the world, and, in particular, NNSTs involved in the huge project of teaching English worldwide, overcome possible feelings of guilt complex likely to arise from a perception that they have been unwittingly acting as quislings in the service of a carefully orchestrated project of self-aggrandizement by the powers that be (Rajagopalan, 1999, 2000). It is important to help NNSTs come to the realization that, provided they take the reins of their professional conduct into their own hands and adopt what Kramsch and Sullivan (1996) refer to as a 'pedagogy of appropriation', whereby they go about the task of teaching the foreign language always keeping in mind 'the need to retain control of its use' (Kramsch & Sullivan, 1996: 211), they can turn things to their own advantage and act as agents of resistance and change (Canagarajah, 1999b; Rajagopalan, 2001b).

## 6.    CONCLUDING REMARKS

As pointed out early on in this paper, the experiment in teacher empowerment that is being reported here is still in its embryonic stage. It is too early to speculate as to what the long-term impact of the ongoing project is going to be. Besides it would be jejune to expect to move mountains by conducting half-a-dozen sessions of 'pep talk', hoping they will help generate enough of a ripple effect across the board. As pointed out already, the project of empowering NNSTs is a long term one and no one in their right senses should expect any concrete results to show up overnight. After all, what we are aiming to do is to pull off the arduous task of intervening decisively is a mindset that is firmly in place, thanks to years of concerted brainwashing.

If anything more realistic than the vaguely-worded promise of future results contained in the foregoing paragraph is to be offered to the reader by way of wrapping up this paper, it can only be a personal note of conviction that there is an urgent need for trying to do something about the plight of NNSTs all over the world. There is, furthermore, an equally important need to convince ourselves that, given the highly ideological nature of the kind of discrimination NNSTs currently face, short of deliberate intervention into the status quo with a view to empowering those on the seamy side of the power divide, nothing should be expected to change significantly or any time soon. This is so because, as has for long been recognized, the tendency for all ideologically infused states of affairs is to reproduce themselves as well as conditions for their perpetuation.

Talk of ideologies reproducing themselves naturally brings to mind the name of Karl Marx, after whose memory we may propose the following motto to round up our discussion of the plight of NNSTs all over the world: 'NNSTs of the world wake up, you have nothing to lose but your nagging inferiority complex'.

## 7.    ACKNOWLEDGMENTS

I am grateful to the CNPq (National Council for Research and Development), a funding agency under Brazil's Ministry of Science and Technology, for financing my research (Process no. 306151/88-0).

## 8.    NOTES

[1] I am assuming here that the world of ESL is typically miles apart. Many ESL countries have their own endonormative standards so that the very distinction between NSTs and NNSTs is, if not altogether neutralized, to a large extent softened or even superseded. In other words, local teachers (call them what you will) are deemed to be better at handling language classes and, more importantly, the locally produced literature in English, than their counterparts contracted off-shore.

[2] The thesis of linguistic imperialism has also come under criticism from different angles. I have myself critiqued its underlying assumption that it is the presence of an alien tongue that institutes inequalities in given societies or, equivalently, that, if it were not for the expansion of English into their midst, the people belonging to those societies would be far happier. I have argued instead (Rajagopalan, 1999) that power inequalities are present even in supposedly 'monolingual' societies, thanks to social stratification etc. Phillipson and other crusaders against the imperialistic advance of English worldwide have also been taken to task more recently by scholars like Janina Brutt-Griffler (2002) for failing to take into account the fact that the state of affairs being decried by them is just as much the result of complicity—and, in some cases, active collusion—by segments of the population at the receiving end. In other words, the imperialistic role of English is not entirely one-sided as might appear at first glimpse; it is actively supported by a handful of 'quislings' who take advantage of the situation.

[3] No doubt, the adulation of the native speaker is not unique to the ELT profession, since the same phenomenon may be easily verified in the teaching of French, Spanish, Japanese—well, you name it (I am grateful to Enric Llurda—personal communication—for this important caveat). Nevertheless, given the unparalleled role of English as the world's number one lingua franca and the extent of the vested interests that are operative in this multi-billion dollar enterprise, the phenomenon is invested with connotations that are probably not readily come across in other comparable cases.

[4] The problem is most acute with NNSTs working in Inner Circle countries (McKay, 2002: 43; Thomas, 1999), followed by those working in EFL contexts (Seidlhofer, 1999; Tang, 1997). In the Outer Circle countries, it is usually a different story. As argued by Agnihotri (1994), in countries like India, speakers of English as a second language in general feel no need whatsoever to model their speech habits on so-called native varieties, the predominant tendency being that of developing and sticking to their own endonormative standards.

[5] This has to do most likely with the reluctance—referred to earlier on in this paper—on the part of NNSTs to admit their own complex of inferiority.

[6] Although the interviews were conducted mostly in Portuguese, there were occasional 'forays' into English, as part of a calculated move designed to verify the respondent's ease in the language. Needless to say, the assessment was purely impressionistic and factors such as the surprise factor, possible difficulties in code-switching etc. were not taken into account.

# 9.   REFERENCES

Agnihotri, R.K. (1994). Sound patterns of Indian English: A sociolinguistic perspective. In R.K. Agnihotri & A.L. Khanna (Eds.), *Second language acquisition: Sociocultural and linguistic aspects of English in India*. New Delhi: Sage. 235-246.

Almeida Filho, J.P. de. (1998). D*imensões comunicativas no ensino de línguas*. Campinas, Brazil: Pontes Editores.

Brutt-Griffler, J. (2002). *World English: A study of its development*. Clevedon: Multilingual Matters.

Canagarajah, A.S. (1999a). Interrogating the 'native speaker fallacy': non-linguistic roots, non-pedagogical results. In G. Braine (Ed.), *Non-native educators in English language teaching*. Mahwah, NJ: Lawrence Erlbaum Associates. 77-92.

Canagarajah, A.S. (1999b). *Resisting linguistic imperialism in English teaching*. Oxford: Oxford University Press.

Consolo, D.A. (1996). Classroom discourse in language studies: A study of oral interaction in EFL lessons in Brazil. Unpublished Ph.D. dissertation. University of Reading, UK.

Cook, V.J. (1999). Going beyond the native speaker in language teaching. *TESOL Quarterly, 33* (2), 185-209.

Davies, A. (2001). Review of Tony Bex and Richard J. Watts (Eds.), Standard English: The widening debate. *Applied Linguistics, 22* (2), 273-282.

Falk, K. (1991). Probationary teachers' needs in their first year at work. Unpublished MA thesis. University of Reading, UK.

Gimenez, T. (1994). Learners becoming teachers: An exploratory study of beliefs held by prospective and practising EFL teachers in Brazil. Unpublished Ph.D. dissertation. Lancaster University, UK.

Graddol, D. (1999). The decline of the native speaker. In D. Graddol & U.H. Meinhof (Eds.), *English in a changing world. AILA Review. Oxford: Catchline/AILA*. 57-68.

Kachru, B.B. (1985). Standards, codification and sociolinguistic realism: The English language in the outer circle. In R. Quirk & H.G. Widdowson (Eds.), *English in the world: Teaching and learning the language and literatures*. Cambridge: Cambridge University Press. 11-30.

Kol, P. & Stoynoff, S. (1995). A status report on English language teaching in Brazil. *TESOL Matters, 5* (1), 5.

Kramsch, C. & Sullivan, P. (1996). Appropriate pedagogy. *ELT Journal, 50* (3), 199-212.

McKay, S.L. (2002). *Teaching English as an international language*. Oxford: Oxford University Press.

Medgyes, P. (1994). *The non-native teacher*. London: Macmillan. (1999) 2nd edition. Ismaning: Max Hueber Verlag.

Mey, J. (1981). 'Right or wrong, my native speaker' Estant les régestes du noble souverain de l'empirie linguistic avec un renvoy au mesme roy. In F. Coulmas (Ed.), *A festschrift for native speaker*. The Hague: Mouton. 69-84.

Pennycook, A. (1994). *The cultural politics of English as an international language*. London: Longman.

Pennycook A. (1998). *English and the discourses of colonialism*. London: Routledge.

Phillipson, R. (1992). Linguistic imperialism. Oxford: Oxford University Press.

Rajagopalan, K. (1997). Linguistics and the myth of nativity: Comments on the controversy over 'new/non-native Englishes'. *Journal of Pragmatics, 27* (2), 225-231.

Rajagopalan, K. (1999). Of EFL teachers, conscience, and cowardice. *ELT Journal, 53* (3), 200-206.

Rajagopalan, K. (2000). Critical pedagogy and linguistic imperialism in the EFL context. *TESOL Journal, 9* (4), 5-6.

Rajagopalan, K. (2001a). ELT classroom as an arena for identity clashes. In M. Grigoletto & A.M.G. Carmagnani (Eds.), *English as a foreign language: Identity, practices, and textuality*. São Paulo, Brazil: Humanitas. 23-29.

Rajagopalan, K. (2001b). Review of A.S. Canagarajah: *Resisting linguistic imperialism in English teaching. Word, 52*, 462-466.

Rajagopalan, K. (2003a). The philosophy of applied linguistics. In A. Davies & C. Elder (Eds.). *Handbook of applied linguistics*. Oxford: Blackwell. 397-420.

Rajagopalan, K. (2003b). Politics of language and the ambivalent role of English in Brazil. *World Englishes, 22*, (2), 91-101.

Rajagopalan, K. (forthcoming-1). 'The concept of 'World English' and its implications for ELT'. *ELT Journal*.

Rajagopalan, K. (forthcoming-2). 'English in South America'. In: B.B. Kachru, Y. Kachru, & C. Nelson (Eds.), *Handbook of World Englishes*. New York: Blackwell.

Rajagopalan, K. & Rajagopalan, C. (forthcoming). The English language in Brazil—a boon or a bane?. In G. Braine. (Ed.). *Teaching English to the world*.

Rampton, M.B.H. (1990). Displacing the native speaker: Expertise, affiliation, and inheritance. *ELT Journal, 44* (2), 97-101.

Seidlhofer, B. (1999). Double standards: Teacher education in the expanding circle. *World Englishes, 18* (2), 233-245.

Selinker, L. (1972). Interlanguage. *IRAL, 10* (3), 209-231.

Selinker, L. (1992). *Rediscovering interlanguage*. London: Longman.

Tang, C. (1997). On the power and status of non-native ESL teachers. *TESOL Quarterly, 31* (3), 577-583.

Thomas, J. (1999). Voices from the periphery: Non-native teachers and issues of credibility. In G. Braine (Ed.), *Non-native educators in English language teaching*. Mahwah, NJ: Lawrence Erlbaum Associates. 5-14.

Van der Geest, T. (1981). How to become a native speaker: One simple way. In F. Coulmas, (Ed.), *A festschrift for native speaker*. The Hague: Mouton. 317-353.

Venuti, L. (1996). Translation and the pedagogy of literature. *College English, 58* (3), 327-344.

Widdowson, H.G. (1994). The ownership of English. *TESOL Quarterly, 28* (2), 377-388.

# APPENDIX A

This questionnaire is part of a research project aimed at assessing the degree of self-confidence of English teachers in their own professional preparedness. The results will be kept in secret (and used for academic purposes only), so too will be the identity of the respondents. Please answer all the questions with utmost frankness.

Name of the Institution (School, University etc.): .....................
Personal data: (Please indicate your option with an 'x')

| **Sex** | Male | | Female | |
|---|---|---|---|---|

| **Age group** | de 20 a 30 ☐ | de 30 a 40 ☐ | de 40 a 50 ☐ | de 50 a 60 ☐ |
|---|---|---|---|---|

Professional Data:

| (1) | How long have you been teaching English? | |
|---|---|---|

| (2) | Which is your favourite teaching level? | Beginners ☐ | Intermediate ☐ | Advanced ☐ |
|---|---|---|---|---|

| (3) | How many years had you studied English before becoming a teacher? | |
|---|---|---|

| (4) | What is your mother tongue? | |
|---|---|---|

| (5) | Have you ever studied/lived in an English-speaking country? Yes  No<br>(a) Which country?                    (b) For how long?<br>(c) Do you feel more at home in English thanks to your having spent some time in an English speaking country?                    Yes        No |
|---|---|

| (6) | Do you feel that you are often being sidelined as a teacher of English for not being a native speaker? | Yes        No |
|---|---|---|

| (7) | What is your biggest worry as a teacher of English in respect of not being a native speaker of the language you teach? (You may tick mark more than one option) | (a) | not knowing the right answers | |
|---|---|---|---|---|
| | | (b) | being 'caught' making mistakes | |
| | | (c) | not being respected as a teacher/professional | |
| | | (d) | not being able to advance in career | |
| | | (e) | thinking that you are always chasing something impossible to achieve | |
| | | (f) | being treated as a second class citizen in the job environment | |

| (8) | Do you think it is possible to do something about the complex of inferiority that many teaches of English feel for not being native speakers of the language? Please explain your position: (If needed, please feel free to use the other side of this sheet) |
|---|---|

# Index

Abelson, R., 86, 105
Ability, 20-21, 30, 51, 55, 64, 68, 107,
    109, 110-111, 116, 122-124, 138,
    144-145, 161, 163, 207, 218, 235,
    251, 258, 267, 270
Accent, 19, 22, 34-35, 39, 50, 135-136,
    138, 141, 144, 149, 156, 162, 184,
    191, 232-233, 253, 255, 269-270, 274,
    278
Accent discrimination, 191
Accuracy, 16, 22, 77, 123, 126, 143, 162,
    207, 215, 219-220, 228, 244
Action research, viii, 283-284, 290
Administrators, 6, 8, 20, 35, 145, 156,
    179, 188, 190
Advanced level, 7, 14, 32, 68, 74, 77,
    110, 137, 148, 181-183, 186, 198,
    205, 211, 214, 247, 273-274, 297
Advantages, viii, 6-7, 18, 26, 28, 32,
    57, 59, 74, 80, 107, 116, 139, 147,
    163-164, 167, 200, 206, 208, 214,
    217, 218-220, 222-223, 228, 234,
    243-245, 248, 252-254, 256, 258-259,
    262, 296, 299-300
Africa, 22
Agnihotri, R., 300-301
Albanian, 158
Alberta, ix, 181, 183, 191
Almeida Filho, J. P. de, 291, 301
Ambiguity, 251-252

America, 22, 67, 96, 126, 141-142, 144,
    218, 249, 288, 302
American culture, 161, 163, 166, 172
American English, 28, 34-36, 38, 41, 43
Amin, N., xi, 187, 191, 269-270, 279
Andrews, S., 109, 124
Anxiety, viii, 7, 74, 76, 174, 233, 270,
    283-284, 287, 289-290
Applied linguistics, 4, 23, 112-113, 115,
    125, 302
Árva, V., xi, 23, 87, 104, 131, 149, 179,
    191, 196, 200, 209, 219, 235
Asher, C., 67, 82
Asia, 16, 21-22, 134, 140, 176, 182, 187,
    254, 269
Assessment, 16-17, 221-222, 224, 232-
    233, 280, 284, 301
Asset, 56, 63, 64, 175
Astor, A., 183, 191, 230, 235
Athanasopoulos, P., 53, 60
Attitude, 5-8, 14-15, 18-19, 23, 41, 43,
    56, 63, 83-84, 105, 110, 131, 145,
    160, 164, 174, 176, 179, 188, 196,
    201, 208, 211, 215, 219, 221-222,
    224, 233, 235, 239, 244-245, 248,
    251-252, 255, 257-260, 262, 281
Austin, J., 86, 104
Australia, 112, 217, 267
Authenticity, 219, 223, 228-229, 285,
    287, 294-295

310

312

# EDUCATIONAL LINGUISTICS

1. J. Leather and J. van Dam (eds.): *Ecology of Language Acquisition*. 2003                   ISBN 1-4020-1017-6
2. P. Kalaja and A.M. Ferreira Barcelos (eds.): *Beliefs about SLA. New Research  Approaches*. 2003                   ISBN 1-4020-1785-5
3. L. van Lier: *The Ecology and Semiotics of Language Learning: A Sociocultural Perspective*. 2004                   ISBN 1-4020-7904-4
4. N. Bartels (ed.): *Applied Linguistics and Language Teacher Education*. 2005                   ISBN 1-4020-7905-2
5. E. Llurda (ed.): *Non-Native Language Teachers: Perceptions, Challenges and Contributions to the Profession*. 2005
                   ISBN 0-387-24566-9